AAT

INTERACTIVE TEXT

Foundation Unit 1

Recording Income and Receipts

In this May 2001 edition

- Layout designed to be easier on the eye - and easy to use
- Clear language and presentation
- Lots of diagrams
- Practical examples
- Icons to guide you through a 'fast track' approach if you wish
- Numerous activities throughout the text to reinforce learning
- Thorough reliable updating of material to 1 May 2001

FOR 2001 AND 2002 DEVOLVED ASSESSMENTS

BPP Publishing
May 2001

First edition June 2000
Second edition May 2001

ISBN 0 7517 6502 3 (Previous edition 0 7517 6205 9)

British Library Cataloguing-in-Publication Data
A catalogue record for this book
is available from the British Library

Published by

BPP Publishing Limited
Aldine House, Aldine Place
London W12 8AW

www.bpp.com

Printed in Great Britain by W M Print
Frederick Street
Walsall WS2 9NE

We are grateful to the Lead Body for Accounting for permission to reproduce extracts from the Standards of Competence for Accounting, and to the AAT for permission to reproduce extracts from the mapping and Guidance Notes.

HOW TO USE THIS INTERACTIVE TEXT

Aims of this Interactive Text

To provide the knowledge and practice to help you succeed in the devolved assessment for Foundation Unit 1 *Recording Income and Receipts.*

To pass the devolved assessment you need a thorough understanding in all areas covered by the standards of competence.

To tie in with the other components of the BPP Effective Study Package to ensure you have the best possible chance of success.

Interactive Text
This covers all you need to know for the devolved assessment for Unit 1 *Recording Income and Receipts.* Icons clearly mark key areas of the text. Numerous activities throughout the text help you practise what you have just learnt.

Devolved Assessment Kit
When you have understood and practised the material in the Interactive Text, you will have the knowledge and experience to tackle the Devolved Assessment Kit for Unit 1 *Recording Income and Receipts*. This aims to get you through the devolved assessment, whether in the form of the AAT simulation or in the workplace.

Recommended approach to this Interactive Text

(a) To achieve competence in Unit 1 (and all the other units), you need to be able to do **everything** specified by the standards. Study the Interactive Text carefully and do not skip any of it.

(b) Learning is an **active** process. Do **all** the activities as you work through the Interactive Text so you can be sure you really understand what you have read.

(c) After you have covered the material in the Interactive Text, work through the **Devolved Assessment Kit**.

(d) Before you take the devolved assessment, check that you still remember the material using the following quick revision plan for each chapter.

  (i) Read through the **chapter learning objectives**. Are there any gaps in your knowledge? If so, study the section again.

  (ii) Read and learn the **key terms**.

  (iii) Look at the devolved **assessment alerts**. These show the sort of things that are likely to come up.

  (iv) Read and learn the **key learning points**, which are a summary of the chapter.

  (v) Do the **quick quiz** again. If you know what you're doing, it shouldn't take long.

  This approach is only a suggestion. Your college may well adapt it to suit your needs.

Remember this is a **practical** course.

(a) Try to relate the material to your experience in the workplace or any other work experience you may have had.

(b) Try to make as many links as you can to your study of the other Units at Foundation level.

(c) Keep this text, (hopefully) you will find it invaluable in your everyday work too!

Unit 1 Recording Income and Receipts

This Unit contains elements previously contained in the old Units 1 and 2. The emphasis is on the practical elements involved in dealing with income and receipts.

The main objectives of Unit 1 are:

- Identify cash and credit transactions
- Record the receipt of income accordingly

The Unit requires a background knowledge of business transactions and the context they occur in. Students need to be able to identify revenue and capital transactions and understand the legal framework. Double entry is a key skill.

FOUNDATION QUALIFICATION STRUCTURE

The competence-based Education and Training Scheme of the Association of Accounting Technicians is based on an analysis of the work of accounting staff in a wide range of industries and types of organisation. The Standards of Competence for Accounting which students are expected to meet are based on this analysis.

The Standards identify the key purpose of the accounting occupation, which is to operate, maintain and improve systems to record, plan, monitor and report on the financial activities of an organisation, and a number of key roles of the occupation. Each key role is subdivided into units of competence, which are further divided into elements of competences. By successfully completing assessments in specified units of competence, students can gain qualifications at NVQ/SVQ levels 2, 3 and 4, which correspond to the AAT Foundation, Intermediate and Technician stages of competence respectively.

Whether you are competent in a Unit is demonstrated by means of:

- *Either* a Central Assessment (set and marked by AAT assessors)
- *Or* a Devolved Assessment (where competence is judged by an Approved Assessment Centre to whom responsibility for this is devolved)
- Or *both* Central *and* Devolved Assessment

Below we set out the overall structure of the Foundation (NVQ/SVQ Level 2) stage, indicating how competence in each Unit is assessed. In the next section there is more detail about the Devolved Assessment for Unit 1.

All units are assessed by Devolved Assessment, and Unit 3 is also assessed by Central Assessment.

NVQ/SVQ Level 2 - Foundation (All units are mandatory)

Unit of competence	Elements of competence
Unit 1 Recording income and receipts	1.1 Process documents relating to goods and services supplied
	1.2 Receive and record receipts
Unit 2 Making and recording payments	2.1 Process documents relating to goods and services received
	2.2 Prepare authorised payments
	2.3 Make and record payments
Unit 3 Preparing ledger balances and an initial trial balance	3.1 Balance bank transactions
	3.2 Prepare ledger balances and control accounts
	3.3 Draft an initial trial balance
Unit 4 Supplying information for management control	4.1 Code and extract information
	4.2 Provide comparisons on costs and income
Unit 20 Working with information technology	20.1 Input, store and output data
	20.2 Minimise risks to data held on a computer system
Unit 22 Monitor and maintain a healthy safe and secure workplace (ASC)	22.1 Monitor and maintain health and safety within the workplace
	22.2 Monitor and maintain the security of the workplace
Unit 23 Achieving personal effectiveness	23.1 Plan and organise own work
	23.2 Establish and maintain working relationships
	23.3 Maintain accounting files and records

UNIT 1 STANDARDS OF COMPETENCE

The structure of the Standards for Unit 1

The Unit commences with a statement of the **knowledge and understanding** which underpin competence in the Unit's elements.

The Unit of Competence is then divided into **elements of competence** describing activities which the individual should be able to perform.

Each element includes:

(a) **A** set of **performance criteria.** This defines what constitutes competent performance.

(b) A **range statement.** This defines the situations, contexts, methods etc in which competence should be displayed.

(c) **Evidence requirements.** These state that competence must be demonstrated consistently, over an appropriate time scale with evidence of performance being provided from the appropriate sources.

(d) **Sources of evidence.** These are suggestions of ways in which you can find evidence to demonstrate that competence. These fall under the headings: 'observed performance; work produced by the candidate; authenticated testimonies from relevant witnesses; personal account of competence; other sources of evidence.' They are reproduced in full in our Devolved Assessment Kit for Unit 1.

The elements of competence for Unit 1 *Recording Income and Receipts* are set out below. Knowledge and understanding required for the unit as a whole are listed first, followed by the performance criteria and range statements for each element. Performance criteria are cross-referenced below to chapters in this Unit 1 *Recording Income and Receipts* Interactive Text.

Unit 1: Recording Income and Receipts

What is the unit about?

This unit relates to the role of invoicing and receiving payments. The first element involves individuals in preparing and checking invoices and credit notes for goods and services supplied, coding them and entering the details in the appropriate primary records and ledger accounts. The element also requires the individual to prepare statements of account. It is expected that individuals will communicate with customers, either in response to their queries or when chasing payments, and these should be handled both politely and effectively.

The second element is concerned with checking and recording receipts. The element requires the individual to deal with receipts in a variety of different forms and, therefore, to complete paying-in documents where necessary. The individual is required to deal with unusual features relating to wrongly completed cheques, out-of-date cheque, debit or credit cards, exceeded credit limits and disagreement with supporting documentation. Where these features are outside of the individual's own area of responsibility the element expects the individual to refer them to their manager or the accountant.

Knowledge and understanding

The business environment

- Types of business transactions and documents involved (Element 1.1)
- Basic law relating to contract law, sales of goods act and document retention policies

(Element 1.1 & 1.2)

- General principles of VAT (Element 1.1)
- Types of discounts (Element 1.1)
- Cheques, including crossings and endorsements (Element 1.2)
- The use of banking documentation (Element 1.2)
- Automated payments: CHAPS, BACS, Direct Debits, Standing Orders (Element 1.2)
- Credit and debit cards (Element 1.2)

Accounting methods

- Double entry bookkeeping (Elements 1.1 & 1.2)
- Methods of coding data (Element 1.1)
- Operation of manual and computerised accounting systems (Elements 1.1 & 1.2)
- Batch control (Element 1.1)
- Relationship between accounting system and the ledger (Elements 1.1 & 1.2)
- Credit card procedures (Element 1.2)
- Methods of handling and storing money, including the security aspects (Element 1.2)
- Petty cash procedures: imprest and non imprest methods; analysis of receipts (Element 1.2)

The organisation

- Relevant understanding of the organisation's accounting systems and administrative systems and procedures (Elements 1.1 & 1.2)
- The nature of the organisation's business transactions (Elements 1.1 & 1.2)
- Organisational procedures for authorisation and coding of sales invoices (Element 1.1)
- Organisational procedures for filing source information (Elements 1.1 & 1.2)
- House style for correspondence (Element 1.1)
- Banking and personal security procedures (Element 1.2)

Element 1.1 Process Documents Relating to Goods and Services Supplied

Performance criteria		Chapters in this Text
1	Invoices and credit notes are prepared in accordance with organisational requirements and checked against source documents	3,4
2	Calculations on invoices and credit notes are checked for accuracy	3,4
3	Invoices and credit notes are correctly authorised and coded before being sent to customers	3,4
4	Invoices and credit notes are entered into primary records according to organisational procedures	5
5	Entries are coded and recorded in the appropriate ledger	3,4,5
6	Statements of account are prepared and sent to debtors	6,10
7	Communications with customers regarding accounts are handled politely and effectively using the relevant source documents	10

Range statement

1 Source documents: quotations; purchase orders; delivery notes; sales orders

2 Calculations: pricing; price extensions; discounts; VAT

3 Primary records: sales daybook; sales journal; returns daybook

4 Ledger: main ledger; subsidiary ledger; integrated ledger

5 Communications: in response to queries; chasing payments

6 Source documents: aged debtors analysis

Element 1.2 Receive and Record Receipts

Performance criteria		Chapters in this Text
1	Receipts are checked against relevant supporting information	6,7,9
2	Receipts are entered in appropriate accounting records	6,9
3	Paying-in documents are correctly prepared and reconciled to relevant records	8
4	Unusual features are identified and either resolved or referred to the appropriate person	7,8,10

Range statement

1 Receipts: cash; cheques; automated payments

2 Accounting records: cash book

3 Unusual features: wrongly completed cheques; out-of-date cheque, credit and debit cards; limits exceeded; disagreement with supporting documentation; under payments; over payments; cheques returned to sender

ASSESSMENT STRATEGY

This unit is assessed by **devolved assessment**.

Devolved Assessment *(More detail can be found in the Devolved Assessment Kit)*

Devolved assessment is a means of collecting evidence of your ability to carry out practical activities and to **operate effectively in the conditions of the workplace** to the standards required. Evidence may be collected at your place of work or at an Approved Assessment Centre by means of simulations of workplace activity, or by a combination of these methods.

If the Approved Assessment Centre is a **workplace** you may be observed carrying out accounting activities as part of your normal work routine. You should collect documentary evidence of the work you have done, or contributed, in an **accounting portfolio**. Evidence collected in a portfolio can be assessed in addition to observed performance or where it is not possible to assess by observation.

Where the Approved Assessment Centre is a **college or training organisation**, devolved assessment will be by means of a combination of the following.

(a) Documentary evidence of activities carried out at the workplace, collected by you in an **accounting portfolio**

(b) Realistic **simulations** of workplace activities; these simulations may take the form of case studies and in-tray exercises and involve the use of primary documents and reference sources

(c) **Projects and assignments** designed to assess the Standards of Competence

If you are unable to provide workplace evidence, you will be able to complete the assessment requirements by the alternative methods listed above.

Part A

The Basics

1 Introduction to double entry

This chapter contains

Learning objectives

On completion of this chapter you will have learned about:

- Types of business transactions and documents involved
- Double entry bookkeeping
- Relevant understanding of the organisation's accounting systems and administrative systems and procedures
- The nature of the organisation's business transactions

1 INTRODUCTION: ACCOUNTING FUNDAMENTALS

1.1 Chapters 1 to 3 of this Interactive Text introduce the **basics of accounting**, particularly the principles of **double entry bookkeeping**. It is important that you understand the topics discussed in the next few chapters. They form a basis for your studies of **financial accounting** at Foundation, Intermediate and Technician levels.

ASSESSMENT ALERT

The material in these chapters will prepare you for the Devolved Assessment for Recording Income and Receipts. Because of the need to build a solid foundation in these topics, you will find when you cover the remaining unit-specific chapters that there is some repetition, as well as amplification. For example, you need to look at the principles of the cash book to understand double entry, but you also need to look at the practical use of the cash book in the context of the performance criteria for Unit 1 *Recording Income and Receipts.*

2 WHAT IS A BUSINESS?

2.1 Before tackling the nuts and bolts of accounting, it is worth considering what we mean when we talk about a **business**. Some ideas are listed below.

- A business is a commercial or industrial concern which exists to deal in the manufacture, resale or **supply of goods and services**.
- A business is an organisation which uses **economic resources** to create goods or services which customers will buy.
- A business is an organisation **providing jobs** for people to work in.
- A business invests money in resources (eg it buys buildings and machinery; it pays employees) in order to make even **more money for its owners.**

2.2 This last definition - investing money to make money - introduces the key idea of **profit**. Businesses vary in character, size and complexity. They range from small businesses (the local shopkeeper or plumber) to very large ones (ICI or BP). But the **objective of earning profit** is common to all of them.

KEY TERM

Profit is the excess of income over expenditure. When expenditure exceeds income, the business is running at a **loss**.

2.3 One of the jobs of an accountant is to **measure** income, expenditure and profit. This is not always straightforward: it can be an inexact science, although the accounting fundamentals of **double entry book-keeping** make sure that there is a firm set of principles underlying everything an accountant does.

2.4 Learning how to account for a business involves building up a clear picture of what a business consists of. We shall start with what a business **owns** and what it **owes** - its **assets** and **liabilities.**

3 ASSETS AND LIABILITIES

Assets

KEY TERM

An **asset** is something of value which a business owns or has the use of.

3.1 Examples of assets are factories, office buildings, warehouses, delivery vans, lorries, plant and machinery, computer equipment, office furniture, cash, goods held in store awaiting sale to customers, and raw materials and components held in store by a manufacturing business for use in production.

Fixed and current assets

3.2 Some assets are held and used by a business for a **long time**. An office building might be occupied for years; similarly, a machine might have a productive life of many years before it wears out. These are referred to as **fixed assets**.

3.3 Other assets are held for only a **short time**. The owner of a newsagent's will have to sell his newspapers on the same day that he gets them. The more quickly a business can sell the goods it has in store, the more profit it is likely to make. We call these **current assets.**

Liabilities

KEY TERM

A **liability** is something which is owed to somebody else.

3.4 '**Liabilities**' is the accounting term for the debts of a business. Debts are owed to **creditors.** Here are some examples of liabilities.

Liability	Description
A **bank loan** or **bank overdraft**	The **liability** is the amount which must eventually be repaid to the **bank**.
Amounts owed to **suppliers** for goods purchased but not yet paid for	A boat builder might buy some timber on credit from a **timber merchant**, which means that the boat builder does not have to pay for the timber until some time after it has been delivered. Until the boat builder pays what he owes, the timber merchant will be his **creditor** for the amount owed.
Taxation owed to the **government**	A business pays tax on its profits but there is a gap in time between when a business earns its profits and becomes liable to pay tax and the time when the tax bill must eventually be paid. The **government** is the business's **creditor** during this time.

4 A BUSINESS IS SEPARATE FROM ITS OWNER(S)

4.1 So far we have spoken of assets and liabilities 'of a business'. We shall see that, in accounting terms, a business is **always a separate entity from its owner(s)**; but there are two aspects to this question: the strict legal position and the convention adopted by accountants.

The legal position

4.2 Many businesses are **limited companies**. The owners of a limited company are its **shareholders**, who may be few in number (as with a small, family-owned company) or numerous (say in the case of a large public company whose shares are quoted on the Stock Exchange).

4.3 The **law recognises a company as a legal entity, quite separate from its owners**.

(a) A company may, in its own name, acquire assets, incur debts, and enter into contracts.

(b) If a company **owns** less than it **owes** (its assets are less than its liabilities), the company as a separate entity might become 'bankrupt', but the owners of the company would not usually be required to pay the debts from their own private resources. The company's debts are not debts of the shareholders, but of the company.

This is **limited liability**: the liability of shareholders to the company is **limited** to the amount they 'put in' to the company (how much the company asks for their shares on issue).

4.4 The case is different, in law, when a business is carried on, not by a company, but by an individual (a **sole trader**) or by a group of individuals (a **partnership**). Suppose that Sonia sets herself up in business as a hairdresser trading under the business name 'Sonia Hair'. The law recognises no distinction between Sonia, the individual, and the business known as 'Sonia Hair'. Any debts of the business which cannot be met from business assets must be met from Sonia's private resources.

4.5 The **law recognises no distinction between the business of a sole trader or partnership and its owner(s).**

Activity 1.1 **Level: Pre-assessment**

Distinguish between the terms 'enterprise', 'business', 'company' and 'firm'.

The accounting convention

4.6 The crucial point, is that **a business must always be treated as a separate entity from its owners when preparing accounts**. This applies whether or not the business is recognised in law as a separate entity, so it applies whether the business is carried on by a company, a sole trader or by a partnership.

Activity 1.2 **Level: Pre-assessment**

Fill in the missing words to make sure you understand the concept of the business as a separate entity and how the law differs from accounting practice.

A business is a _______ entity, distinct from its _______ . This applies to _______ businesses. However, the law only recognises a _______ as a legal entity separate from its ___________ . The liability of shareholders to the company is _______ to the amount the company asks them to pay for their shares.

5 THE ACCOUNTING EQUATION

5.1 A business is a separate entity from its owners, so:

- The business can owe money to, or be owed money by, its owners
- And the assets and liabilities of the business are separate from the assets and liabilities of the owners.

This is a fundamental rule of accounting: **the assets and liabilities of a business must always be equal** (**the accounting equation**). Let's demonstrate this with an example, which we will build up during this chapter.

5.2 EXAMPLE: THE ACCOUNTING EQUATION

On 1 July 20X7, Petula opens a flower stall in the market, to sell flowers and potted plants. She has saved up some money and has £2,500 to put into her business.

When the business is set up, an 'accountant's picture' can be drawn of what it **owns** and what it **owes**. The business begins by **owning** the cash that Petula has put into it, £2,500. But does it **owe** anything? The answer is **yes**.

The business is a separate entity in accounting terms. It has obtained its **assets**, in this example cash, from its owner, Petula. **It owes this amount of money to its owner.** If Petula changed her mind and decided not to go into business after all, the business would be dissolved by the 'repayment' of the cash by the business to Petula.

5.3 The money put into a business by its owners is **capital**. As long as that money is invested, **accountants will treat the capital as money owed to the proprietor by the business**.

KEY TERM

Capital is an investment of money (funds) with the intention of earning a return. A business proprietor invests capital with the intention of earning **profit**. The business owes the capital and the profit to the proprietor.

5.4 Capital invested is a form of **liability.** Adapting this to the idea that liabilities and assets are always equal amounts, we can state the accounting equation as follows.

THE ACCOUNTING EQUATION 1

Assets = Capital + Liabilities

5.5 For Petula, as at 1 July 20X7:

Assets	=	*Capital*	+	*Liabilities*
£2,500 cash		£2,500 owed to Petula		£0

5.6 EXAMPLE CONTINUED: DIFFERENT ASSETS

Petula uses some of the money invested to buy a market stall from Mark, who is retiring from his fruit and vegetables business. The cost of the stall is £1,800.

She buys some flowers and potted plants from a trader in the New Covent Garden wholesale market, at a cost of £650.

This leaves £50 in cash, after paying for the stall and goods for resale, out of the original £2,500. Petula keeps £30 in the bank and draws out £20 in small change. She is now ready for her first day of market trading on 3 July 20X7. How does the accounting equation look now?

5.7 SOLUTION

The assets and liabilities of the business have now altered. At 3 July, before trading begins, the state of her business is as follows.

Assets		=	*Capital*	+	*Liabilities*
	£				
Stall	1,800		£2,500		£0
Flowers and plants	650				
Cash at bank	30				
Cash in hand	20				
	2,500				

5.8 EXAMPLE CONTINUED: PROFIT INTRODUCED

On 3 July Petula has a very successful day. She is able to sell all of her flowers and plants, for £900 cash.

Since Petula has sold goods costing £650 to earn revenue of £900, we can say that she has earned a **profit** of £(900 – 650) = £250 on the day's trading. How do we show this in the accounting equation?

5.9 SOLUTION

Profit, like capital, belongs to the owners of a business: it's why they invested in the first place. In this case, the £250 belongs to Petula. However, so long as the **business retains the profits, and does not pay anything out to its owners, the retained profits are accounted for as an addition to the proprietor's capital:** they become part of that capital.

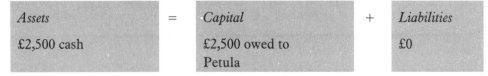

Assets		=	*Capital*		+	*Liabilities*
	£			£		
Stall	1,800		Capital introduced	2,500		
Flowers and plants	0		Retained profit	250		
Cash in hand and at bank £(30 + 20 + 900)	950					
	2,750			2,750		£0

5.10 So we could expand the accounting equation as follows.

THE ACCOUNTING EQUATION 2

Assets = (Capital introduced + Retained profits) + Liabilities

Increase in net assets

KEY TERM

Net assets = Total assets – Total liabilities

5.11 We can re-arrange the accounting equation to help us to calculate the total capital balance, which we have seen is the sum of capital introduced plus retained profit.

Assets – Liabilities	=	Capital
Net assets	=	Capital

5.12 At the beginning and then at the end of 3 July 20X7 Petula's financial position was as follows.

	Net assets	=		*Capital*
(a) At the beginning of the day:	£(2,500 – 0)	=		£2,500
(b) At the end of the day:	£(2,750 – 0)	=		£2,750
Increase in net assets	250	=	Retained profit for day	250

5.13 We can now state various principles.

- At any point in time, a business's **net assets** represent the **capital introduced** by the owner plus the business's **retained profit** to that point in time.
- At a later point in time, the **increase** in the business's net assets represents the additional **profit made** in the intervening period.
- **Total** net assets at that later point represent the capital introduced by the owner plus the business's **increased** retained profit.

For example:

		£m			£m			£m
1 Jan	Net assets	170	=	Capital introduced	20	+	Retained profit	150
1 Jan-31 Dec	Increase in net assets	34	=				Profit made in year	34
31 Dec	Total net assets	204	=	Capital introduced	20	+	Total retained profit	184

Drawings

KEY TERM

Drawings are amounts of money taken out of a business by its owner.

5.14 EXAMPLE CONTINUED: DRAWINGS

Since Petula has made a profit of £250 from her first day's work, she might draw some of the profits out of the business. After all, business owners, like everyone else, need income for living expenses. Petula decides to pay herself £180, in what she thinks of as 'wages', as a reward for her day's work.

But because she is the business's **owner,** the £180 is **not** an expense to be deducted before the figure of profit is arrived at. In other words, it would be **incorrect** to calculate the profit earned by the business as follows.

	£
Profit on sale of flowers etc	250
Less 'wages' paid to Petula as drawings	180
Profit earned by business (incorrect)	70

This is because **any amounts paid by a business to its proprietor are treated by accountants as withdrawals of profit (drawings),** and not as expenses incurred by the business. In the case of Petula's business, the true position is that the profit **earned** is the £250 surplus on sale of flowers, but the profit **retained** in the business is £(250 – 180) = £70.

	£
Profit earned by business	250
Less profit withdrawn by Petula	180
Profit retained in the business	70

The drawings are taken in cash, and so the business loses £180 of its cash assets. After the drawings have been made, the accounting equation would be restated.

Assets		=	*Capital*		+	*Liabilities*
	£			£		
Stall	1,800		Capital introduced	2,500		
Flowers and plants	0		Profit earned	250		
Cash £(950 – 180)	770		Less drawings	(180)		
	2,570			2,570		£0

The increase in net assets since trading operations began is now only £(2,570 – 2,500) = £70, which is the amount of the retained profits.

5.15 So **profits are capital as long as they are retained in the business**. When they are paid out as drawings, the business suffers a **reduction in capital**.

5.16 We can therefore restate the accounting equation again.

THE ACCOUNTING EQUATION 3

Assets = Capital introduced + (Earned profit – Drawings) + Liabilities

5.17 These examples have illustrated that the basic equation (Assets = Capital + Liabilities) always holds good. Any transaction affecting the business has a **dual effect** as shown in the table below.

	Asset	=	*Capital*	+	*Liabilities*
	Increase		Increase		
or	Increase				Increase
or			Increase		Decrease
or			Decrease		Increase
or	Decrease		Decrease		
or	Decrease				Decrease

Activity 1.3 — Level: Pre-assessment

Consider each of the transactions below, and mark on the grid which area will be increased and which decreased by the transaction. We have done the first one for you.

(a) The bank tells the business it no longer owes the bank £100 in bank charges.
(b) The business finds it has been overcharged £50 for some furniture it bought on credit.
(c) A gas bill of £200 is received by the business.
(d) The owner withdraws £500 from the business.
(e) Cash is introduced into the business by its owner.
(f) A car is bought by the business, for payment in 1 month's time.

Transaction	=	*Assets*	=	*Capital*	+	*Liabilities*
a				Increase		Decrease
b						
c						
d						
e						
f						

6 THE BUSINESS EQUATION

6.1 The business equation is a further development of the accounting equation which gives a definition of profits earned. The example of Petula has shown that **the amount of profit earned in a time period can be related to the increase in the net assets of the business, the drawings of profits by the proprietor** and **the introduction of new capital.**

6.2 We know that: *Accounting equation*

Assets	=	Capital	+	Liabilities	1

which is the same as:

Assets	=	Capital introduced + Retained profits	+	Liabilities	2

which is the same as:

Assets	=	Capital introduced + Profit earned – Drawings	+	Liabilities	3

6.3 As time goes on, **retained profit** (shown as profit earned less drawings) builds up the amount of capital in the business - it becomes **part of the opening balance of capital**. As we proceed through another period of trading, additional profit will (hopefully) be earned. So we should restate the accounting equation again:

THE ACCOUNTING EQUATION 4

Assets = Capital introduced

+ Liabilities

+ Profit retained in previous periods

+ Profit earned in current period

− Drawings

6.4 Let's see how this works in the case of Petula.

6.5 EXAMPLE CONTINUED: MORE PROFIT EARNED

The next market day is on 10 July, and Petula gets ready by buying more flowers and plants for cash, at a cost of £740. She was not feeling well, however, and so she decided to accept the offer of help for the day from her cousin, Loukis. She agrees to pay him a wage of £40 at the end of the day.

Trading on 10 July is again very brisk, and Petula and Loukis sell all their goods for £1,100 cash. Petula pays Loukis his wage of £40 and draws out £200 for herself. How do these transactions affect Petula's capital?

6.6 SOLUTION

The accounting equation before trading begins on 10 July, and after trading ends on 10 July, can be set out as follows.

(a) *Before trading begins*

Assets		=	*Capital*		+	*Liabilities*
	£			£		
Stall	1,800		Capital introduced	2,500		
Flowers and plants	740		Retained profit	70		
Cash £(770 – 740)	30					
	2,570			2,570		£0

(b) *After trading ends*

On 10 July, all the goods are sold for £1,100 cash, and Loukis is paid £40. The profit for the day is £320, computed as follows.

		£	£
Sales			1,100
Less:	cost of goods sold	740	
	Loukis's wage	40	
			780
Profit			320

Petula withdraws £200 of this profit for her personal use.

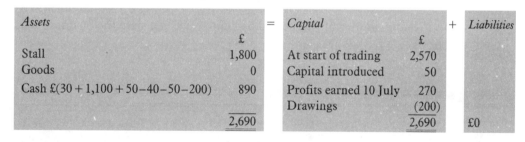

Assets		=	Capital		+	Liabilities
				£		
Stall	1,800		At beginning of 10 July	2,570		
Flowers and plant	0		Profits earned on 10 July	320		
Cash £(30 + 1,100 – 40 – 200)	890		Less drawings	(200)		
	2,690			2,690		£0

More capital introduced

6.7 When a business is doing well, the owner is very likely to **invest more money** in it in the hope of making even more profit. We need to include this in our accounting equation too: in doing so, we will arrive at the **business equation**, which allows us to compute profit from analysing the increase in net assets of the business, drawings and new capital introduced.

6.8 EXAMPLE: MORE CAPITAL INTRODUCED

On 10 July, in addition to all the other transactions, Petula decides to hire a van for £50 to transport the flowers and plants, paying for the hire with her own cash. How would this affect the accounting equation at the end of 10 July?

6.9 SOLUTION

After trading ends

On 10 July, all the goods are sold for £1,100 cash, Loukis is paid £40 and the van cost £50. Profit for the day is £270:

		£	£
Sales			1,100
Less:	cost of goods sold	740	
	Loukis's wage	40	
	van hire	50	
			830
			270

Petula withdraws £200 for her personal use.

Assets		=	Capital		+	Liabilities
	£			£		
Stall	1,800		At start of trading	2,570		
Goods	0		Capital introduced	50		
Cash £(30 + 1,100 + 50 – 40 – 50 – 200)	890		Profits earned 10 July	270		
			Drawings	(200)		
	2,690			2,690		£0

6.10 So new capital introduced should also be brought into the accounting equation.

THE ACCOUNTING EQUATION 5

Assets = Capital introduced in previous periods
+ Liabilities
+ Profit retained in previous periods
+ Profit earned in current period
+ Capital introduced in current period
– Drawings in current period

6.11 If we put Petula's figures from Paragraph 6.9 into this, we get:

	£		£		£
Assets	2,690	= Capital introduced in previous periods	2,500	+	0
		+ Profit retained in previous periods	70		
		+ Profit earned in current period	270		
		+ Capital introduced in current period	50		
		– Drawings in current period	(200)		
	2,690		2,690		0

The business equation

6.12 We are now ready to see how profit earned in a period can be expressed simply in terms of transactions within the period.

PREVIOUS PERIODS	Assets at start of period	=	Capital introduced in previous periods + Profit retained in previous periods	+	Liabilities at start of period
			+		
CURRENT PERIOD	Increase/decrease in assets (I)	=	Profit earned in current period (P) + Capital introduced in current period (C) – Drawings in current period (D)	+	Increase/decrease in liabilities (I)
			=		
END OF CURRENT PERIOD	Total assets at end of period	=	Total capital at end of period	+	Liabilities at end of period

6.13 Concentrating on the current period box above, we can state the business equation as follows.

THE BUSINESS EQUATION

Profit earned in current period	=	Increase/decrease in net assets in current period*	+ Drawings in current period	– Capital introduced in current period
P	=	I	+ D	– C

*This is the net figure of the increase/decrease in assets less the increase/decrease in liabilities.

6.14 Let's see how Petula's figures for 10 July plug into this equation.

Profit = Increase in net assets + Drawings – Capital introduced
= £(2,690 – 2,570) + £200 – £50
= £270

6.15 You may be a little concerned about why the **capital introduced in the period** is a **negative figure** in the equation. This is because when a business is given new capital, there will be an increase in the net assets of the business without any profits being earned. This means, say, that if a proprietor puts an extra £5,000 into his business the profit from the transaction, according to the business equation, would be P = £5,000 + 0 – £5,000 = £0.

We saw with Petula that the £50 cash introduced was added to assets (cash) in the accounting equation in Paragraph 6.9 but was also added to capital:

P = £50 + 0 – £50 = 0

7 CREDITORS AND DEBTORS

Credit transactions

7.1 So far we have been concentrating on **capital** (including profits) and certain types of **asset** (cash, goods for resale, fixed assets). We shall now look at two important items which arise when goods and services are purchased or sold as part of a **credit transaction: debtors and creditors**.

KEY TERMS

- A **cash transaction** is a sale or purchase when cash changes hands at the same time as the goods or services concerned.
- A **credit transaction** is a sale or a purchase which occurs some time **earlier** than cash is received or paid.

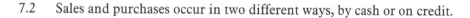

7.2 Sales and purchases occur in two different ways, by cash or on credit.

(a) A **sale** takes place at one of two points in time.

- **Cash sales**. If the sale is for cash, the sale occurs when goods or services are given in exchange for immediate payment, in notes and coins, or by cheque or plastic card.
- **Credit sales** (goods are ordered and delivered before payment is received). If it is on credit, the sale occurs when the business sends out an invoice for the goods or services supplied; cash is received later.

(b) A **purchase** also takes place at one of two points in time.

- **Purchases for cash**. If the goods are paid for in cash then the purchase occurs when the goods and cash exchange hands.
- **Purchases on credit**. If the goods are bought on credit, the purchase normally occurs when the business receives the goods, accompanied by an invoice from the supplier. Cash is paid later.

7.3 With credit transactions, the **point in time when a sale or purchase is recognised in the accounts of the business** is *not* the same as **the point in time when cash is eventually received or paid** for the sale or purchase. There is a **gap** in time between the sale or purchase and the eventual cash settlement. (It is possible that something might happen during that time which results in the amount of cash eventually paid (if any) being different from the original value of the sale or purchase on the invoice.)

Creditors

KEY TERMS

- A **creditor** is a person to whom a business **owes** money. A creditor is a **liability** of the business.
- A **trade creditor** is a person to whom a business owes money for debts incurred in the course of trading operations. The term might refer to debts which arise from the purchase of materials, components or goods for resale.

7.4 It is a common business practice to make purchases on **credit terms**, with a promise to pay within 30 days, or two months or three months of the date of the purchase. For example, if A buys goods costing £2,000 on credit from B, B might send A an invoice for £2,000, dated say 1 March, with credit terms that payment must be made within 30 days. If A then delays payment until 31 March, B will be a creditor of A between 1 and 31 March, for £2,000.

We will be looking at **invoices** in more detail in later chapters.

Debtors

KEY TERMS

- A **debtor** is a person who owes the business money. A debtor is an **asset** of a business (the right to receive payment is owned by the business).
- A **trade debtor** is a person who owes the business money for debts incurred in the course of trading operations ie because the business has sold its goods or services.

7.5 Just as a business might buy goods on credit, so too might it sell goods to customers on credit. For example, suppose that C sells goods on credit to D for £6,000 on terms that the debt must be settled within two months of the invoice date, 1 October. If D does not pay the £6,000 until 30 November, D will be a debtor of C for £6,000 from 1 October until 30 November.

7.6 This should serve as a useful summary.

CREDIT TRANSACTIONS	
SALES by the business to a customer	PURCHASES by the business from a supplier
↓ creates a DEBTOR a customer who owes money to the business	↓ creates a CREDITOR a supplier who is owed money by the business
↓ recorded as an ASSET of the business	↓ recorded as a LIABILITY of the business
↓ settled when the business RECEIVES CASH	↓ settled when the business PAYS CASH

7.7 EXAMPLE CONTINUED: DEBTORS AND CREDITORS

The example of Petula's market stall will be continued further, by looking at the following transactions in the week to 17 July 20X7.

(a) Petula realises that she is going to need more money in the business and so she makes the following arrangements.

   (i) She invests a further £250 of her own capital.

   (ii) Her Uncle Zappa lends her £500. Uncle Zappa tells her that she can repay the loan whenever she likes, but in the meantime she must pay him interest of £5 per week each week at the end of the market day. They agree that it will probably be a long time before the loan is eventually repaid.

(b) She is very pleased with the progress of her business, and decides that she can afford to buy a second-hand van to pick up flowers and plants from her supplier and bring them to her stall in the market. She finds a car dealer, Arthur, who agrees to sell her a van on credit for £700. Petula agrees to pay for the van after 30 days' trial use.

(c) During the week before the next market day (which is on 17 July), Petula's Uncle Iggy asks whether she would sell him some garden gnomes and furniture for his garden. Petula tells him that she will look for a supplier. After some investigations, she buys what Uncle Iggy has asked for, paying £300 in cash to the supplier. Uncle Iggy accepts delivery of the goods and agrees to pay £350 at a later date.

(d) The next market day approaches, and Petula buys flowers and plants costing £800. Of these purchases £750 are paid in cash, with the remaining £50 on seven days' credit. Petula decides to use Loukis's services again as an assistant on market day, at an agreed wage of £40.

(e) For the third market day running, on 17 July, Petula succeeds in selling all her goods, earning revenue of £1,250 (all in cash). She takes out drawings of £240 for her week's work. She pays Loukis £40 in cash. She decides to make the interest payment to her Uncle Zappa the next time she sees him.

(f) There were no van expenses.

First of all we want to state the accounting equations:

(a) After Petula and Uncle Zappa have put more money into the business

(b) After the purchase of the van

(c) After the sale of goods to Uncle Iggy

(d) After the purchase of goods for the weekly market

(e) At the end of the day's trading on 17 July, and after drawings have been withdrawn from profit

Then we are going to state the business equation showing profit earned during the week ended 17 July.

7.8 SOLUTION

This solution deals with each transaction one at a time in chronological order, highlighting the numbers that change each time with an asterisk*. (In practice, it would be possible to do one set of calculations which combines the results of all the transactions, but we shall come to this 'shortcut' method later.)

(a) The addition of Petula's extra capital and Uncle Zappa's loan.

Uncle Zappa's loan is long term, but he is not an owner of the business, even though he has made an investment of a loan to it. He would only become an owner if Petula offered him a partnership in the business. To the business, Uncle Zappa is a long-term creditor, and his investment is a **liability** of the business - it is not business capital.

The accounting equation after £(250 + 500) = £750 cash is put into the business will be:

Assets		=	*Capital*		+	*Liabilities*	
	£			£			£
Stall	1,800		As at end of 10 July	2,690		Loan	*500
Goods	0		Additional capital	*250			
Cash £(890 + 750*)	*1,640						
	3,440			2,940			500

(b) The purchase of the van (cost £700) is on credit, so Petula doesn't have to pay until later.

Assets		=	*Capital*		+	*Liabilities*	
	£			£			£
Stall	1,800		As at end of 10 July	2,690		Loan	500
Van	*700		Additional capital	250		Creditor	*700
Cash	1,640						
	4,140			2,940			1,200

(c) The sale of goods to Uncle Iggy is on credit (£350), the cost to the business being £300 (cash paid). Uncle Iggy, because he is paying later, is shown as a debtor.

Assets		= *Capital*		+ *Liabilities*	
	£		£		£
Stall	1,800	As at end of 10 July	2,690	Loan	500
Van	700	Additional capital	250	Creditor	700
Debtors	*350	Profit on sale to Uncle Iggy	*50		
Cash £(1,640 – 300*)	*1,340				
	4,190		2,990		1,200

(d) After the purchase of goods for the weekly market (£750 paid in cash and £50 of purchases on credit) we have:

Assets		= *Capital*		+ *Liabilities*	
	£		£		£
Stall	1,800	As at end of 10 July	2,690	Loan	500
Van	700	Additional capital	250	Creditor for car	700
Goods	*800	Profit on sale to Uncle Iggy	50	Creditor for goods	*50
Debtor	350				
Cash £(1,340 – 750*)	*590				
	4,240		2,990		1,250

(e) After market trading on 17 July. Sales of goods costing £800 earned revenues of £1,250. Loukis's wages were £40 (paid), Uncle Zappa's interest charge is £5 (not paid yet) and drawings out of profits were £240 (paid). The profit for 17 July may be calculated as follows, taking the full £5 of interest as a cost on that day.

	£	£
Sales		1,250
Cost of goods sold	800	
Wages	40	
Interest	5	
		845
Profits earned on 17 July		405

Assets		= *Capital*		+ *Liabilities*	
	£		£		£
Stall	1,800	As at end of 10 July	2,690	Loan	500
Van	700	Additional capital	250	Creditor for van	700
Goods	*0			Creditor for Goods	50
Debtor	350				
Cash £(590 + 1,250* – 40* – 240*)	*1,560	Profit for week (405 + 50)	*455	Creditor for interest payment	*5
		Drawings	*(240)		
	4,410		3,155		1,255

7.9 The increase in the net assets of the business during the week was as follows.

	£
Net assets as at the end of 17 July £(4,410 – 1,255)	3,155
Net assets as at the end of 10 July	2,690
Increase in net assets in week	465

The business equation for the week ended 17 July is as follows. (Remember that extra capital of £250 was invested by Petula.)

$$
\begin{aligned}
P &= I + D - C \\
&= £465 + £240 - £250 \\
&= £455
\end{aligned}
$$

This confirms the calculation of total profit.

Activity 1.4 **Level: Pre-assessment**

Liza has £2,500 of capital invested in her business. Of this, only £1,750 has been provided by herself, the balance being provided by a loan of £750 from Phil. What are the implications of this for the accounting equation?

Hint. The answer is not necessarily clear cut. There are different ways of looking at Phil's investment.

8 DOUBLE ENTRY BOOK-KEEPING

ASSESSMENT ALERT

You will always be asked to demonstrate your knowledge of double entry book-keeping in the Devolved Assessment.

8.1 Since the **total of liabilities plus capital is always equal to total assets,** any transaction has a **dual effect** - if it changes the amount of total assets it also changes the total liabilities plus capital, and *vice versa*. Alternatively, a transaction might use up assets to obtain other assets of the same value. For example, if a business pays £50 in cash for some goods, its total assets will be unchanged. Cash falls by £50, the value of goods in stock rises by £50.

8.2 There are two sides to every business transaction. From this concept has developed the system of accounting known as the 'double entry' system of bookkeeping. Every transaction is recorded twice in the accounts.

KEY TERM

Double entry book-keeping is the system of accounting which reflects the fact that:

- Every financial transaction gives rise to two accounting entries, one a debit and the other a credit.
- The total value of **debit entries** is therefore always equal at any time to the total value of **credit entries.**

8.3 Each asset, liability, item of expense or item of income has a **ledger account** in which debits and credits are made. Which account receives the credit entry and which receives the debit depends on the nature of the transaction.

8.4 Below is a summary. Later in the text we shall look again in detail at double entry.

DEBIT To own/have ↓	**CREDIT** To owe ↓
AN ASSET INCREASES eg new office furniture	AN ASSET DECREASES eg pay out cash
CAPITAL/ A LIABILITY DECREASES eg pay a creditor	CAPITAL/A LIABILITY INCREASES eg buy goods on credit
INCOME DECREASES eg cancel a sale	INCOME INCREASES eg make a sale
AN EXPENSE INCREASES eg incur advertising costs	AN EXPENSE DECREASES eg cancel a purchase
Left hand side	**Right hand side**

Activity 1.5 **Level: Pre-assessment**

Try to explain the dual effects of each of the following transactions.

(a) A business receives a loan of £5,000 from its bank
(b) A business pays £800 cash to purchase a stock of goods for resale
(c) The proprietor of a business removes £50 from the till to buy her husband a birthday present
(d) A business sells goods costing £300 at a profit of £140
(e) A business repays a £5,000 bank loan, plus interest of £270

Key learning points

- In order to achieve competence in the Devolved Assessment for Unit 1 it is vital that you acquire a thorough understanding of the **principles of double entry bookkeeping.**
- A **business** may be defined in various ways. Its purpose is to make a **profit** for its owner(s).
- **Profit** is the excess of income over expenditure.
- A business **owns assets** and **owes liabilities**.
- For accounting purposes it is important to keep business assets and liabilities **separate** from the personal assets and liabilities of the owners.
- **Assets** are items belonging to a business and used in the running of the business. They may be **fixed** (such as machinery or office premises), or **current** (such as stock, debtors and cash).
- **Liabilities** are sums of money owed by a business to outsiders such as a bank or a trade creditor.
- **Assets = Capital + Liabilities** (the accounting equation).
- **P = I + D – C** (the business equation).
- Double entry book-keeping requires that every transaction has two accounting entries, a **debit** and a **credit.**

Quick quiz

1 What is a business's prime objective?

2 Define profit.

3 What is an asset?

4 What is a liability?

5 How does the accounting view of the relationship between a business and its owner differ from the strictly legal view?

6 State the basic accounting equation.

7 What is capital?

8 What are drawings? Where do they fit in the accounting equation?

9 What does the business equation attempt to show?

10 What is the main difference between a cash and a credit transaction?

11 What is a creditor? What is a debtor?

12 Define double entry book-keeping.

Answers to quick quiz

1 A business's prime objective is earning a profit.

2 Profit is the excess of income over expenditure.

3 An asset is something valuable which a business owns or has the use of.

4 A liability is something which is owed to someone else.

5 In accounting a business is always treated as a separate entity from its owners, even though in law there is not always a distinction (in the cases of a sole trader and a partnership).

6 Assets = Capital + Liabilities.

7 Capital is the investment of funds with the intention of earning a profit.

8 Drawings are the amounts of money taken out of a business by its owner. In the accounting equation drawings are a reduction of capital.

9 The business equation describes the relationship between a business's increase in net assets in a period, the profit earned, drawings taken and capital introduced.

10 The main difference between a cash and a credit transaction is simply a matter of time - cash changes hands immediately in a cash transaction, whereas in a credit one it changes hands some time after the initial sale/purchase takes place.

11 A creditor is a person that a business owes money to. A debtor is a person who owes a business money.

12 Double entry book-keeping is a system of accounting which reflects the fact that every financial transaction gives rise to two equal accounting entries, a debit and a credit.

2 Capital and revenue items

This chapter contains

1 Introduction to financial statements
2 The balance sheet
3 Fixed assets
4 Current assets
5 Liabilities
6 The profit and loss account
7 So what goes where? - capital and revenue items

Learning objectives

On completion of this chapter you will have learned about:

- Relevant understanding of the organisation's accounting systems and administrative systems and procedures
- The nature of the organisation's business transactions

1 INTRODUCTION TO FINANCIAL STATEMENTS

1.1 In Chapter 1 you were introduced to the idea of the accounting and business equations. If you understand these, you should have little difficulty in getting to grips with the concepts of the **balance sheet** and the **profit and loss account**.

ASSESSMENT ALERT

Strictly speaking, you do not need to know about these two statements, but an overview will give you a better understanding of book-keeping and double entry. It will also make clearer the distinction between capital and revenue transactions, discussed in Section 7, which is likely to come up in Devolved Assessments regularly.

2 THE BALANCE SHEET

KEY TERM

A **balance sheet** is a statement of the assets, liabilities and capital of a business at a given moment in time. It is like a 'snapshot' photograph, since it captures on paper a still image, frozen at a single moment in time, of something which is dynamic and continually changing. Typically, a balance sheet is prepared to show the assets, liabilities and capital as at the **end** of the accounting period to which the financial statements relate.

2.1 A **balance sheet** is very similar to the **accounting equation**.

Assets = Capital introduced + Retained profit – Liabilities

There are only two differences between a balance sheet and the accounting equation.

(a) The manner or **format** in which the assets and liabilities are presented
(b) The extra **detail** which is contained in a balance sheet

2.2 A balance sheet is divided into two halves, usually showing **capital** in one half and **net assets** (ie assets less liabilities) in the other.

NAME OF BUSINESS
BALANCE SHEET AS AT (DATE)

	£
Assets	X
Less liabilities	X
Net assets	X
Capital	X

The total value in one half of the balance sheet will equal the total value in the other half. You should understand this from the **accounting equation**.

2.3 For many organisations, the way in which assets and liabilities are categorised and presented in a balance sheet is a matter of choice, and you may come across different formats. The format below should help you see how a typical balance sheet is compiled.

XYZ
BALANCE SHEET AS AT 31 DECEMBER 20X7

	£	£
Fixed assets		
Land and buildings	X	
Plant and machinery	X	
Fixtures and fittings	X	
		X
Current assets		
Stock	X	
Debtors	X	
Cash at bank and in hand	X	
	A	
Current liabilities		
Bank overdraft	X	
Trade creditors	X	
	B	
Net current assets (A – B)		X
Long-term liabilities		(X)
Net assets		C
Capital		
Proprietor's capital		X
Retained profits (including previous and current year profits)		X
		C

3 FIXED ASSETS

3.1 Assets in the balance sheet are divided into **fixed** and **current** assets, as we saw in Chapter 1.

> **KEY TERM**
>
> A **fixed asset** is an asset acquired for use within the business (rather than for selling to a customer), with a view to earning income or making profits from its use, either directly or indirectly, over more than one accounting period.

Examples are as follows. These are only ideas; you may well be able to think of other assets.

Industry	Example of fixed asset
Manufacturing	A production machine, because it makes goods which are then sold.
Service	Equipment used by employees giving service to customers, such as testing machines and ramps in a garage, and furniture in a hotel.

3.2 To be classed as a fixed asset in the balance sheet of a business, an item must satisfy two further conditions.

(a) It must be **used by the business**. For example, the proprietor's own house would not normally appear on the business balance sheet.

(b) The asset must have a **'life' in use of more than one year** (strictly, more than one 'accounting period', which might be more or less than one year).

4 CURRENT ASSETS

KEY TERM

Current assets are *either*:

- Items owned by the business with the intention of turning them into cash within one year (stocks of goods, and debtors)
- Cash, including money in the bank, owned by the business

Assets are 'current' in the sense that they are continually flowing through the business.

Activity 2.1 **Level: Pre-assessment**

The type of asset held by of a business depends on the nature of its trading activities. Try to imagine what the main assets might be in the accounts of:

(a) A steel manufacturer
(b) A bank.

4.1 EXAMPLE: TURNING STOCK AND DEBTORS INTO CASH WITHIN ONE YEAR

Let us suppose that a trader, Chris, runs a business selling cars, and has a showroom which he stocks with cars for sale. He obtains the cars from a manufacturer, and pays for them cash on delivery (COD).

(a) If he sells a car in a **cash sale**, the 'goods' are immediately converted back into cash (hopefully more cash than he paid for them, making a profit). This cash might then be used to buy more cars for sale.

(b) If he sells a car in a **credit sale**, expecting payment in 14 days time, the car will be given to the customer who then becomes a **debtor** of the business. Eventually, the debtor will pay what he owes, and Chris will receive cash. The cash might then be used to buy more cars for sale.

4.2 The cars, debtors and cash are all current assets. Why?

(a) The cars (**goods**) held in stock for re-sale are current assets, because Chris intends to sell them within one year, in the normal course of trade.

(b) The **debtor** is a current asset, as he is expected to pay what he owes in 14 days.

(c) **Cash** is a current asset.

4.3 The transactions described above could be shown as a **cash cycle**.

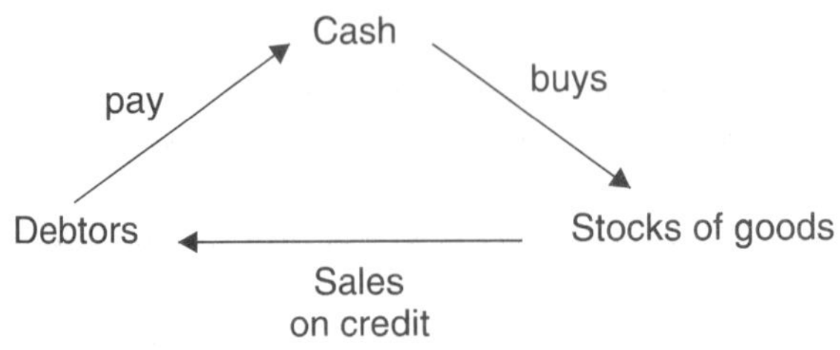

Cash is used to buy goods which are sold. Sales on credit create debtors, but eventually cash is earned from the sales. Some, perhaps most, of the cash will then be used to replenish stocks.

Activity 2.2 **Level: Pre-assessment**

Which of the following assets falls into the 'fixed' category and which should be treated as 'current'?

Asset	Business	Current or fixed
Van	Delivery firm	
Machine	Manufacturer	
Car	Car trader	

---

5 LIABILITIES

5.1 In the case of liabilities, the main distinction is made between:

- **Current** liabilities
- **Long-term** liabilities

Current liabilities

KEY TERM

Current liabilities are debts of the business that must be paid within a fairly short period of time (by convention, within one year).

5.2 Examples of current liabilities include **loans** repayable in one year, **bank overdrafts, trade creditors** and **taxation payable**.

5.3 Some may argue that a **bank overdraft** is not a current liability, because a business is usually able to negotiate an overdraft facility for a long period of time. However, you should normally expect to account for an overdraft as a current liability, since banks usually reserve the right to have repayment on demand.

Activity 2.3 **Level: Pre-assessment**

Try to classify the following items as long-term assets ('fixed assets'), short-term assets ('current assets') or liabilities.

(a) A PC used in the accounts department of a retail store
(b) A PC on sale in an office equipment shop
(c) Wages due to be paid to staff at the end of the week
(d) A van for sale in a motor dealer's showroom
(e) A delivery van used in a grocer's business
(f) An amount owing to a bank for a loan for the acquisition of a van, to be repaid over 9 months

---

Long-term liabilities

KEY TERM

Long-term liabilities are debts which are not payable within the 'short term'. Any liability which is not current must be long-term. Just as 'short-term' by convention means one year or less, 'long-term' means more than one year.

5.4 Examples of long-term liabilities are bank or venture capital fund loans **repayable after more than one year**.

Capital

5.5 The make-up of the 'capital' section of the balance sheet will vary, depending on the legal nature of the business. It will include **amounts invested** by the owner(s) in the business, plus **profits earned and retained** by the business

Activity 2.4 **Level: Pre-assessment**

Reproduced below is an example of a balance sheet

MANDERS LTD
BALANCE SHEET AS AT 31 DECEMBER 20X7

	£	£
Fixed assets		
Land and buildings	50,000	
Plant and machinery	28,000	
Fixtures and fittings	7,500	
		85,500
Current assets		
Stocks	6,200	
Debtors	7,100	
Cash at bank and in hand	2,500	
	15,800	
Creditors: amounts falling due within one year		
Bank overdraft	1,700	
Trade creditors	4,900	
	6,600	
Net current assets		9,200
Total assets less current liabilities		94,700
Capital		
Proprietor's capital		30,000
Retained profits		64,700
		94,700

Using the figures in the balance sheet above, check that the accounting equation holds good in the form: Assets = Capital + Liabilities.

6 THE PROFIT AND LOSS ACCOUNT

KEY TERM

The **profit and loss account** is a statement which matches the **revenue** earned in a period with the **costs** incurred in earning it. It is usual to distinguish between a **gross profit** (sales less cost of goods sold) and a **net profit** (being the gross profit less the expenses of selling, distribution, administration etc). If costs exceed revenue the business has made a **loss.**

6.1 Any organisation needs income (or revenue) from one or more sources. A **business** will **sell** its **goods or services** to **customers** in exchange for **cash**.

6.2 The income generated will be used to finance the activities of the business which incur **costs**: purchasing raw materials for use in manufacturing goods, purchasing ready-made goods for onward sale, purchasing equipment, paying expenses such as staff salaries, stationery, lighting and heating, rent and so on.

6.3 **Revenue** less **costs** result in a **profit or loss.** Periodically the organisation will prepare a **trading and profit and loss account**.

The trading, profit and loss account

6.4 Many businesses try to distinguish between a **gross profit** earned on trading, and a **net profit**. They prepare a statement called a **trading, profit and loss account.**

(a) In the first part of the statement (the **trading account**) revenue from selling goods and services is compared with direct costs of acquiring, producing or supplying the goods sold to arrive at a **gross profit figure**.

(b) From this, deductions are made in the second half of the statement (the **profit and loss account**) in respect of indirect costs (overheads) to arrive at a **net profit figure**.

6.5 As with the balance sheet earlier in this chapter, it may help you to focus on the content of the profit and loss account if you have an example in front of you.

XYZ
TRADING, PROFIT AND LOSS ACCOUNT
FOR THE YEAR ENDED 31 DECEMBER 20X7

	£	£
Sales		X
Cost of sales		X
Gross profit		X
Selling costs	X	
Distribution costs	X	
Administration expenses	X	
		X
Profit retained for the current year		X

The trading account

KEY TERMS

- The **trading account** shows the gross profit for the accounting period.
- **Gross profit** is the difference between:
  - The value of sales
  - The purchase cost or production cost of the goods sold

6.6 Different businesses will have different items shown as the cost of goods sold.

Business	Cost of goods sold
Retail	Purchase cost of goods bought from suppliers
Manufacturing	Cost of raw materials in the finished goods made, **plus** the cost of the labour required to make the goods, and often **plus** an amount of production 'overhead' costs

The profit and loss account

KEY TERMS

- The **profit and loss account** shows the net profit of the business.
- The **net profit** is:
  - The gross profit
  - **Plus** any other income from sources other than the sale of goods
  - **Minus** other 'overhead' expenses of the business which are not included in the cost of goods sold, mainly selling, distribution and administration expenses.

6.7 Typical expenses falling into the **overhead category** are as follows.

Overhead expenses	Include
Selling	• Salaries of a sales director and sales management • Salaries and commissions of salesmen • Travelling and entertainment expenses of salesmen • Marketing costs (eg advertising and sales promotion expenses) • Discounts allowed to customers for early payment of their debts
Distribution	The costs of getting goods to customers, such as the costs of running and maintaining delivery vans
Administration	The expenses of providing management and administration for the business, for example, rent and rates, insurance, telephone and postage, stationery

Activity 2.5 **Level: Pre-assessment**

Suggest three items which might be included in administration expenses.

6.8 EXAMPLE: TRADING, PROFIT AND LOSS ACCOUNT

On 1 June 20X7, Mr Whippy commenced trading as an ice-cream salesman, selling ice-creams from a van.

(a) He borrowed £2,000 from his bank, and the interest cost of the loan was £25 per month.

(b) He rented the van at a cost of £1,000 for three months. Running expenses for the van averaged £300 per month.

(c) He hired a part-time helper at a cost of £100 per month.

(d) His main business was to sell ice-cream to customers in the street, but he also did some special catering arrangements for business customers, supplying ice-creams for office parties. Sales to these customers were usually on credit.

(e) For the three months to 31 August 20X7, his total sales were:

  (i) Cash sales £8,900
  (ii) Credit sales £1,100 (all paid by 31 August 20X7)

(f) He purchased his ice-cream from a local manufacturer, Melted Ltd. The cost of purchases in the three months to 31 August 20X7 was £6,200, and at 31 August he had sold all of it. He still owed £700 to Melted Ltd for unpaid purchases on credit.

(g) He used his own home for his office work. Telephone and postage expenses for the three months to 31 August were £150.

(h) During the period he paid himself £300 per month.

We need to prepare a trading and profit and loss account for the three months 1 June - 31 August 20X7.

6.9 SOLUTION

MR WHIPPY
TRADING AND PROFIT AND LOSS ACCOUNT
FOR THE THREE MONTHS ENDED 31 AUGUST 20X7

	£	£
Sales (8,900 + 1,100) (e)		10,000
Cost of sales (f)		– 6,200
Gross profit		3,800
Expenses		
Wages (c)	300	
Van rental (b)	1,000	
Van expenses (b)	900	
Telephone and postage (g)	150	
Interest charges (a)	75	
		2,425
Net profit earned in the period (transferred to the balance sheet)		1,375

Note the following points.

(1) The **net profit** is the profit for the period, and it is transferred to the balance sheet of the business as part of the proprietor's capital.

(2) **Drawings** are withdrawals of profit and not expenses. They must not be included in the profit and loss account. In this example, the payments that Mr Whippy makes to himself (£900) are drawings. **These are shown as a reduction in the profit and loss account figure on the face of the balance sheet.**

(3) The cost of sales is £6,200, even though £700 of the costs have not yet been paid for and Melted Ltd is still a creditor for £700 in the balance sheet.

Activity 2.6 — Level: Pre-assessment

Having arrived at a net profit figure, see if you can draw up a balance sheet for Mr Whippy. Don't panic - fill in the figures below.

Step 1 *Cash*

	£
Borrowed from bank 1 June 20X7	
(a) Interest charges	
(b) Van hire	
Van running expenses	
(c) Part-time helper	
(e) Cash sales	
Credit sales	
(f) Purchase of ice cream	
(g) Telephone and postage	
(h) Drawings	
Balance in hand at 31 August 20X7	

Step 2 *Accounting equation at 1 June 20X7*

Assets	£	=	*Capital*	£	+	*Liabilities*	£
Cash				0		Bank loan	

Accounting equation at 31 August 20X7

Assets	£	=	*Capital*	£	+	*Liabilities*	£
Cash			Profit			Bank loan	
			Drawings			Melted Ltd	

Step 3 *Business equation (to check profit figure)*

P	=	I	+	D	–	C
P	=	£	+	£	–	£0

Step 4 Prepare balance sheet.

MR WHIPPY
BALANCE SHEET AS AT 31 AUGUST 20X7

	£	£
Current assets		
Cash	3175	
Current liabilities	2,000	
Bank loan	700	
Trade creditors		
	2,700	
Net assets		475
Capital		
Proprietor's opening capital		0
Net profit for period		1,375
Drawings		− 900
		475

7 SO WHAT GOES WHERE? - CAPITAL AND REVENUE ITEMS

7.1 You have seen how the profit and loss account and balance sheet are developed, and how they are linked via the accounting equation. What you will still be concerned about is how we distinguish between items which appear in the **calculation of profit**, and those which belong on the **balance sheet**.

7.2 Consider the following examples.

(a) A business sells goods worth £20,000 (for cash) during one month, and during the same month borrows £10,000 from a bank. Its total receipts for the month are therefore £30,000.

(b) A business spends £15,000 buying some land, and receives £1,000 rent from the tenant farmer in the year.

How would these amounts be accounted for in the profit and loss account and/or balance sheet?

7.3 The answer is as follows.

(a) (i) The £20,000 of sales appear as **sales** in the **trading, profit and loss account** and as an **asset** (cash) in the **balance sheet**.

(ii) The £10,000 borrowed will not be shown in the profit and loss account, but will be shown as an **asset** (cash) and a **liability** (loan) of £10,000 in the **balance sheet**.

(b) (i) The cost of the land will not be an expense in the profit and loss account. It will appear as a **fixed asset** in the **balance sheet**. Paying out the cash will decrease an **asset** (cash) in the **balance sheet.**

(ii) The rent of £1,000 will appear as **income** of the business in the **profit and loss account,** and as an **asset** (cash) in the **balance sheet.**

7.4 So how do we make these decisions? To try to make them we must now turn our attention to the distinction between **capital** and **revenue** items.

Capital and revenue expenditure

KEY TERMS

- **Capital expenditure** is expenditure which results in the acquisition of fixed assets, or an improvement in their earning capacity.
  - Capital expenditure on fixed assets results in the appearance of a fixed asset in the **balance sheet** of the business.
  - Capital expenditure is **not** charged as an expense in the **profit and loss account**.
- **Revenue expenditure** is expenditure which is incurred *either*:
  - For the purpose of the trade of the business, including expenditure classified as selling and distribution expenses, administration expenses and finance charges
  - To maintain the *existing* earning capacity of fixed assets, eg repairs to fixed assets

Revenue expenditure is shown in the **profit and loss account of a period,** provided that it relates to the trading activity and sales of that particular period. If it carries over into the next period, revenue expenditure would appear as a **current asset** in the balance sheet.

7.5 EXAMPLE: REVENUE EXPENDITURE

If a business buys ten widgets for £200 (£20 each) and sells eight of them during an accounting period, it will have two widgets left at the end of the period. The full £200 is **revenue expenditure** but only (8 × £20) = £160 is a cost of goods sold during the period. The remaining £40 (cost of two units) will be included in the **balance sheet** in the stock of goods held - as a **current asset** valued at £40.

Capital income and revenue income

KEY TERMS

- **Capital income** is the proceeds from the sale of non-trading assets (ie proceeds from the sale of fixed assets). The profits (or losses) from the sale of fixed assets are included in the **profit and loss account** of a business, for the accounting period in which the sale takes place.
- **Revenue income** is income derived from:
  - The sale of trading assets, such as goods bought or made for resale
  - Rent, interest and dividends received from fixed assets held by the business.

Revenue income appears in the **profit and loss account.**

Additional capital, additional loans and the repayment of existing loans

7.6 The categorisation of capital and revenue items given above does not mention raising additional capital from the owner of the business, or raising and repaying loans. These are transactions which either:

(a) Add to the cash **assets** of the business, thereby creating a corresponding **capital** or a **liability**.

(b) Or when a loan is repaid, reduce the **liabilities** (loan) and the **assets** (cash) of the business.

From your understanding of the accounting equation, you should see that these transactions would be reported through the balance sheet, **not** the profit and loss account.

Why is the distinction between capital and revenue items important?

7.7 Since **revenue expenditure** and **capital expenditure** are accounted for in different ways (in the **profit and loss account** and **balance sheet** respectively), the correct and consistent calculation of profit for any accounting period depends on the correct and consistent classification of items as revenue or capital. Failure to classify items correctly will lead to misleading profit figures.

ASSESSMENT ALERT

Questions on the distinction between revenue and capital items are likely to come up in assessment for this Unit, so make sure you attempt the next two activities.

Activity 2.7 **Level: Pre-assessment**

Complete the missing words to ensure you fully understand the difference between capital and revenue items.

Revenue expenditure results from the purchase of goods and services that will either:

(a) Be __________ fully in the accounting period in which they are ________, and so be a cost or expense in the trading, profit and loss account.

(b) Or result in a ________ asset as at the end of the accounting period (because the goods or services have not yet been consumed or made use of).

Capital expenditure results in the purchase or improvement of ________ assets, which are assets that will provide benefits to the business in more than ________ accounting period, and which are not acquired with a view to being resold in the normal course of trade. The cost of purchased fixed assets is not charged to the trading, profit and loss account of the period in which the purchase occurs.

Activity 2.8 **Level: Assessment**

State whether each of the following items should be classified as 'capital' or 'revenue' expenditure or income for the purpose of preparing the trading, profit and loss account and the balance sheet of the business.

(a) Purchase of leasehold premises capital

(b) Solicitors' fees in connection with the purchase of leasehold premises capital

(c) Costs of adding extra storage capacity to a mainframe computer used by the business capital

(d) Computer repair and maintenance costs

(e) Profit on the sale of an office building

(f) Revenue from sales by credit card

(g) Cost of new machinery

(h) Customs duty charged on the machinery when imported into the country

(i) 'Carriage' costs of transporting the new machinery from the supplier's factory to the premises of the business purchasing the machinery

(j) Cost of installing the new machinery in the premises of the business

(k) Wages of the machine operators

Key learning points

- The purpose of this chapter has been to introduce the characteristics of the balance sheet and the trading, profit and loss account so you can understand the distinction between **capital and revenue items** more easily.
- A **balance sheet** is a statement of the financial position of a business at a given moment in time.
- A **trading, profit and loss account** is a financial statement showing in detail how the profit or loss of a period has been made.
- A distinction is made in the balance sheet between **long-term liabilities** and **current liabilities,** and between **fixed assets** and **current assets.**
- **Fixed assets** are those acquired for long-term use within the business.
- 'Current' means 'within one year'. **Current assets** are expected to be converted into cash within one year. **Current liabilities** are debts which are payable within one year.
- An important distinction is made between **capital** and **revenue** items. If these are not identified correctly, then the resulting **profit figure** will be wrong and misleading.

Quick quiz

1. What is a balance sheet?
2. How long does a business keep a fixed asset?
3. What are current liabilities?
4. Is a bank overdraft a current liability?
5. What is a profit and loss account?
6. Distinguish between the trading account and the profit and loss account.
7. Distinguish between capital expenditure and revenue expenditure.

Answers to quick quiz

1. A balance sheet is a listing of asset and liability balances on a certain date. The balance sheet gives a 'snapshot' of the net worth of the company at a single point in time.
2. At least one accounting period and usually several.
3. Amounts owed which must be paid soon, usually within one year.
4. Yes, usually, because it is repayable on demand.

5 A profit and loss account matches revenue with the costs incurred in earning it.

6 The trading account shows the gross profit; the profit and loss account shows net profit (gross profit plus non-trading income, less overhead expenses).

7 Capital expenditure results in a fixed asset appearing on the balance sheet. Revenue expenditure is trading expenditure or expenditure in maintaining fixed assets, which appears in the profit and loss account.

3 Documenting business transactions

This chapter contains

Learning objectives

On completion of this chapter you will have learned about:

- Operation of manual and computerised accounting systems
- Types of business transactions and documents involved
- Types of discounts
- General principles of VAT
- Relevant understanding of the organisation's accounting systems and administrative systems and procedures
- The nature of the organisations business transactions
- Methods of coding data
- Batch control

Performance criteria

1.1.1 Invoices and credit notes are prepared in accordance with organisational requirements and checked against source documents

1.1.2 Calculations on invoices and credit notes are checked for accuracy

1.1.3 Invoices and credit notes are correctly authorised and coded before being sent to customers

1.1.5 Entries are coded and recorded in the appropriate ledger

Range statement

1.1.1 Source documents: quotations; purchase orders; delivery notes; sales orders

1.1.2 Calculations: pricing; price extensions; discounts; VAT

1 INTRODUCTION

1.1 With the help of Petula and Mr Whippy we have come a long way: from the nature of a business to preparing a profit and loss account and balance sheet, via the accounting and business equations and a brief look at double-entry book-keeping.

1.2 What we have to consider now is how a real business, operating from year to year with numerous different transactions, succeeds in preparing a profit and loss account and balance sheet. Each transaction will need **documenting, recording, summarising** and **presenting** so that, when we look at sales figures in the profit and loss account, we are seeing the result of hundreds, thousands or even millions of individual sales to different customers.

2 DOCUMENTING BUSINESS TRANSACTIONS

Business transactions

2.1 Whenever property changes hands there has been a **business transaction**. The simplest form of business transaction is a cash transaction.

KEY TERM

A **cash transaction** is one where the buyer pays cash to the seller at the time goods or services are transferred.

In a **credit transaction,** as we saw in Chapter 1, there is a time-lag between the sale/purchase taking place and cash changing hands.

External documentation

2.2 It is usual to record a business transaction on a **document**. The amount of documentation required will vary depending on the type of transaction and the people involved.

(a) If you buy a **small item** from a market stall and pay cash, it is unlikely that any documents would change hands unless you ask for a receipt.

(b) If you were having a **central heating system** installed, the paperwork involved might include the following. (This is summarised on the diagram following Paragraph 2.3)

(i) Firstly, you get in touch with the central heating business either by phone, or by **letter of enquiry**.

(ii) The central heating business will probably send round a sales engineer, to visit you. He will take a look at your residence and estimate how much work needs to be done.

You will receive a **quotation** detailing the price.

(iii) Asking for a quotation does not commit you to anything. Should you wish to proceed with the quotation, the next thing you might do is **send a letter accepting the quotation**. You may, on the other hand, be required to sign a more formal **sales order document**, which you will return to the business.

You should receive an **acknowledgement**.

(iv) The **sales order** you have signed will be used by the central heating business as evidence of what you require. It gives them the 'go-ahead' to prepare and carry out the work.

(v) A great deal of **internal documentation** will then be prepared. A record must be kept of the process of the installation and its costs. Also, the business might keep other documents. We will look at internal documentation in Paragraph 2.5.

(vi) Your central heating system has now been installed. The central heating staff will ask you to sign a **delivery note**.

(vii) The delivery note will be evidence to the business that the job has been completed. This is then taken to the accounts department for review. Eventually you will be sent a **bill or invoice**.

If you are charged too much, you will receive a **credit note**.

(viii) At the end of the agreed period of credit that the business has allowed you, you will pay the invoice by **cheque.**

(ix) The company, on receipt of your cheque, will ensure that it is banked, and recorded in the internal **books of account.**

2.3 Let us put all this in a picture of the **external documentation** involved. We will not examine what happens *inside* the central heating business yet, but just look at the system as a whole.

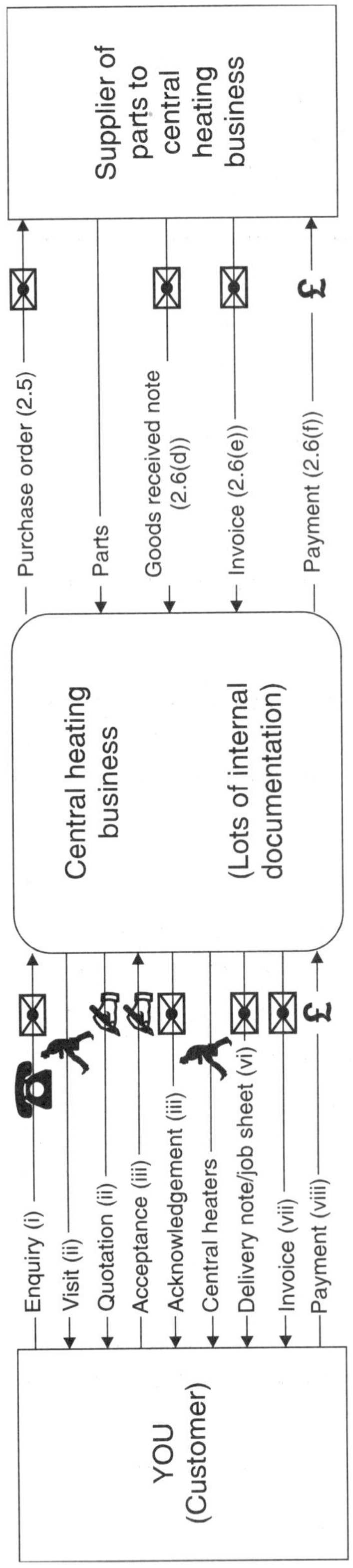

External documentation

2.4 In this one business transaction, then, there has already been a large amount of **paperwork**. It is quite possible that some of this paperwork will not be paperwork at all. It might be automated, and the majority of the transactions will be carried out by **computer**. No matter: **the principles are the same**.

Activity 3.1 **Level: Pre-assessment**

(a) A friend of yours who has no knowledge of accounting matters has asked you to explain the difference between a cash transaction and a credit transaction. What would you say to him?

(b) State what documentation you would expect to change hands in the following circumstances.

(i) You buy a CD from a shop, paying cash
(ii) You have double glazing installed

Internal documentation

2.5 Internal documents needed would include **purchase orders**, if some parts had to be purchased from other suppliers. A similar set of documents to the ones described above, but this time between the central heating business and its suppliers, would then be necessary.

2.6 In addition there will be several other internal documents.

(a) **Stock lists,** to check that all the parts for the central heating system are available. Each part will be identified by its own specific code number.

(b) **Supplier lists,** to trace from the code numbers of the parts which supplier manufactures which item of stock.

(c) **Staff schedules**. The central heating business's engineers will travel from job to job, and it is probable that the right mix of qualified staff must be booked. They will record the actual hours they spend on a **timesheet**.

(d) **Goods received notes.** When the parts ordered have been received, a goods received note might be raised, as formal notification, and for input to the business's own accounting system.

(e) **Invoices.** The business will receive an invoice from its supplier which will be used to update the business's accounting records. A **credit note** may be required.

(f) **Cheques.** The business will eventually pay the supplier by cheque.

2.7 Are more documents involved? Plenty! This is for several reasons.

(a) Yours will not have been the only central heating system installed. The organisation will have hundreds of transactions to schedule, to keep track of, to account for and to keep on a list of **who owes it money**.

(b) The central heating business might also need a list of people **to whom it owes money** (the suppliers of parts for example).

(c) The central heating business needs to ensure that it has enough **cash at the right times** to pay its bills, and to pay its employees.

(d) Comparing what it earns with what it costs is important, as the business hopes to make a **profit**.

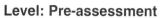

2.8 The diagram below summarises the **internal documentation** required by the central heating business.

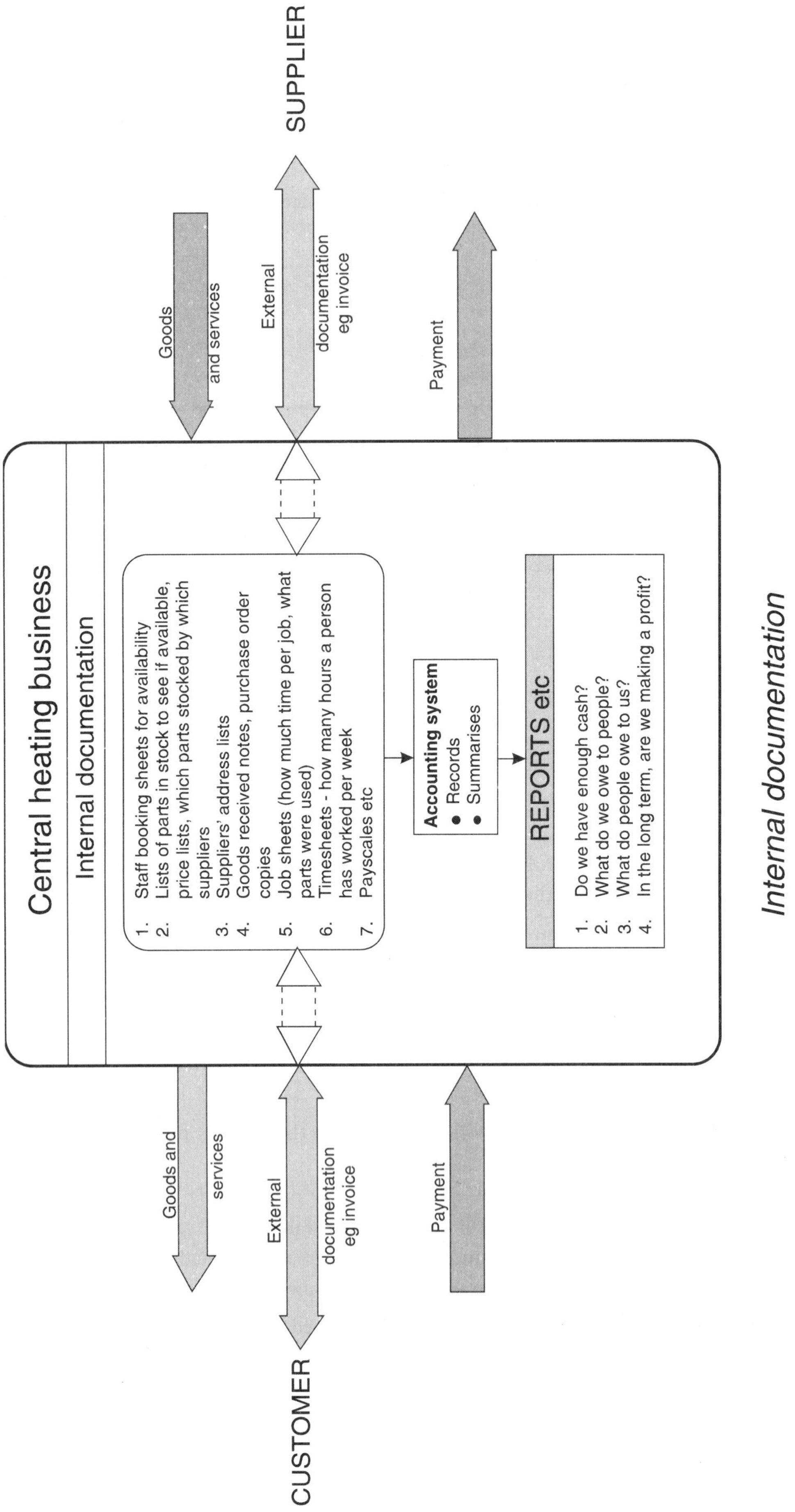

What does the accounting system actually do?

> **KEY TERM**
>
> The purpose of the **accounting system** is to **record, summarise** and **present** the information contained in the documentation generated by transactions.

2.9 In the case of the central heating business, this would entail the following.

(a) The workers who installed the central heating system will expect to be paid. If they are paid an hourly rate, then the *total* number of hours they work in a period must be aggregated.

> This is the job of the **payroll system**, and is covered in Unit 2.

(b) At defined periods the accounting system produces lists of:

- Those who owe the business money (debtors).
- Those to whom the business owes money (creditors).

> This is the job of the **sales ledger** and **purchase** (or **bought**) **ledger** systems.

(c) The accounting system will keep track of the business's resources of **cash,** and the funds in the bank account.

(d) Finally, the accounting system will be used to provide periodic information to management.

2.10 Most of the documents described in Paragraph 2.2 are covered in detail in this Interactive Text. In this chapter we will concentrate on two very important types of document, **invoices** and **credit notes**, as examples of the sort of accounting information contained in business documentation.

3 INVOICES AND CREDIT NOTES

3.1 As an example of the importance of documents in organisations, let us examine the use of the **invoice**. Documents, as we have seen, are created when contact is made between customer and supplier.

(a) **Sales order:** a customer writes out an order or signs an order for goods or services he wishes to buy.

(b) **Purchase order:** a business places an order with another business for the purchase of goods or services, such as material supplies.

The invoice

3.2 **Invoices** are created when there is a sale or a purchase. Remember that what is a **sale** to one business is a **purchase** to the individual or business in receipt of the goods. The details on the invoice should agree with what was on the purchase/sales order.

KEY TERM

An **invoice** is a demand for payment

3.3 Three different uses of the invoice can be described.

Transaction	Example	Document best described as
A transaction is **settled immediately in cash**, with the invoice created as evidence of expense/receipt of payment	Manager paying cash for a business meal in a restaurant	Receipt: invoice marked by restaurant as 'paid with thanks'
An invoice is sent from seller to buyer, and is **paid on receipt of the goods** using cheque or cash	Delivery of new car to company	Cash on delivery (COD) invoice
An invoice is sent after goods have been delivered, with request to **pay within a certain time**	Delivery of raw materials from long-standing supplier on usual credit terms	Credit invoice

3.4 Although you may find it helpful to think of the receipt, the COD invoice and the credit invoice, you will find that usually people refer only to **receipts** (for cash transactions, such as buying a newspaper) and **invoices** (for credit transactions). Remember, however, that not all documents described as invoices are invoices on **credit terms** - they may need to be settled immediately.

What does an invoice show?

3.5 The invoice below is a fairly typical example of a demand for payment from a seller (Bangles Ltd) to a purchaser (ABC Ltd).

BANGLES LTD (a)

Jewel House
Richmans Road
LONDON SE1N 5AB

INVOICE

Invoice Number: 123456 (c)
Date: 01/08/97(d)
Tax Point: 01/08/97(h)
Account Number: 3365

DELIVER TO	INVOICE TO:	
ABC Ltd 112 Peters Square Weyford Kent CR2 2TA (b)	Same address	Telephone Number 0207 123 4567 VAT Registration Number 457 4635 19 Northern Bank plc Code 20-25-42 Account Number 957023

Item Code	Description	Quantity	Unit Price £	Net Amount £
Your order number: 2490				
13579A	Desks (e)	30 (f)	250.00	7,500.00
	Delivery	1	100.00	100.00
			SALES VALUE:	7,600.00
			VAT AT 17.5%:	1,330.00
			AMOUNT PAYABLE:	8,930.00 (g)

(a) Name and address of the seller
(b) Name and address of the purchaser
(c) Invoice number, so that the business can keep track of all the invoices it sends out.
(d) Date of the transaction
(e) Description of what is being sold
(f) Quantity and unit price of what has been sold (30 desks at £250 a desk)
(g) Total amount of the invoice including (in the UK) any details of VAT
(h) The tax point for VAT purposes (see Section 8 of this chapter)

3.6 Points to note about the invoice shown above include the following.

(a) **Delivery address.** Businesses sometimes want goods delivered to somewhere other than their own premises. In this example, ABC Ltd might want the desks delivered directly to one of their own customers.

(b) **Referencing.** A business usually keeps a record of its orders, just as it does of its sales. In this case, ABC Ltd's order number was 2490. Bangles Ltd puts the order number on the invoice so that ABC Ltd can quickly see which order the invoice relates to.

(c) **Unit price.** In our example, desks were £250.00 each, but sometimes goods are sold in batches of, say, 20. If that is the case, then something like '£6 for 20' will be put in the unit price column. The amount of the invoice is calculated in the usual way.

Other information often found on invoices

3.7 Sometimes, the **date by which payment is due**, and other terms of sale, are included on the face of the invoice. 'Net 30 days' means that payment is due 30 days after the date of delivery.

3.8 'FOB' stands for '**free on board**', and may be found on import or export invoices. 'FOB shipping point' means that the supplier pays all costs of carriage (shipping, insurance and freight for example) up to the point of shipping but the customer will have to pay any subsequent carriage costs.

3.9 Two other phrases you may find on an invoice are as follows.

(a) **Ex works.** This means that the price excludes the cost of delivery.

(b) **E & O E.** This stands for 'errors and omissions excepted', meaning that the supplier reserves the right to make alterations to the details as shown on the invoice should any prove at a later date to be incorrect.

Invoice copies

3.10 Invoice forms for different businesses will be designed in different ways, although they all show the same sort of information. Another thing they have in common is that there are usually **several copies of the invoice**.

3.11 Businesses may use as many as four **copies of an invoice**, often as follows.

Copy	Location	Purpose of invoice copy
1	Sent to the **purchaser**	Request to pay for the goods, as we have seen
2	Kept as a **file copy**	Partly to keep records straight, and partly so that the business can prove it made out the invoice in the first place. (In a large business, both the sales and accounts departments may keep copy sales invoices.)
3	**Delivery note** sent to customer for signature, and then retained by seller	Whoever delivers the goods to the purchaser asks the purchaser to sign the note as proof that the goods have actually been delivered. The delivery note is then brought back to the supplier's business and matched with the file copy as proof of the validity of the sale.
4	**Advice note** signed and kept by purchaser	Rather like the delivery note, this goes with the goods but instead of being brought back to the supplier, it is left with the purchaser. The idea is that the purchaser's storekeeper uses it as a sort of checklist to make sure that the goods delivered are the same as those on the invoice.

Note that either copy 3 or copy 4 may be used by the selling business as a 'picking list' for an order, so it can be sure it packs up the required quantities.

Sales order sets

3.12 Another common approach is to use multi-part **sales order sets** so the seller can keep track of the order.

Copy	Location	Purpose of sales order copy
1	Sent to customer	Confirming order
2	Sent to warehouse	Arranging delivery to customer
3	Kept in sales dept	Dealing with customer queries
4	Passed to 'accounts'	Raising an invoice
5	Sent with goods	Acting as advice note for customer to keep
6	Sent with goods	Acting as delivery note - signed by customer and retained by seller
7	Kept in warehouse	Dealing with customer queries

3.13 Multi-part **purchase order sets** follow the same pattern so the purchaser can keep track of his order.

Copy	Location	Purpose of purchase order copy
1	Sent to supplier	To place, or confirm an earlier telephone, order
2	Kept in purchasing department *or* warehouse	For reference, and to compare with supplier's advice and delivery notes
3	Accounts department	To match against invoice and goods received note when delivered

Activity 3.2 **Level: Pre-assessment**

(a) A multi-part sales order set completed on receipt of a customer order may have as many as seven copies. State the possible destination and purpose of each copy.

(b) A multi-part purchase order set generally consists of only three copies. State the usual purpose and destination of each copy.

The credit note

KEY TERM

A **credit note** is used by a seller to cancel part or all of previously issued invoice(s).

3.14 A seller might sometimes give the purchaser a **credit note**, so that the total amount payable to the seller is the value of the unpaid invoice **minus** the amount of the credit note.

3.15 Credit notes can be treated like **negative invoices**. They should be matched with the seller's invoices and when the invoices to the seller are paid, the cheque should be made up for the value of the invoices **minus** the credit notes.

3.16 EXAMPLE: INVOICE AND CREDIT NOTE

ABC Ltd has received an invoice from its supplier, Keats Supplies Ltd, for office stationery. There has been some dispute with the supplier about the goods, and the supplier has issued a credit note. The invoice and credit note are held in the accounts department's file of unpaid invoices, and are as shown on the next page.

If the accounts department prepares a cheque for payment on 24 April 20X7, the amount of the cheque will be £470 less £117.50 = £352.50.

The cheque counterfoil could include a note of the invoice number (123678) and credit note number (2045). Both the invoice and credit note should be stamped, PAID and CLAIMED respectively, with the date of payment (24/4/X7).

KEATS SUPPLIES LTD

15 Great Way
Hending
Kent KN5 3TX

INVOICE

Invoice Number:	123678
Date:	25th March 19X7
Tax Point:	25/03/X7
Account Number:	B138

Attention: J Smith
ABC Ltd
112 Peters Square
Weyford
Kent CR2 2TA

AUTHORISED
JS
25/3/X7
Credit to follow

Quantity	Code	Description	Unit Price £	Net Amount £
200	X12345Y	Ring Binders	2.00	400.00

TOTAL GOODS:	400.00
VAT AT 17.5%:	70.00
AMOUNT PAYABLE:	470.00
TERMS:	30 Days Net

VAT Registration Number 345 7654 32

KEATS SUPPLIES LTD

15 Great Way
Hending
Kent KN5 3TX

CREDIT NOTE

Credit Note Number: 2045
Date: 6 April 19X7
Tax Point: 06/04/X7
Account Number: B138

AUTHORISED
JS
6/4/X7

Attention: J Smith
ABC Ltd
112 Peters Square
Weyford
Kent CR2 2TA

Quantity	Code	Description	Unit Price £	Net Amount £
50	X12345Y	Ring Binders	2.00	100.00

TOTAL GOODS:	100.00
VAT AT 17.5%:	17.50
AMOUNT PAYABLE:	117.50

VAT Registration Number 345 7654 32

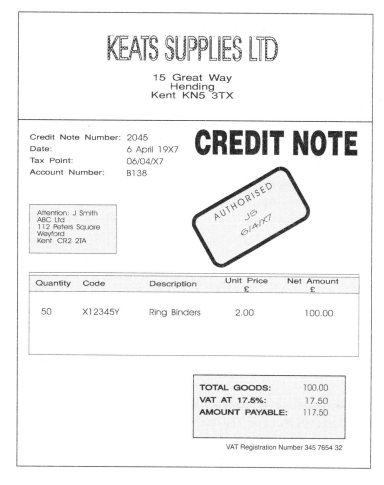

3.17 Some other documents are sometimes used in connection with sales and purchases.

Document	Purpose
Debit note	A debit note is issued by a customer to a supplier as a means of formally requesting a credit note. A supplier might also issue a **debit note** instead of an invoice in order to adjust upwards the amount of an invoice already issued.
Goods received note (GRNs)	Goods received notes (GRNs) are filled in to record a receipt of goods, most commonly in a warehouse. They may be used instead of (or in addition to) suppliers' advice notes. Often the accounts department will want to see the relevant GRN before paying a supplier's invoice. Even where GRNs are not routinely used, the details of a consignment from a supplier which arrives without an advice note must always be recorded.

Proforma invoices

3.18 When a customer does not want credit and/or wishes to pay in advance for goods, he may request a **proforma invoice** from the supplier.

- This will show all the details of the sale as we have seen on invoices above, but will not be entered into the seller's books of account - it is a dummy invoice
- The customer will create a cheque or get the cash to pay the proforma invoice

- When the seller receives the cash or cheque it creates a real invoice which is recorded as normal. Because it is paid immediately the invoice is effectively a COD (cash on delivery) invoice.

3.19 Proforma invoices are vital for a **seller** who cannot settle in advance of despatch but which has customers who do not want credit and need an 'invoice' against which to raise payment (and because their procedures do not permit payment except against invoice).

3.20 Many **importing buyers** (ie buyers who require goods from a seller overseas) require proforma invoices so that payment (often by bank transfer) and export/import documentation can be prepared for despatch. **Buyers** whose credit is not good also have little choice but to pay against proforma invoices.

4 METHODS OF CODING DATA

4.1 Each account in an accounting system has a **unique code** which is what will be used to identify the correct account for a posting (to be keyed into the computer if the system is computerised). If there were two debtors called John Smith, you could only tell their accounts apart by the fact the accounts had a different code.

4.2 Coding also saves time in copying out data because **codes are shorter** than 'longhand' descriptions. For the same reason, and also to save storage space, computer systems make use of coded data.

4.3 In accounting systems, the most obvious examples of codes are as follows.

- Customer account numbers
- Supplier account numbers
- General ledger account numbers
- Employee reference numbers
- Stock item codes

These are all codes a business sets up and applies internally. External codes which affect the business include **bank account numbers** and **bank sort codes**.

4.4 Various coding systems (or combinations of them) may be used when designing codes. The systems are described below.

Sequence codes

4.5 **Sequence codes** make no attempt to classify the item to be coded. It is simply given the next available number in a rising sequence. New items can only be inserted at the end of the list and therefore the codes for similar items may be very different.

(a) For example:

1 = saucepans
2 = kettles
3 = pianos
4 = dusters

(b) Sequence codes are rarely used when a large number of items are involved, except for document numbering (eg invoice numbers).

Block codes

4.6 **Block codes** provide a different sequence for each different group of items. For example for a particular firm, customers may be divided up according to area:

South East	code numbers 10,000-19,999
South West	code numbers 20,000-29,999
Wales	code numbers 30,000-39,999

The coding of customer accounts is then sequential within each block.

Significant digit codes

4.7 **Significant digit codes** incorporate some digit(s) which is (are) part of the descriptions of the item being coded. An example is:

5000	Electric light bulbs
5025	25 watt
5040	40 watt
5060	60 watt
5100	100 watt
etc	

Hierarchical codes

4.8 **Hierarchical codes** are allocated on the basis of a tree structure where the interrelationship between the items is of the paramount importance. A well known example is the Universal Decimal Code used by most libraries. For example:

5	Business
5 2	Finance
5 2 1	Cost accounting
5 2 1.4	Standard costing
5 2 1.4 7	Variance analysis
5 2 1.4 7 3	Fixed overhead variances

Faceted codes

4.9 **Faceted codes** are made up of a number of sections, each section of the code representing a different feature of the item. For example in a clothing store there might be a code based on the following facets.

Garment type	*Customer type*	*Colour*	*Size*	*Style*

If SU stood for suit, M for man and B for blue, a garment could be given the code SU M B 40 17. Similarly ND F W 14 23 could stand for a woman's white nightdress size 14, style 23. One of the great advantages of this system is that the type of item can be recognised from the code.

Faceted codes may be entirely numeric. For example, a large international company may allocate code numbers for each sales representative on the basis that:

Digit 1	Continent (eg America - 1, Europe - 2)
Digits 2/3	Country (eg England - 06)

Digit 4 Area (eg North - 3)
Digits 5/6 Representative's name (eg Mr J Walker - 14)

The code number may be expressed as 2/06/3/14.

Coding in the general ledger

4.10 A general ledger will consist of a **large number of coded accounts**. For example, part of a general ledger might be as follows.

Account code	Account name
100200	Plant and machinery (cost)
100300	Motor vehicles (cost)
300000	Total debtors
400000	Total creditors
500130	Wages and salaries
500140	Rent and rates
500150	Advertising expenses
500160	Bank charges
500170	Motor expenses
500180	Telephone expenses
600000	Sales
700000	Cash

4.11 A business will choose its own codes for its general ledger accounts. The codes given in the above table are purely imaginary.

Activity 3.3 **Level: Pre-assessment**

State what type of code is being used in paragraph 4.10 above. Explain your answer.

5 MANUAL AND COMPUTERISED SYSTEMS

5.1 We have looked at the way an accounting system is organised in the last few sections. It is important to realise that all of the books of prime entry and the ledgers may be either hand-written books or computer records. Most businesses now use computers, ranging in size from one PC used by a one-man business to huge mainframe computer systems used by multi-national companies.

5.2 All computer activity can be divided into three processes.

Process	Activity
Input	Entering data from original documents
Processing	Entering up books and ledgers and generally sorting the input information
Output	Producing any report desired by the managers of the business, including financial statements

Activity 3.4 **Level: Assessment**

Your friend Ivan Issue believes that computerised accounting systems are more trouble than they are worth because 'you never know what is going on inside that funny box'.

Task

Explain briefly why computers might be useful in accounting.

Computers are discussed in detail in the Unit 20 Working With Information Technology Interactive Text.

6 BATCH PROCESSING AND CONTROL TOTALS

KEY TERM

Batch processing is where similar transactions are gathered into batches, and then each batch is sorted and processed by the computer.

6.1 Rather than inputting individual invoices into a computer for processing, which would be time consuming and expensive, invoices can be gathered into a **batch** and **input and processed all together**. Batches can vary in size, depending on the type and volume of transactions and on any limit imposed by the system on batch sizes. This type of processing is less time consuming than **transaction processing,** where transactions are processed individually as they arise.

KEY TERM

Control totals are used to make sure that there have been no errors when the batch is input. A control total is used to make sure that the total value of transactions input is the same as that previously calculated.

6.2 As an example, say a batch of 30 sales invoices has a manually calculated total value of £42,378.47. When the batch is input, the computer adds up the total value of the invoices input and produces a total of £42,378.47. The control totals agree and therefore no further action is required.

6.3 Should the control total **not agree** then checks would have to be carried out until the difference was found. It might be the case that an invoice had accidentally not been entered or the manual total had been incorrectly calculated.

7 DISCOUNTS, REBATES AND ALLOWANCES

KEY TERM

A **discount** is a reduction in the price of goods below the amount at which those goods would normally be sold to other customers of the supplier.

Types of discount

7.1 There are two types of discount.

Type of discount	Description	Timing	Status
Trade discount	A reduction in the **cost of goods** owing to the nature of the trading transaction. It usually results from buying goods in bulk. For example: (a) A customer might be quoted a price of £1 per unit for a particular item, but a lower price of, say, 95 pence per unit if the item is bought in quantities of, say, 100 units or more at a time. (b) An important customer or a regular customer might be offered a discount on all the goods he buys, regardless of the size of each individual order, because the total volume of his purchases over time is so large. Customers who receive trade discounts are often other business customers, but not always.	Given on supplier's invoice	Permanent
Cash (sometimes called settlement) discount	A reduction in the **amount payable** to the supplier, in return for immediate or very early payment in cash, rather than purchase on credit. For example, a supplier might charge £1,000 for goods, but offer a cash discount of, say, 10% if the goods are paid for immediately in cash, 5% if they are paid for within 7 days of the invoice date but payment in full within 30 days. In this case the invoice would show '10% 0 days, 5% 7 days, net 30 days', indicating these terms.	Given for immediate or very prompt payment	Withdrawn if payment not received within time period stated

7.2 The distinction between trade and cash discounts is important as they are accounted for differently.

7.3 EXAMPLE: DISCOUNTS

Maurice trades widely in his district. In particular, he has three suppliers.

(a) Martin is in the same business as Maurice and offers 5% trade discount.

(b) Sol offers a trade discount of 7% on amounts *in excess of* £100 (ie the trade discount does not apply to the first £100).

(c) Tony offers a 10% cash discount for immediate payment or a 5% cash discount for all items paid for within 30 days of purchase.

In January 20X7, Maurice makes purchases of goods worth the following amounts before discounts have been deducted.

(a) From Martin: £400
(b) From Sol: £700

(c) From Tony: £350 cash
£700 to be paid on 14.1.X7 for goods purchased on 3.1.X7

Calculate how much Maurice has received as discounts in January. How much were trade and cash discounts?

7.4 SOLUTION

		£	
From Martin	£400 × 5%	20	Trade
From Sol	(£700 – £100) × 7%	42	Trade
From Tony	£350 × 10%	35	Cash: immediate
	£700 × 5%	35	Cash: prompt
		132	

Accounting for trade discounts

KEY TERM

A **trade discount** is a reduction in the amount of money *demanded* from a customer.

7.5 If a trade discount is **received** by a business for goods purchased from a supplier, the **amount of money demanded from the business** by the supplier will be **net** of discount (ie it will be the normal sales value less the discount).

If a trade discount is **allowed** by a business for goods sold to a customer, the amount of money demanded by the business will be after deduction of the discount.

Accounting for cash discounts

KEY TERM

A **cash discount** is an *optional* reduction in the amount of money *payable* by a customer.

Cash discounts received

7.6 Taking advantage of a cash discount is a matter of **financing policy**, not of **trading policy**. This is because the discount is **optional**.

7.7 EXAMPLE: OPTIONAL CASH DISCOUNTS RECEIVED

Suppose that A buys goods from B, on the understanding that A will be allowed a period of credit before having to pay for the goods. The terms of the transaction might be as follows.

Date of sale: 1 July 20X7

Credit period allowed: 30 days

Invoice price of the goods (the invoice will be issued at this price when the goods are delivered): £2,000

Cash discount offered: 4% for immediate payment

A has the choice between:

(a) Holding on to the £2,000 for 30 days and then paying the full amount.
(b) Paying £2,000 less 4% (a total of £1,920) now.

This is a financing decision about whether it is worthwhile for A to save £80 by paying its debts sooner, or whether she can employ her cash more usefully for 30 days, and pay the debt at the latest acceptable moment.

Assume that if A pays now, her bank account would go overdrawn for a month. The bank would charge an overdraft fee of £50 together with interest of 1.6% per month (also charged on the overdraft fee). A currently has £150 in the bank (and has an agreed overdraft facility). Assuming no other transactions, what should A do? Work it out before looking at the solution.

7.8 SOLUTION

A pays now, so the bank account will be as follows.

		£
Funds		150.00
Less:	payment	(1,920.00)
	overdraft fee	(50.00)
Overdraft		(1,820.00)
Interest (1.6% × £1,820) added at end of the month		29.12

Whereas the discount is worth £80, bank charges and interest of £50 + £29.12 will be incurred. However, the amount of the discount is still worth more than the bank charges by 88p. A should therefore take advantage of the discount offered by B.

Cash discounts allowed

7.9 The same principle is applied in accounting for cash discounts given (allowed) to customers. Goods are sold at a trade price, and the offer of a cash discount on that price is a matter of **financing policy** for the selling business and not a matter of trading policy.

7.10 Allowing cash discounts to customers, as opposed to receiving discounts from suppliers, is subject to similar considerations.

(a) It may be worth your while to **receive an amount of cash now**, as you can earn more in **interest** on it than you would lose by offering the discount.

(b) If you are in a **precarious financial position**, your bank manager might be happier to see the money now rather than later (and you might save money on overdraft interest and bank charges).

(c) You may be concerned that the **customer's own financial position** is insecure. Accepting cash now, rather than more later, means that at least the money is securely yours.

Activity 3.5 — Level: Assessment

Quickpay purchases goods with a list price of £22,000. The supplier offers a 10% trade discount, and a 2½% cash discount for payment within 20 days.

Tasks

Note. Ignore VAT.

(a) Calculate the amount Quickpay will have to pay if it delays longer than 20 days before paying.

(b) Calculate the amount the business will pay if it pays within 20 days.

7.11 Businesses may be offered other kinds of 'discounts' as incentives, to encourage them to buy in bulk or even just to stop them buying goods from other businesses. **Rebates** and **allowances** are not as common and they are only mentioned briefly here.

(a) An example of a **rebate** is where the gas company will lower its overall tariff for customers who use over a certain number of units per year. The rebate will be given in the form of either:

- A reduction in the bills for the following year
- A cheque for the calculated rebate amount

(b) An example of an **allowance** is where, if a certain number of units are ordered at one time, then a few extra units are given free of charge. For instance, if a record shop orders 50 compact discs, then another five may be sent **free of charge.**

8 VAT (VALUE ADDED TAX)

8.1 Many business transactions involve VAT (Value Added Tax), and most invoices, like the one shown earlier, show any VAT charged separately.

KEY TERMS

- **VAT** is a tax levied on the sale of goods and services. It is administered by HM Customs & Excise, but most of the work of collecting the tax falls on VAT-registered businesses, which hand the tax they collect over to the authorities.
- **Output tax**: VAT charged on goods and services sold by a business (that is, the business 'output').
- **Input tax**: VAT paid on goods and services bought in by a business.

8.2 VAT is charged by all members of the European Union (EU), though at different rates. Some countries, for example, charge 5% for some kinds of product and 10% on others.

8.3 In the UK there are two rates of VAT.

(a) **Standard rate**. This is nearly always 17½% of the value of the goods (in a few cases, it has been reduced to 5% by the Government). So, if you sell a standard rated item which is worth £100 you must also charge £17.50 in tax, so that the total paid by your customer will be £117.50. (Note that the prices you pay in shops generally **include** VAT.)

(b) **Zero-rate**. This is 0%.

Not all goods and services have VAT on them. **Exempt items** are not part of the VAT system.

Calculating VAT

8.4 If a product has a **net price** of, say £120 and VAT is to be added, then it is just a question of working out 17½% of £120.

$$\text{VAT} = £120 \times 17.5/100$$
$$= £21$$

8.5 The **gross price** of the product is therefore £120 + £21 = £141. **It is always true that gross price = net price + VAT.**

	£
Purchaser pays gross price	141
Customs and Excise take VAT	(21)
Seller keeps net price	120

If you are given the gross price of a product (say, £282), then you can work out the VAT which it includes by multiplying by 17.5/117.5 (or 7/47).

$$£282 \times 17.5/117.5 = £42$$

Therefore the net price must be £282 – £42 = £240.

8.6 Where the calculation involves pence then the rule you should apply (unless told otherwise in a Devolved Assessment) is to round **down to the nearest penny**. For example

	£
Net price	25.75
VAT at 17½% (£25.75 ×17½% = £4.50625)	4.50
	30.25

Activity 3.6 **Level: Pre-assessment**

The gross price of product A is £705.60 and the net price of product B is £480.95. What is the VAT charged on each product?

Input and output VAT

8.7 Usually output VAT (on sales) exceeds input VAT (on purchases). The excess is paid over to Customs & Excise. If output VAT is less than input VAT in a period, Customs & Excise will refund the difference to the business. In other words, if a business pays out more in VAT than it receives from customers it will be paid back the difference.

Output tax received	Input tax paid	Total	Treatment
£1,000	£(900)	£100 received	Pay to C&E
£900	£(1,000)	£(100) paid	Refund from C&E

8.8 EXAMPLE: INPUT AND OUTPUT TAX

A company sells goods for £35,250 including VAT in a quarter (three months of a year). It buys goods for £32,900 including VAT. What amount will it pay to or receive from HM Customs & Excise for the quarter?

8.9 SOLUTION

The **output tax** will be:

	£
$£35{,}250 \times \dfrac{17.5}{117.5} =$	5,250
The **input tax** will be:	
$£32{,}900 \times \dfrac{17.5}{117.5} =$	4,900
The tax **payable** is the output tax less the input tax =	350

ASSESSMENT ALERT

Remember that, in the Devolved Assessment, if you come up with a figure which runs to more than two decimal places when you apply the VAT fraction, you should simply **round down** to the nearest penny (unless told otherwise).

Some practical aspects of VAT

Registration

8.10 It would not be easy for HM Customs & Excise to administer and collect VAT if *all* businesses had to account for it. For this reason, **only businesses with at least a certain turnover or level of sales must register**. The limits change quite frequently, but at the time of writing, a business or company must register for VAT if the level of sales for the last 12 months was £52,000 or higher. Also, if the business expects turnover of £52,000 in the next 30 days then it must register for VAT.

Administrative time

8.11 VAT affects a large proportion of businesses in the UK (and in other European countries) and it is something that a business will have to spend quite a lot of time administering. There are several reasons for this.

(a) Most businesses will account to HM Customs & Excise for their transactions involving VAT **every quarter**. There is a special scheme which allows accounting on an annual basis but normally, every quarter, someone will have to sit down and work out the VAT position of the business.

(b) All transactions which are recorded involving VAT will have to show **separately** the net price, VAT and the gross price. This increases the **time taken to record** the transactions of the business.

(c) Accounting for VAT will have an effect on **cash flow**, whether the business is a net payer of VAT or a net receiver.

(d) Failure to comply with all the rules relating to VAT will lead to **large penalties**. HM Customs & Excise has far more wide-ranging and punishing powers than the Inland Revenue.

Discounts and VAT

8.12 If a **cash discount** is offered for prompt payment of the invoice, VAT is computed on the amount **after** deducting the discount (at the highest rate offered), even if the discount is not taken.

ASSESSMENT ALERT

The interaction of VAT and discounts comes up frequently in the Devolved Assessment.

Activity 3.7 **Level: Assessment**

For Activity 3.5 above recalculate your answers for (a) and (b) if VAT was charged at the standard rate.

Credit cards

8.13 If a trader charges **different prices** to customers paying with credit cards and those paying by other means, the VAT due on each standard rated sale is the full amount paid by the customer × 7/47.

8.14 There are some circumstances in which traders are *not* allowed to reclaim VAT paid on their inputs. In such cases, the trader must bear the cost of VAT and account for it accordingly. The most important of these is where the inputs are **non-deductible**, eg motor cars.

Documentation and VAT

8.15 We have already looked at invoices and some other documentation. There are special rules relating to the content of an invoice if it is to be used as a proof of purchase (or sale) for reclaiming VAT - a **VAT invoice**.

BANGLES LTD

Jewel House
Richmans Road
LONDON SE1N 5AB

INVOICE

Invoice Number: 123456
Date: 01/08/X7
Tax Point: 01/08/X7 (a)
Account Number: 3365

DELIVER TO
ABC Ltd
112 Peters Square
Weyford
Kent CR2 2TA

INVOICE TO:
Same address

Telephone Number 0207 123 4567
VAT Registration Number 457 4635 19 (b)
Northern Bank plc Code 20-25-42
Account Number 957023

Item Code	Description	Quantity	Unit Price £	Net Amount £
Your order number: 2490				
13579A	Desks	30	250.00	7,500.00
	Delivery	1	100.00	100.00
			SALES VALUE:	7,600.00
			VAT AT 17.5%:	(c) 1,330.00
			AMOUNT PAYABLE:	8,930.00

8.16 Note the following contents which are necessary for the invoice to be a 'VAT invoice'.

(a) **Tax point**. This determines when the transaction has taken place for VAT purposes; it is normally the invoice date. Note that, for cash transactions, the tax point for VAT purposes is the date the transaction took place.

(b) **VAT registration number** of the supplier. This is to prove to HM Customs & Excise that the purchase was from a real supplier of standard rated goods.

(c) **VAT rate**. The correct rate must be applied to each type of goods; if the goods are zero-rated then the rate would be shown as 0%.

Key learning points

- Business transactions are of two main types: **cash** and **credit**.
- **Invoices** and **credit notes** are important documents which must contain specific information.
- There are two kinds of **discount**.

- **Trade discount**: a reduction in the cost of goods
- **Cash (or settlement) discount**: a reduction in the amount payable to the supplier

- VAT rules can be quite complex but the main points to remember are:
  - **Output VAT** is charged on sales and **input VAT** is incurred on purchases
  - **VAT invoices** must contain specific pieces of information

Quick quiz

1. What type of document would a business raise to give a customer a price for something?
2. Why should a business raise a goods received note?
3. What is an invoice?
4. What information is usually shown on an invoice?
5. What does E&OE on an invoice mean?
6. What is input tax and what is output tax?
7. What is a VAT 'tax point'?

Answers to quick quiz

1. A quotation
2. A GRN acts as notification that the goods have been received (complete and in good condition) and it can be used to input the information into the business's accounting system.
3. An invoice is a demand for payment.
4. (a) Name and address of the seller
   (b) Name and address of the purchaser
   (c) Invoice number, so that the business can keep track of all the invoices it sends out
   (d) Date of the transaction
   (e) Description of what is being sold
   (f) Quantity and unit price of what has been sold
   (g) Total amount of the invoice including any details of VAT
   (h) The tax point for VAT purposes
5. Errors and omissions excepted, ie the supplier can alter any incorrect details on the invoice.
6. Input tax is VAT paid on purchases; output tax is VAT charged on sales.
7. A 'tax point' determines the date a transaction has taken place for VAT purposes.

Part B

Accounting for Sales

4 Invoicing and issuing credit notes

This chapter contains

1 Documenting the supply of goods and services

2 The invoice

3 Credit notes and debit notes

4 Customer credit limits

5 Generation of invoices and credit notes by computer

Learning objectives

On completion of this chapter you will have learned about:

- Types of business transactions and documents involved
- Methods of coding data
- Organisational procedures for authorisation and coding of sales invoices
- Operation of manual and computerised accounting systems

Performance criteria

1.1.1 Invoices and credit notes are prepared in accordance with organisational requirements and checked against source documents

1.1.2 Calculations on invoices and credit notes are checked for accuracy

1.1.3 Invoices and credit notes are correctly authorised and coded before being sent to customers

1.1.5 Entries are coded and recorded in the appropriate ledger

Range statement

1.1.1 Source documents: quotations; purchase orders; delivery notes; sales orders

1.1.2 Calculations: pricing; price extensions; discounts; VAT

Chapter 4 scenario – Workbase Office Supplies Ltd. This scenario applies to all the activities in this chapter.

At Workbase Office Supplies where you work as an accounting assistant, customer discounts are allowed in accordance with the list provided in appendix b at the end of the chapter.

1 DOCUMENTING THE SUPPLY OF GOODS AND SERVICES

The contract

1.1 Basic aspects of the **law of contract** are covered in Chapter 11. We will briefly summarise the legal aspects of trading here.

- Whenever a business (the **supplier**) agrees to supply goods or services to another business or individual (the **customer**), it is entering into a **legally binding contract with the customer**.
- A contract may be either in **writing** or **spoken** (oral), and becomes legally binding at the point at which the two parties **agree**.

Documenting a business transaction

1.2 Whenever a business transaction takes place, involving sales or purchases, receiving or paying money, or owing or being owed money, it is usual for the transaction to be recorded on a **document**.

1.3 The amount of documentation involved in a business transaction will vary according to the kind of transaction and whoever is involved in it.

- When a **shop** makes a small sale to you or me it may be that **no documentation at all** changes hands unless we ask for or are given a till receipt.
- Transactions **between businesses** are more likely to involve a number of **documents of different types**, depending on the procedures of the business involved.

Raising an invoice

1.4 One way for a business transaction to take place is for a buyer of goods or services to pay cash to the seller at the time the goods or services are supplied (a cash transaction).

> **KEY TERM**
>
> In a **credit transaction** the buyer does not pay for the goods or services until some time after they have been supplied.

1.5 When a business sells goods on credit to a customer, it 'raises' an invoice.

> **KEY TERM**
>
> The **invoice** is a formal demand for the customer to pay what is owed. The invoice is an important document in what may be a whole series of documents involved in supplying goods or services.

We look in more detail later in this chapter at what needs to be shown on an invoice.

What documents come before the invoice?

1.6 A credit sale may involve some or all of the following business documents leading up to the raising of an invoice:

letter of enquiry	quotation	purchase order	order acknowledgement	delivery note advice note	invoice

1.7 In the following paragraphs we explain the purpose of each of these documents. We also provide examples of what some of these documents might look like. Bear in mind, however, that although an invoice *must* show certain things, **there is no standard format for any of the various kinds of documents**, and organisations vary in the way they use them.

1.8 For example, while a supplier of **goods** will probably find it useful to send a delivery note with a consignment of goods, a supplier of **services** (eg someone offering professional services, such as a solicitor or accountant, or an office cleaning company) is unlikely to have a use for a delivery note in the supply of their services.

The letter of enquiry and quotation

1.9 Someone who wants to buy goods which a business sells may send a **letter of enquiry** to the seller to find out the price at which the seller is prepared to supply the goods.

In reply, the seller will send back a **quotation** giving details of the price at which the goods are offered.

ANYWHERE REMOVALS LIMITED

64 Luton Road, Dunford DN4 4PN

Telephone (01990) 42254 Fax (01990) 42401 VAT Reg No 943 441417

Pickett (Handling Equipment) Ltd
Unit 7
Western Industrial Estate
Dunford
DN2 7RJ

7 March 20X2

Dear Sirs

I shall be grateful if you will send me as soon as possible your quotation for the supply of the items listed below. Your quotation should indicate the delivery period.

6 x Medium weight sack trucks
2 x Low loading platform trucks

Yours faithfully

M Stephens

M Stephens (Mr)
General Manager

Registered office: 64 Luton Road, Dunford DN4 4PN *Registered in England No 9482472*

Pickett (Handling Equipment) Limited
Unit 7 Western Industrial Estate
Dunford DN2 7RJ
Tel: (01990) 72101 Fax: (01990) 72980 VAT Reg No 982 721349

11 March 20X2

Mr M Stephens
Anywhere Removals Ltd
64 Luton Road
Dunford DN4 4PN

Dear Mr Stephens

QUOTATION

Thank you for your letter dated 7 March 20X2. We are pleased to be able to provide a quotation as follows. This quotation is valid for a period of three months from the date of this letter, after which a new quotation will be supplied on request.

6 Medium weight sack trucks, Cat No ST 200 @ £52.50 each. 25mm 14 gauge steel tube. 30cm x 15cm toe plate. 98cm high x 48cm wide. 20cm cushion tyres. Available in blue or red.

2 Low loading platform trucks, Cat No PT 410 @ £116.80 each. 200kg capacity. Wheels 200mm x 50mm cushion tyres with roller bearings and two 125mm swivel castors. Timber platform. 107cm long x 61cm wide. Available in red only.

The above prices are subject to VAT at the standard rate of 17.5%.

Yours sincerely,

P Morley

P Morley
Sales Manager

Registered Office: 4 Arkwright Road, London E16 4PQ Registered in England No 2182417

1.10 The documents may be in some other **form**.

- In some businesses, a **standard printed form** may be available to use as a letter of enquiry.
- Instead of sending a quotation in the form of a letter, the seller might send a **pre-printed list** or catalogue giving details of product descriptions and prices.

1.11 Where a business has dealt with the seller before, the business may already know the seller's current prices and there will be **no need for a quotation to be asked for.** In such cases, the purchaser may start the process of buying the goods with a **purchase order**.

The purchase order

1.12 If the buyer finds the seller's quotation satisfactory, he or she will send a **purchase order** to the seller. The purchase order might look like the example shown here.

ANYWHERE REMOVALS LIMITED

64 Luton Road Dunford DN4 4PN

Telephone (01990) 42254 Fax (01990) 42401 VAT Reg No 943 441417

Purchase order NO: 9607

Pickett (Handling Equipment) Ltd
Unit 7
Western Industrial Estate
Dunford
DN2 7RJ

14 March 20X2

Quantity	Cat. No.	Description	Unit price £	Total price £
6	ST 200	Medium weight sack trucks (colour red)	52.50	315.00
2	PT 410	Low loading platform trucks	116.80	233.60
				548.60
		VAT @ 17.5%		96.00
		Total		644.60

Delivery to:
Anywhere Removals Ltd 64 Luton Road Dunford DN4 4PN

Delivery within 7 days, carriage paid

M Stephens

M Stephens
General Manager

Sellers' order forms

1.13 Rather than sending its own order form, a customer may use an **order form produced by the selling firm** along with their catalogue or price list.

- This will be particularly appropriate if the products are of a specialised nature and need to be identified by highly specific product codes.
- It helps to make sure that the buyer **includes all of the details required**.
- It also helps to **speed** along the processing of orders if the people doing the processing are dealing with their own standardised form rather than the various styles and formats of customers' purchase order forms.
- The form can also be matched with **despatch documents** and **invoices** which are in a similar format.

1.14 **Computers** can be used to read details on the orders if they are in a certain form. This can be achieved by using one of two different types of forms which are machine readable.

- **Optical Character Recognition** (OCR) forms
- **Optical Mark Recognition** (OMR) forms

Stock records may be updated as well as part of the process.

1.15 An example of an **OMR order form** is set out below. The customer account number is entered manually, while the marks to show what quantities are required are machine-read. Most of M&N's customers order quantities of under ten of each of the items at a time. If a customer wants to order more than nine of any item, the number must be input manually.

M&N CLEANING SUPPLIES LTD
FERRY LANE OXFORD OX2 9RL

ORDER FORM

DELIVER TO: ....

....

....

A/C No. ☐ ☐ ☐ ☐ ☐ ☐

DATE ☐ ☐ ☐ ☐ ☐ ☐ (D D M M Y Y)

Your order will be machine read. Using black ink, please show your requirements with a mark [—] for the appropriate quantity. If you require more than nine of any item, please mark [—] on the far right column [(0)] and write in the number required.

Item	Pack Size	Quantity required	More than (9)
C Cleaner	1 litre	[(1)] [(2)] [(3)] [(4)] [(5)] [(6)] [(7)] [(8)] [(9)]	[(0)] ☐☐
	2 litre	[(1)] [(2)] [(3)] [(4)] [(5)] [(6)] [(7)] [(8)] [(9)]	[(0)] ☐☐
Bleach	1 litre	[(1)] [(2)] [(3)] [(4)] [(5)] [(6)] [(7)] [(8)] [(9)]	[(0)] ☐☐
	5 litre	[(1)] [(2)] [(3)] [(4)] [(5)] [(6)] [(7)] [(8)] [(9)]	[(0)] ☐☐
Detergent	small	[(1)] [(2)] [(3)] [(4)] [(5)] [(6)] [(7)] [(8)] [(9)]	[(0)] ☐☐
	large	[(1)] [(2)] [(3)] [(4)] [(5)] [(6)] [(7)] [(8)] [(9)]	[(0)] ☐☐
K-Cloths	small	[(1)] [(2)] [(3)] [(4)] [(5)] [(6)] [(7)] [(8)] [(9)]	[(0)] ☐☐
	large	[(1)] [(2)] [(3)] [(4)] [(5)] [(6)] [(7)] [(8)] [(9)]	[(0)] ☐☐
Bin liners	small	[(1)] [(2)] [(3)] [(4)] [(5)] [(6)] [(7)] [(8)] [(9)]	[(0)] ☐☐
	large	[(1)] [(2)] [(3)] [(4)] [(5)] [(6)] [(7)] [(8)] [(9)]	[(0)] ☐☐
F Polish	1 litre	[(1)] [(2)] [(3)] [(4)] [(5)] [(6)] [(7)] [(8)] [(9)]	[(0)] ☐☐
	2 litre	[(1)] [(2)] [(3)] [(4)] [(5)] [(6)] [(7)] [(8)] [(9)]	[(0)] ☐☐

Internal sales orders

1.16 Even a business which receives written orders from customers on customers' own purchase order forms may choose to make out its own internal **sales order form** for each order, on which the **details of the customers' order** will be entered. It can then be filed with the corresponding customer purchase order. Sales order forms have the following benefits in addition to those noted in paragraph 1.13 above.

- The internal sales order serves as a **record that a customer's order has been received.**
- **Prenumbering** the internal sales order forms will help in controlling orders coming into the business: for example, it should make it easy to see which order came in first.

Order acknowledgement

1.17

Step 1 An **order acknowledgement** is sent by the seller to the buyer in order to confirm:

- That the order has been **received**
- That the goods required **can be supplied**
- **When** the goods are expected to be delivered

Step 2 When the buyer receives the acknowledgement, he or she will check that it agrees with the order.

1.18 An order acknowledgement is often written in the form of a **letter**, thanking the buyer for the order and repeating the details of the goods ordered and how they are to be delivered.

Multi-part stationery

1.19 In some businesses, the order acknowledgement is produced as part of a multi-part stationery set.

- The details of the order are copied onto **each document in the set.**
- Each part is pre-printed with a description of the **type of document** it represents (eg 'order acknowledgement', 'invoice').
- Each part may be made in a different colour of paper, so that each can be easily identified.

Sales order set

1.20 An order acknowledgement may be produced as part of a **sales order set** which might be made up as follows.

Copy	Description	Function
1	Order acknowledgement	Sent to the customer
2	File copy (sales)	Kept in the sales department to help deal with **customer queries.**
3	File copy (accounts)	Passed to the **accounts office** for retention awaiting a signed delivery note and subsequently the preparation of an invoice.
4	Delivery note	Whoever delivers the goods to the purchaser asks the purchaser (or his storekeeper) to sign the note as proof that the goods have actually been delivered. The delivery note is then brought back to the supplier's premises to be matched with the accounts copy so that the invoice can be raised.
5	Advice note	This is like a delivery note in that it goes to the purchaser, but instead of being brought back to the supplier, it is left with the purchaser (or his storekeeper). The storekeeper may then use this to make sure that the goods delivered are the same as those shown on the invoice.
6	Despatch note	The storekeeper will enter the date when the goods are despatched to the customer, and the despatch note will be kept in the warehouse for the warehouse records, in case of query.

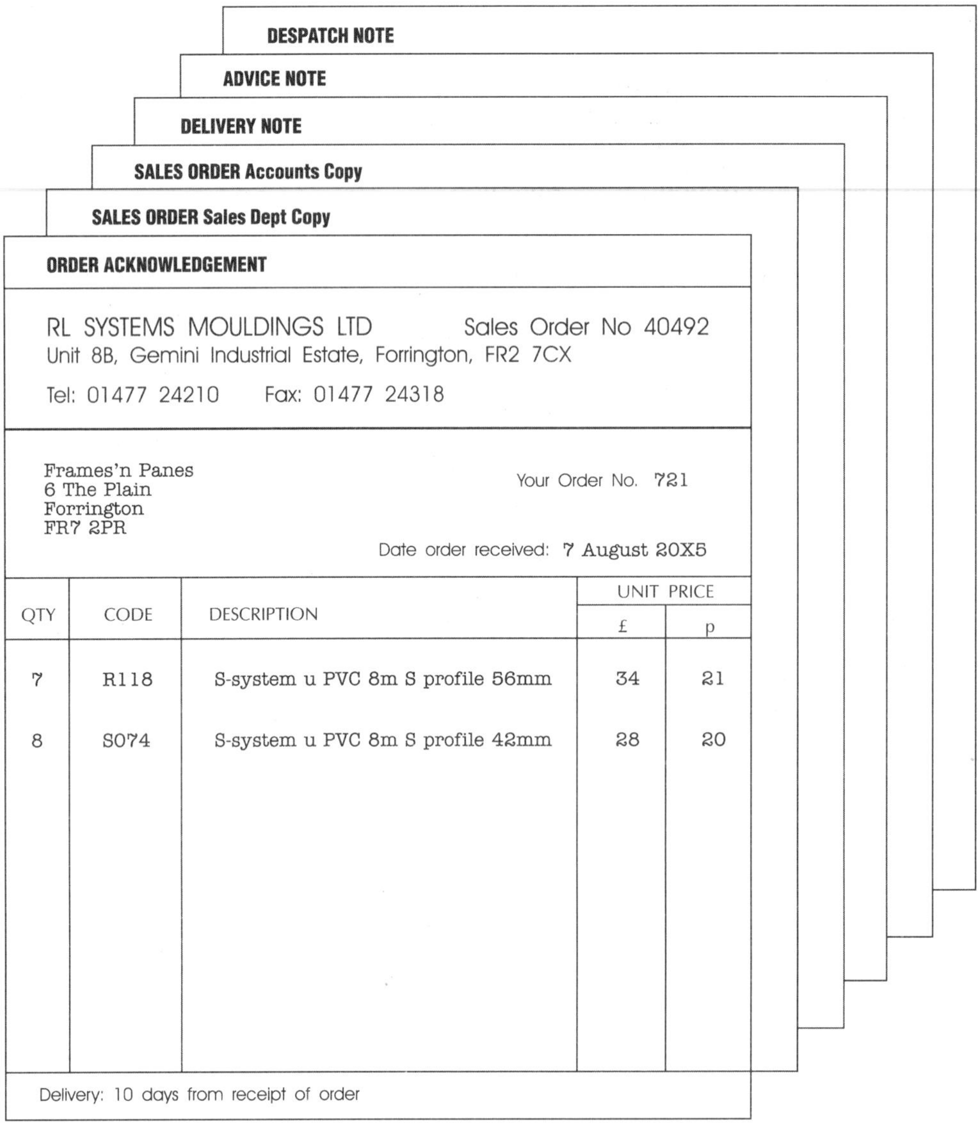

DESPATCH NOTE

ADVICE NOTE

DELIVERY NOTE

SALES ORDER Accounts Copy

SALES ORDER Sales Dept Copy

ORDER ACKNOWLEDGEMENT

RL SYSTEMS MOULDINGS LTD Sales Order No 40492
Unit 8B, Gemini Industrial Estate, Forrington, FR2 7CX
Tel: 01477 24210 Fax: 01477 24318

Frames'n Panes
6 The Plain
Forrington
FR7 2PR

Your Order No. 721

Date order received: 7 August 20X5

QTY	CODE	DESCRIPTION	UNIT PRICE £	p
7	R118	S-system u PVC 8m S profile 56mm	34	21
8	S074	S-system u PVC 8m S profile 42mm	28	20

Delivery: 10 days from receipt of order

1.21 On the **delivery note copy**, a box at the bottom will be used for obtaining the signature of the person receiving the goods. For example, the copy may be pre-printed with the words:

'Date of delivery .... Goods received in good condition .... Signed ....'

Similarly, the advice note may be signed by the storekeeper and the **despatch note copy** for the warehouse will probably have a pre-printed space on which to enter the date/time of despatch.

Invoice set

1.22 Another common approach is for the supplier to use a **multi-part invoice set.**

Copy	Description	Function
1	Invoice	Sent to the purchaser as a request to pay for the goods.
2	Copy invoice	Kept by the supplier for his records and will probably be kept on file in order of invoice number. The supplier may need it as proof that he made out the invoice in the first place and the auditors may need to inspect copy sales invoices during the annual audit. In a large business, both the sales department and the accounts department may keep copy sales invoices.
3	Delivery note	As above.
4	Advice note	As above.

1.23 Similar information can be entered on to a multi-part invoice set as on an invoice produced in any other way (eg as a single document). We will now look at the information found on an invoice.

2 THE INVOICE

KEY TERM

An **invoice** is a demand for payment.

What does an invoice show?

2.1 The information shown on an **invoice** normally includes the following.

(a) **Name and address** of seller

(b) Name and address of purchaser

(c) The **date** of the sale

(d) The **tax point** - the date of the transaction for VAT purposes (normally the invoice date, although it may be a different date under certain circumstances)

(e) A **description** of what has been sold

(f) The **quantity** and the **price per unit** of what has been sold (for example, 450 wooden rulers at 12p each)

(g) Details of any **trade discounts** which are being given (for example, 10% reduction in cost if buying over 2,000 wooden rulers)

(h) The **total amount of the invoice** including details of any VAT

(i) If the seller is registered for VAT, the **VAT registration number** of the seller will be shown

(j) The date by which the payment is due, and other **terms** of sale

2.2 The invoice might look something like the one shown here, which is cross-referenced to the standard features above.

STUDENT SUPPLIES LIMITED

(a) 123 Factory Street Worktown London W19 4NB
Tel: 0208 123 4567 Fax: 0208 123 4589

INVOICE

Invoice Number: 1496

Your Order Number: 3365

INVOICE TO:	DELIVER TO:	
Westshire County Council 46 Chamber Street Camberwick Green CG2 4SP (b)	Brilliant Primary School School Road Booktown BK1 1AA	Date of Invoice/Taxpoint : (d) 9 May 20X5 Date of Supply : (c) 6 May 20X5

ITEM CODE	QUANTITY	DESCRIPTION	UNIT PRICE £	AMOUNT £
17004	450 (f)	12" Wooden rulers (e)	0.12 (f)	54.00

SALES VALUE: 54.00
VAT AT 17.5%: 8.97

(i) VAT No 245 8269 41 (j) Terms: 5/7, n/30 (h) AMOUNT PAYABLE: 62.97

2.3 Here are some points to note about this invoice.

- Businesses sometimes want goods delivered to somewhere other than their own premises. In this example, although the county council might pay for the rulers, it is the school which actually needs them, so there is a different **delivery address.**
- A business usually keeps a record of its orders, just as it does of its sales. In this case, the purchaser's **order number** was 3365. Student Supplies puts the order number on the invoice so that the county council can quickly see which order the invoice relates to.
- In our example, rulers were 12p each, but sometimes goods are sold in batches of, say 20. If that is the case, then something like '£2 for 20' will be

put in the **unit price** column. The amount of the invoice is calculated in the usual way.

- ◦ '5/7' means that if payment is made within seven days then a **discount** of 5% of the invoice total may be deducted as a cash discount.

  ◦ 'n/30' stands for 'net 30 days' and means that payment is to be made within 30 days of the invoice date (ie these are the **credit terms**).

> Remember that the VAT has been calculated on the amount less discount: £54.00 × 95% × 17.5% = £8.97 (rounded down). This continues to apply even when the discount is not taken because the invoice is paid after 7 days.

2.4 Other terms which you may come across on invoices include the following.

- **E & OE.** These letters may be printed at the bottom of an invoice. They stand for the words 'Errors and omissions excepted'. These words are saying that the seller reserves the right to correct any errors made on the invoice or any omissions from it at some later date (for example, if a keyboard operator enters an incorrect amount on the invoice).
- **Carriage paid.** This means that the invoice price includes delivery of the goods to the buyer.
- **Ex works.** The invoice price does not include delivery, and the purchaser must therefore arrange transport.
- **Cash on delivery** or **COD.** The goods will have to be paid for in cash at the time of delivery to the buyer's premises.
- **FOB**. These letters stand for the words 'free on board' and may be found on import or export invoices. They indicate that prices exclude transport costs. 'FOB shipping point' means that the supplier pays all costs of carriage (shipping, insurance and freight for example) up to the point of shipping but the customer has to pay any carriage costs from that point on.
- **CIF.** This contrasts with FOB and indicates that transport costs are included in prices. (The letters stand for 'cost, insurance, freight' or 'charged in full'.)
- **Proforma.** A proforma invoice includes all the details of a normal invoice but is not recorded in the accounting system. It is like a dummy invoice. A proforma is usually raised when goods are not sold on credit, that is when cash must be received before, or at the time of, delivery. Having a proforma allows the customer to prepare the necessary documentation to pay for the goods, but means that the seller does not record the sale until it is sure of being realised in cash.

2.5 Invoice forms of different businesses will be **designed in different ways**, although they all show the same sort of information.

Numbering of invoices

2.6 It is usual for a business to **sequentially number the sales invoices** it issues so that it can keep track of all the invoices it sends out.

2.7 A business will want to ensure that blank invoice forms are not misused by someone who is trying to obtain money dishonestly. There may be **security**

procedures to ensure this, such as keeping blank invoices locked in a cupboard and maintaining registers of invoice forms. Any spoiled invoice forms should be kept, so that it can be proved (to the auditors or others) that the forms involved have not gone astray.

Discounts

2.8 There is a distinction between trade discounts and cash discounts.

Discount	Characteristic
Trade	Offered to particular customers or groups of customers. The discount is deducted from the selling price of the goods and services when the sales invoice is prepared. It **reduces the cost of the goods.**
Cash	Offered if the customer pays within a certain specified period. It **reduces the amount payable.**

VAT and discounts

2.9 This is a good point at which to refresh your memory about the **calculation of VAT and discounts**.

2.10 Where a **trade discount** is allowed, the discount is deducted **before** VAT is calculated.

For example, Bouncy Beds Ltd buys ten beds from Sleepsoft Ltd. The list price is £124.00 per bed, but Sleepsoft offers a 20% trade discount to Bouncy, a valued customer. The invoice sets out the following details.

Quantity	*Description*	*Unit price*	*Amount*
		£	£
10	BL40 Beds	124.00	1,240.00
	Discount 20%		248.00
			992.00

2.11 Where a **cash discount** is allowed, the VAT is calculated on the lowest amount which a customer can pay.

For example, as well as the 20% trade discount, Sleepsoft Ltd might also offer Bouncy Beds Ltd a 2% discount for payment within 30 days.

(a) The VAT-exclusive amount payable within 30 days is £972.16 (£992 × (100 – 2)%).

(b) VAT is therefore calculated on this amount, giving £170.12.

(c) The amount invoiced is £992 plus £170.12 VAT = £1,162.12.

(d) The customer may either pay the full amount invoiced of £1,162.12, or, if paying within 30 days, £972.16 plus £170.12 VAT = £1,142.28.

2.12 Thus on the Student Supplies invoice, VAT is £8.97, which is 17.5% of £54 × 95%, as a cash discount of 5% is offered for payment within 7 days.

Checks over invoicing

2.13 We have looked at the information necessary for an invoice to be made up. A business will want to have **checking procedures** which ensure that the invoices it sends out are correct.

2.14 The various checks which are needed will depend upon how the business is organised and on what information is included on an invoice. These checks might include the following.

Details	Agree with	Yes or no?
Customer's name and address and customer account code (if shown on the invoice)	'Master list' of the customers of the business	
Product details	Customer's purchase order	
Product details	Despatch note (showing what goods were sent)	
Each product description	Product code number or catalogue number stated on the invoice	
Unit price stated on the invoice	Price list of the business (or with any quotation, if given)	
Level of discount stated (if any)	Records of discounts allowed for various customers etc	
Calculations of 'quantity × unit price = amount'	Calculator	
Calculations of any discounts, VAT and totals	Calculator	

2.15 Ideally, there should be **segregation of duties** so that the three areas of order acceptance, control and despatch of goods and preparation of invoices are the jobs of separate people in the organisation.

Activity 4.1 — Level: Pre-assessment

A batch of delivery notes shows that goods have been supplied by Workbase Office Supplies Ltd to the order of ten customers as follows. 'Goods total' indicates the total value of the goods at list prices before discounts and VAT.

	Customer	*Goods total*
		£
1	Conduit Insurance Co plc	94.92
2	Bowser & Bowser	125.20
3	Wendy Homes (Southern) Ltd	242.10
4	Roundabout Supplies Ltd	572.63
5	Pike & Perch	421.74
6	Flowex Filters Ltd	62.00
7	United Craft Distributors Ltd	160.60
8	Underwood Dairies	34.17
9	Brittan's Farm Management Ltd	721.47
10	Lexicon Translators	84.89

Task

By reference to Appendix B at the end of this chapter, indicate the discount percentage due for each order. Then calculate the amount of discount for each order and the net total before VAT for each order. *Note.* Discount amounts are rounded to the nearest penny.

Activity 4.2 — Level: Assessment

Goods are to be supplied by Workbase Office Supplies to satisfy purchase orders, the details of which are given on the following pages.

Tasks

(a) You are required to prepare sales invoices for each of the three purchase orders detailed below, making reference to the following appendices at the end of this chapter.

Appendix A Catalogue and price list
Appendix B List of customer discounts and credit limits

Use the blank invoice forms given here for your solution. Your invoices should be numbered from 7010 onwards, and dated 30 April 20X7. All goods supplied are subject to VAT at the standard rate of 17½%.

(b) An extract from the Workbase Office Supplies procedures manual reads as follows.

> An invoice (or invoices) must be prepared for every order. If the invoice (or invoices) prepared to satisfy a particular order:
>
> 1. result(s) in an invoice value, before VAT, of £800; or
> 2. result(s) in the customer's credit limit being breached,
>
> it should be referred to the Sales Manager.
>
> Goods should not be despatched to customers who have exceeded their credit limit, until they have reduced their debt, so that the credit limit will not be exceeded.

Considering what the procedures manual says:

(i) Which of the invoices should you refer to the Sales Manager?
(ii) Which would be delayed?

Further information

Credit limits can be found in Appendix B following the key learning points for this chapter.

Fawsley's & Co Ltd currently owes you: £500
Keats and Joyce owes you: £900

Rabbit Fast Food Franchises Ltd owes you: nothing

Purchase orders (part (a))

PURCHASE ORDER **No 3017**

FAWSLEY'S & CO LTD
74 Green bank Road
Blackley
Liverpool L6 4NP

Tel: 0151-721-4221
Fax: 01512-721-4211

Workbase Office Supplies Ltd
63 Conduit Street
Liverpool L1 6NN

7 April 20X7

Qty	*Ref No*	*Description*	*Unit price*
1	A87724	Tara 6-tray file trolley	£65.00
1	A87725	Tara 12-tray file trolley	£94.00
18	A87821	Tara Tower filing tray	£4.92
1	F10577	Ambience 9-drawer card filing cabinet	£484.50
2	F58110	Ambico 6-shelf unit	£126.00

KEATS & JOYCE

Estate Agents and Valuers, 24 Fore Street, Bourneley L24 6PN
Tel: 01442 92914 Fax: 01442 92422

Workbase Office Supplies Limited
63 Conduit Street
Liverpool L1 6NN

14 April 20X7

Dear Sirs

Please supply the following items to the above address:

3 x Heavy duty 2-hole 8cm gauge perforators
10 x 'Mini-punch' perforators
12 x Fine point Hi-lite black Jumbo markers
24 x 'B' Office Star pencils
36 x 'HB' Office Star pencils

Yours sincerely

James Keats

James Keats

A telephone order was received from Rabbit Fast Food Franchises Ltd for three 'Chequers' 474E Typist's chairs. Two were ordered in Fern and one in Charcoal. The order was later confirmed by fax. The company's address is 62 Hellon Avenue, Bourneley, L24 6BS.

Invoice form

WORKBASE OFFICE SUPPLIES LTD

63 Conduit Street
Liverpool L1 6NN

Telephone: 0151-432 2222
Fax: 0151-432 2210

VAT Reg No. 924 4614 29

Invoice No.

Account No.

Date/Tax point

Product code	*Description*	*Quantity*	*Unit price* £ p	*Total amount* £ p

Comments:	NET TOTAL	
	VAT @ 17 ½%	
	GRAND TOTAL	

Registered Office: 63 Conduit Street, Liverpool L1 6NN   Registered No: 822 4742

WORKBASE OFFICE SUPPLIES LTD

Invoice No.

63 Conduit Street
Liverpool L1 6NN

Telephone: 0151-432 2222
Fax: 0151-432 2210

Account No.

VAT Reg No. 924 4614 29

Date/Tax point

Product code	*Description*	*Quantity*	*Unit price* £ p	*Total amount* £ p

Comments:

NET TOTAL	
VAT @ 17 ½%	
GRAND TOTAL	

Registered Office: 63 Conduit Street, Liverpool L1 6NN

Registered No: 822 4742

BPP PUBLISHING

WORKBASE OFFICE SUPPLIES LTD

63 Conduit Street
Liverpool L1 6NN

Telephone: 0151-432 2222
Fax: 0151-432 2210

VAT Reg No. 924 4614 29

Invoice No.

Account No.

Date/Tax point

Product code	*Description*	*Quantity*	*Unit price* £ p	*Total amount* £ p

Comments:	NET TOTAL	
	VAT @ 17 ½%	
	GRAND TOTAL	

Registered Office: 63 Conduit Street, Liverpool L1 6NN — Registered No: 822 4742

3 CREDIT NOTES AND DEBIT NOTES

The credit note

3.1 Using our earlier example of the Student Supplies' invoice (see Paragraphs 2.2 and 2.3 of this chapter), suppose that Student Supplies sent out its invoice for 450 rulers, but the typist accidentally typed in a total of £162.97, instead of £62.97. The county council has been **overcharged** by £100. What is Student Supplies to do?

3.2 Alternatively, suppose that when the primary school received the rulers, it found that 120 of the rulers had been broken in the post and that it was going to send the broken ones back. Although the County Council has received an invoice for £62.97, it has no intention of paying that amount, because 120 of the rulers were **useless**. Again, what is Student Supplies to do?

3.3 The answer is that the supplier (in this case, Student Supplies) sends out a **credit note**.

KEY TERM

A **credit note** is a document subtracting an amount from an invoice (or invoices) which have already been sent.

A credit note is sometimes printed in red to distinguish it from an invoice. Otherwise, it will be made out in much the same way as an invoice, but with less detail and with a 'Credit Note Number' instead of an 'Invoice Number'.

3.4 For example, in the case described in Paragraph 3.2 above, the credit note issued might look like this.

STUDENT SUPPLIES LIMITED

123 Factory Street Worktown London W19 4NB
Tel: 0208 123 4567 Fax: 0208 123 4589

CREDIT NOTE

Credit Note No: 83
Re: Invoice No: 1496

CREDIT TO:
Westshire County Council
46 Chamber Street
Camberwick Green
CG2 4SP

Date of credit/Taxpoint : 10 May 20X7

ITEM CODE	QUANTITY	DESCRIPTION	UNIT PRICE £	AMOUNT £
17004	120	12" Wooden rulers	0.12	14.40
		VAT at 17.5%		2.39
		Total credit		16.79

Reason for credit
Goods damaged in transit. Original order no. 3365 (Brilliant Primary School).
Returns note number 42.
VAT No 245 8269 41 Terms:5/7, n/30

VAT and discounts on credit notes

3.5 Where a cash discount is applied on the original invoice, **VAT is calculated** on credit notes on the **lowest amount** which the customer could have paid. In the example above, VAT is calculated as **£14.40 × 95% × 17.5% = £2.39**, because of the cash discount offered on the original invoice.

Checks over credit notes

3.6 Just as it is important to ensure that invoices are correct, it is important to have **checks on the credit notes** which are issued too.

3.7 Some of the checks listed for invoices (Paragraph 2.14), for example the arithmetical checks, are relevant to credit notes too. In the case of a credit note, checking to a despatch document will not apply. The equivalent check in the case of a credit note issued when goods are returned will be to agree the details of the credit note to the **goods returned note**.

3.8 But what if the credit note is not being given for goods returned? We have noted above that a credit note might be necessary in the case of a **clerical error**. Goods being **lost in transit** might also result in a credit note being needed. In neither of these cases will there be 'goods returned documents' with which the credit note can be checked.

3.9 The fact that a credit note may be issued for various reasons, some of which do not involve the actual return of goods, means that many businesses will have fairly **strict procedures over the issue of credit notes**. Credit notes should require the **special authorisation of a senior member of staff**, who will examine what evidence there is for credit being granted before signing the authorisation.

3.10 If an **incorrect invoice** is issued then a credit note may be issued for the total amount of that invoice. A new invoice can then be raised for the correct amount.

Reasons for issuing credit notes

3.11 Reasons for issuing a credit note include the following.

- When a customer returns **faulty** or **damaged goods**
- When a customer returns perfect goods under a **sale or return agreement** with the supplier
- When a **clerical error** is made on the invoice resulting in the customer being overcharged
- When **fewer items have been delivered than have been invoiced**
- To **settle a dispute** with the customer
- To credit the customer for perfect returned goods when the supplier **has specifically agreed** to do so

The debit note

3.12 A **debit note** might be issued by a **supplier** instead of raising a new invoice to adjust an invoice already issued **upwards** (for example because **more goods** were delivered than were invoiced). This is also commonly achieved by issuing a revised invoice after a credit or debit note has been raised for internal purposes only (to keep records straight).

3.13 More commonly, a debit note is issued by a **customer** as a means of **formally requesting a credit note from the supplier**. In this case a debit note is a 'memorandum' item and therefore it is not used to record a transaction in the accounting system.

Activity 4.3 — Level: Assessment

The two invoices below have been prepared by a colleague of yours at Workbase Office Supplies Ltd and passed to you for checking before they are sent out.

Task

You are required to amend (where possible) any errors apparent on the invoices. If there is not sufficient information to amend the invoice, indicate what the error is without amending it.

Your checks should cover the following points.

(i) Are the prices correct? The Catalogue and Price List is provided in Appendix A of this chapter.

(ii) Has any discount due been correctly calculated? The List of Customer Discounts is provided at Appendix B.

(iii) Has VAT been calculated correctly at the standard rate of 17½%?

(iv) Are other details on the invoice correct?

You may assume that product descriptions and quantities are correct, as these have been agreed to purchase orders and despatch notes.

WORKBASE OFFICE SUPPLIES LTD

63 Conduit Street
Liverpool L1 6NN

Telephone: 0151-432 2222
Fax: 0151-432 2210

VAT Reg No. 924 4614 29

Invoice No. 7064

Order No. 6057

Account No. W001

Date/Tax point 4 May 20X7

Whiterock Publishing Ltd
74 Whiterock Road
Manor Park
Liverpool
L24 7BJ

Product code	*Description*	*Quantity*	*Unit price* £ p		*Total amount* £ p	
F74700	Exeter 420L Executive Chair (Colour: Oatmeal)	2	296	00	296	00
F71610	Chequers 474E Typist's chair (Colour: Charcoal)	1	136	00	136	00
			Goods total		412	00
			Less 15% discount		61	80
			NET TOTAL		350	20
			VAT @ 17 ½%		61	28
			GRAND TOTAL		411	48

Registered Office: 63 Conduit Street, Liverpool L1 6NN   Registered No: 822 4742

WORKBASE OFFICE SUPPLIES LTD

63 Conduit Street
Liverpool L1 6NN

Telephone: 0151-432 2222
Fax: 0151-432 2210

VAT Reg No. 924 4614 29

Invoice No.

Order No. 624

Account No. C011

Date/Tax point 4 May 20X7

Coals of Newcastle Ltd
25A Hive Street
Newcastle-upon-Tyne
NE4 6PR

Product code	*Description*	*Quantity*	*Unit price* £ p	*Total amount* £ p
F55650	Stakkaform 1200 Workstation base unit	1	85 15	85 15
F10430	Ambience multidrawer filing cabinet (colour: coffee/cream)	1	186 20	186 20
A22588	Perfex 600F 4-hole fixed punch	5	20 47	81 88
			NET TOTAL	271 35
			VAT @ 17 ½%	47 49
			GRAND TOTAL	223 86

Registered Office: 63 Conduit Street, Liverpool L1 6NN Registered No: 822 4742

Activity 4.4 Level: Assessment

Imagine that you are working in the sales department of Workbase Office Supplies Ltd.

(a) Mr Bunny of Rabbit Fast Food Franchises telephones you on 4 May 20X7. He says that one of the Chequers 474E Typist's Chairs in Fern (Invoice No 7012) in Activity 4.2) is faulty. The fabric has not been correctly fixed to the seat, and he asks you to arrange for it to be collected.

You consult your supervisor, telling her that there are currently no more stocks of item F71620. It is agreed that the chair should be collected from the customer and that full credit should be given for the item.

(b) Mrs French, of Lexicon Translators, 67 Back Lane, Mountford L22 7FE (account number L004), calls to tell you that she has received eight Priory System 3 Triple tier tray sets in Grey. She ordered that number of the sets in Slate Blue, but the details were incorrectly transcribed from the purchase order on to the multi-part invoice set (Invoice Number 7038) which includes the delivery note. As a result, eight Grey sets were despatched and invoiced to Lexicon Translators. Mrs French requires the items delivered to be replaced by the correct items. The procedures of your firm do not permit the despatch of goods without a delivery note.

Task

Consider what action is necessary in each case.

If appropriate, prepare a credit note to be issued to the customer, assuming that the next credit note number to be issued is C422, and the date of issue is 9 May 20X7. If you consider that it is not appropriate to issue a credit note, state what alternative action you would recommend, giving reasons.

Two credit note forms are provided below. You are not required to prepare invoices for goods replacing any items for which credit is being given.

Credit note forms

WORKBASE OFFICE SUPPLIES LTD **Credit Note No.**

63 Conduit Street
Liverpool L1 6NN

Telephone: 0151-432 2222
Fax: 0151-432 2210

VAT Reg No. 924 4614 29

Account No.

Date/Tax point

Product code	*Description*	*Quantity*	*Unit price* £ p	*Total amount* £ p

Reasons for credit:	NET TOTAL	
	VAT @ 17 ½ %	
	TOTAL CREDIT	

Registered Office: 63 Conduit Street, Liverpool L1 6NN Registered No: 822 4742

WORKBASE OFFICE SUPPLIES LTD

63 Conduit Street
Liverpool L1 6NN

Telephone: 0151-432 2222
Fax: 0151-432 2210

VAT Reg No. 924 4614 29

Credit Note No.

Account No.

Date/Tax point

Product code	*Description*	*Quantity*	*Unit price* £ p	*Total amount* £ p

Reasons for credit:	NET TOTAL	
	VAT @ 17 ½%	
	TOTAL CREDIT	

Registered Office: 63 Conduit Street, Liverpool L1 6NN   Registered No: 822 4742

4 CUSTOMER CREDIT LIMITS

What are customer credit limits?

4.1 When a business supplies goods or services on credit it puts itself into a position in which **it is owed money**. The business faces the risk that the purchaser may not eventually pay for the goods and services, for example if the purchaser goes bankrupt. It makes sense for a business to set a **credit limit.**

KEY TERM

Credit limits are set on the **value** of goods or services a business is prepared to supply on credit to any individual customer. Many businesses set such limits for each of its credit customers, so that a list can be drawn up of all the customers with a credit limit against each customer name.

For example, a new customer might only have a credit limit of £100, while an established one may have £10,000. In either case, the total credit extended by the business to the respective customers must not exceed those limits.

Setting a credit limit

4.2
- A credit limit for a customer will be set by **senior staff** in the organisation.
- Some businesses pay to receive reports on customers from a **credit reference agency** which will help to indicate how 'creditworthy' the customer is - in other words, how safe it is to allow a certain amount of credit to the customer.

Taking credit limits into account

4.3 The customer's **credit limit** needs to be considered when a customer's order is processed. **An order received from a customer should not be accepted if supplying and invoicing that order would mean that the customer owed more to the business than the amount of the credit limit.** How records are kept of the total amount which a customer owes will be discussed in later chapters of this text.

4.4 In some organisations, a clerical assistant receiving an order which would lead to the customer's owing more than his or her credit limit will be expected to refer the order to a supervisor, who may then need to refer the matter to a manager. Turning the order down straight away might cause offence or ill will with the customer and the manager may want to consider **revising the credit limit**.

4.5 **Checking customer credit limits when orders are received from customers** is another of the checks (or 'controls') which a business is likely to have over supplying goods and services on credit.

5 GENERATION OF INVOICES AND CREDIT NOTES BY COMPUTER

Working with computerised systems

5.1 Nowadays most businesses, including smaller ones, use computers for accounting.

5.2 The most important thing to bear in mind if you are ever confronted with a computerised accounting system - whether it be in an assessment or in real life - is that **in theory it is just the same as a manual system**. The difference is that the various books of account have become invisible. They are now inside the computer, ready to be called upon, and the computer has taken on the chores of entering and posting all the original data.

How are computers used in invoicing?

5.3 You should remember that, in computer terminology, a **file** is a collection of data having some common features. For example, a price list or a customer list may be held as a computer file.

5.4 An **invoicing program** operates by making use of two data files:

(a) The **customer file**, containing the name, address and account number of the customer.

(b) The **product file**, containing descriptions, unit quantities and selling prices of each product which the business sells.

Step 1 The computer operator enters the **customer account number.** This will bring the name, address and any other necessary details on to the screen.

Step 2 The operator can then enter **product codes and quantities** to be supplied.

Step 3 The program **calculates any discount due, VAT** and the **total** amount of the invoice.

Step 4 The invoice may be **printed out** immediately, or it may be stored on disk for printing later with a batch of invoices.

5.5 The procedure for producing **credit notes** will be similar. The computer operator will key in the reason for credit, to be entered on the credit note.

Reports produced by an invoicing program

5.6 An invoicing program may produce various reports which a business may need from time to time. Examples include the following.

- Lists of customers by geographical area
- Details of the sales of different products
- A list of products sold
- An analysis of sales to different customers (perhaps by geographical area)

Key learning points

- A **credit transaction** takes place when the seller of goods or services does not expect to be paid for the goods or services until some time after they have been supplied. The seller sends an **invoice** to the customer. The invoice is a demand for the customer to pay the amount owed, usually by a certain date.

- Documents which may be involved in a supply of goods include an **initial letter of enquiry**, a **quotation**, an **order** and an **order acknowledgement**. When the goods are supplied, a **delivery note** is signed by the customer as proof of the delivery and an **advice note** may be left with the customer for his or her records. **Multi-part stationery sets** are often used to provide many of these documents, and such sets may also include the invoice.

- An invoice is usually numbered, and gives the seller's **VAT** registration number. Any **trade discount** will be subtracted from the price of goods before VAT is added. A VAT registered business must charge VAT. The standard rate of VAT which applies to most goods and services in the UK is 17½%.

- **Checks over the invoices** raised by a business could include repeating invoice calculations originally performed by the person who completed the invoice. Invoices may need to be checked to orders and to despatch documents, and prices agreed to price lists. Ideally, there should be **segregation of duties** so that the three areas of order acceptance, control and despatch of goods, and invoice preparation, are the job of separate people in the organisation.

- A **credit note** will need to be issued if a customer has been charged too much. Reasons for credit include errors in invoicing and goods damaged or lost in transit. Credit notes may require special authorisation.

- A business needs to place limits on the credit it allows to customers. Orders should not be accepted if they would result in customer **credit limits** being exceeded.

- In a **computer-based system** invoices and credit notes may be produced using an invoicing program. The invoice or credit note will be created from:

  - Information in the customer file
  - Information in the product file
  - Details keyed in by the computer operator

Chapter 4: Appendix A

Workbase Office Supplies Limited

Quality products for your office environment

Catalogue and price list

[Extracts from the catalogue are set out below]

		Code no
OFFICE FURNITURE		
Exeter 420L Executive chair		
	Oatmeal	F74700
	Fern	F74710
	Charcoal	F74720
Chequers 472E Conference chair		
	Oatmeal	F76400
	Charcoal	F76410
Chequers 474E Typist's chair		
	Paprika	F71600
	Oatmeal	F71610
	Fern	F71620
	Charcoal	F71630
Ambience multidrawer filing cabinets		
	Grey	F10420
	Coffee/cream	F10430
Ambience card filing cabinet		
	For 6" × 4" cards (9 drawers) - grey	F10577
	For 8" × 5" cards (7 drawers) - grey	F10579

Stakkaform shelving units

These units offer a combined filing and working area for computer operators. Available in two sizes, the top and base units may be purchased together or the base unit may be purchased separately.

	600 workstation top and base unit	F55540
	600 workstation base unit	F55550
	1200 workstation top and base unit	F55640
	1200 workstation base unit	F55650

Ambico shelving

Steel posts and polyester-coated steel shelves, adjustable at 1" intervals

	6-shelf unit	F58110
	12-shelf unit	F58120
	18-shelf unit	F58130

	Code no
OFFICE ACCESSORIES	
Tara file trolleys	
Available in three sizes. Trays not included	
Holds 6 'Tower 300' filing trays	A87724
Holds 12 'Tower 300' filing trays	A87725
Holds 6 'Tower 400' filing trays	A87726
Tara filing trays	
Tower 300	A87821
Tower 400	A87822
Prior System 3 tripe tier tray sets	
Smoke	A89810
Grey	A89811
Slate blue	A89812
Perfex punches and perforators	
420 heavy duty perforator. Two-hole, 8cm gauge	A22410
340 medium duty perforator. Two-hole, 8cm gauge	A22421
120 mini-punch. Capacity: 8 sheets	A22500
600F 4-hole fixed punch	A22588
PENS, PENCILS AND MARKERS	
Ultrapoint ball pens	
Fine point. Black. Pack of 50	G12342
Fine point. Blue. Pack of 50	G12343
Fine point. Red. Pack of 50	G12344
Fine point. Green. Pack of 12	G12345
Medium point. Black. Pack of 50	G12352
Medium point. Blue. Pack of 50	G12353
Medium point. Red. Pack of 50	G12354
Medium point. Green. Pack of 12	G12355
HI-lite Jumbo markers	
Chisel point. Black	G14385
Chisel point. Red	G14386
Fine point. Black	G14392
Fine point. Red	G14393
Two-colour marker. Black and red	G14384
Office Star pencils. The popular general office pencil	
Supplied in packs of 12	
4B	G14001
HB	G14000
3H	G14002
B	G14003
2H	G14004

Workbase Office Supplies Limited

Price list

Prices exclude VAT • Please use the product codes shown • Products are supplied singly unless otherwise stated • All goods are carriage paid

The prices of items listed in the catalogue extracts are set out below

Code no	*Price* £
A22410	23.45
A22421	10.92
A22500	1.64
A22588	20.47
A87724	65.00
A87725	94.00
A87726	82.00
A87821	4.92
A87822	6.13
A89810	14.27
A89811	14.27
A89812	14.27
F10420	186.20
F10430	186.20
F10577	484.50
F10579	464.00
F55540	189.90
F55550	85.15
F55640	276.50
F55650	104.25
F58110	126.00
F58120	226.00
F58130	338.00
F71600	136.00
F71610	136.00
F71620	136.00
F71630	136.00
F74700	296.00
F74710	296.00
F74720	296.00
F76400	212.00
F76410	212.00
G12342	6.08
G12343	6.08
G12344	6.08
G12345	1.45
G12352	6.08
G12353	6.08
G12354	6.08
G12355	1.45

Code no	*Price* £
G14000	2.58
G14001	2.58
G14002	2.58
G14003	2.58
G14004	2.58
G14384	1.71
G14385	1.21
G14386	1.21
G14392	0.94
G14393	0.94

Chapter 4: Appendix B

Workbase Office Supplies Limited

List of customer discounts and credit limits

For internal use only

	Account no	*% Discount*	*Credit limit*
			£
Rabbit Fast Food Franchises Ltd	R001	25	500
Bowser & Bowser	B020	25	500
Roundabout Supplies Ltd	R002	20	500
Underwood Dairies	U001	20	500
Brittan's Farm Management Ltd	B007	20	500
Keats & Joyce	K010	15	1,000
Rank & Co	R005	15	750
Conduit Insurance Co plc	C002	15	500
John Cotton (Grantley) Ltd	C008	10	500
Whiterock Publishing Ltd	W011	10	500

- All credit customers not on the above list are entitled to a 10% discount on the full value of orders over £100.
- Workbase Office Supplies Ltd has a special arrangement with Fawsley's (account no: F003) whereby Fawsley's have a credit limit of £2,000.

Quick quiz

1 What is a credit transaction?

2 Name three documents which come before an invoice.

3 What is multi-part stationery?

4 What is meant by the 'tax point'?

5 What does 'ex works' mean?

6 What is the rule about VAT and discounts?

7 What is a credit note?

8 What is a debit note?

Answers to quick quiz

1 A transaction in which the buyer does not pay for the goods or services until some time after they have been supplied.

2 (i) A letter of enquiry
(ii) A quotation
(iii) A purchase order
(iv) An acknowledgement
(v) A delivery note or advice note

3 Sets of stationery pre-printed with the type of document represented, eg invoice, acknowledgement. The details of the order are copied onto each part in the set.

4 The date of the transaction for VAT purposes.

5 The invoice price does not include delivery.

6 The VAT is calculated on the amount net of the discount, regardless of whether the discount is taken.

7 A document subtracting an amount from an invoice already sent.

8 A document issued by a supplier to adjust an invoice already issued upwards or as a formal demand for a credit note.

5 Sales and sales returns day books

This chapter contains

Learning objectives

On completion of this chapter you will have learned about:

- Organisational procedures for authorisation and coding of sales invoices
- Organisational procedures for filing source information
- Relationship between accounting system and the ledger

Performance criteria

1.1.4 Invoices and credit notes are entered into primary records according to organisational procedures

1.1.5 Entries are coded and recorded in the appropriate ledger

Range statement

1.1.3 Primary records: sales day book; sales journal; returns day book

1.1.4 Ledger: main ledger; subsidiary ledger; integrated ledger

Chapter 5 scenario – Diners' Suppliers Ltd. This scenario applies to all the activities in this chapter.

Diners' Suppliers Ltd is a wholesaler of crockery, glassware, electrical appliances and sundry other goods for the kitchen and home.

Sales are classified into the following categories:

C	crockery
G	glassware
E	electrical appliances
X	sundry

All of the company's supplies are standard-rated for VAT purposes. The standard rate of VAT is 17½ %.

1 WHAT IS THE SALES DAY BOOK?

The need for the sales day book

1.1 A business will obviously want to make sure that it **receives the money due for all of the sales which it makes**. To do this it needs to:

(a) Raise invoices for all of the goods and services which it sells on credit
(b) Issue invoices to the right customer
(c) Keep track of the invoices and credit notes which it has raised.

1.2 In other words, **the business will need records which show:**

(a) **When and who it should ask for money**.

(b) The **total sales** it has made so that it can see how well it is doing as a business.

The business will therefore need to have some way of **recording** and **summarising** the contents of the invoices and credit notes, which are called 'source documents'.

The function of the sales day book

KEY TERM

The **sales day book** is used to keep a list of all the invoices and credit notes sent out to customers each day. One alternative name for this list is the sales journal; you may also come across other names for a listing which serves the same purpose.

1.3 Because a transaction is recorded in the sales day book before being recorded elsewhere, the sales day book is sometimes referred to as a '**book of prime entry**' or a '**primary record**'.

1.4 The term 'book' is used because that is the form which these records generally used to and sometimes still do take. But it is worth bearing in mind that, nowadays, books of prime entry are often not actual books, but are rather files hidden in the memory of a computer. **Nevertheless, the principles of how transactions are recorded remain the same whether the records used are computerised or manual.**

1.5 EXAMPLE: SALES DAY BOOK

An extract from the sales day book of Boot and Shoe Supplies appears as follows.

Date	*Invoice number*	*Customer*	*Net total*	*VAT*	*Gross total*
			£	£	£
10.1.X5	20247	S Jones	172.00	30.10	202.10
	20248	Abbey Supplies Ltd	84.50	14.78	99.28
	20249	Cook & Co	292.70	51.22	343.92
	20250	Texas Ltd	172.00	30.10	202.10
	20251	Dinham Shoes	74.75	13.08	87.83
	20252	Mentor Ltd	272.05	47.60	319.65
	Totals		1,068.00	186.88	1,254.88

1.6
- The items listed in the day book should follow an **unbroken numerical sequence**, usually by invoice number.
- Numbers of **spoiled invoices** should be entered too, with blanks in the 'amounts' columns and/or a note as cancelled under 'customer', so that it is clearly recorded that no invoice with that number has been raised.

Activity 5.1 — Level: Assessment

Task

Complete and total the proforma sales day book from Diners' Supplies Ltd on page 107 in respect of the following transactions. The customer's name follows the invoice number.

17/3/X7 Invoice I2060 - Kirby Kitchenware

Product description	*Amount (inc VAT)*
	£
Bostonware plates	68.15
Wine glasses	72.85
	141.00

17/3/X7 Invoice I2061 – Boddington Kitchens Ltd

Product description	*Amount (inc VAT)*
	£
Electric toasting forks	42.03
Electric salt/pepper mills	30.92
Glassware	65.00
Sundry items	13.67
	151.62

17/3/X7 Invoice I2062 - Invoice form spoiled

17/3/X7 Invoice I2063 - Placesetters Ltd

Product description	*Amount (inc VAT)*
	£
Electric salt/pepper mills	30.92
Glassware (various)	40.50
Tablemats (sundry)	32.69
	104.11

18/3/X7 Invoice I2064 - Anston Mayne

Product description	*Amount (inc VAT)*
	£
Wine glasses	141.00

18/3/X7 Invoice I2065 - Nye & Co

Product description	*Amount (inc VAT)*
	£
Plates 9"	48.62
Saucers 5"	10.45
	59.07

18/3/X7 Invoice I2066 - Dindins Ltd

Product description	*Amount (inc VAT)*
	£
Electric plate cleaners	37.10
Sundry	8.88
	45.98

18/3/X7 Invoice I2067 - Major John Design

Product description	*Amount (inc VAT)*
	£
Crockery (various)	45.30
Glassware (various)	45.30
	90.60

Further information

Customer account numbers are as follows.

Anston Mayne	A01
Boddington Kitchens Ltd	B09
Dindins Ltd	D06
Fuller Crockery	F03
Kirby Kitchenware	K02
Major John Design	M09
Nye & Co	N04
Placesetters Ltd	P11

Tutorial note. You can ignore the rounding rules for VAT in this exercise.

DINERS' SUPPLIES - SALES DAY BOOK

Date	Invoice No.	Customer No.	Total	C	G	E	X	VAT
	TOTAL							

2 WHAT IS THE SALES RETURNS DAY BOOK?

KEY TERM

The **sales returns day book** is a chronological listing of sales returns. It records the value of goods returned to the business by buyers, dealt with by the issue of credit notes.

2.1 An entry from the sales returns day book of Boot and Shoe Supplies looks like this.

Date	*Credit note number*	*Customer*	*Net total* £	*VAT* £	*Gross total* £
10.1.X7	C2214	Pediform Ltd	29.40	5.14	34.54

2.2 Some sales returns day books may have a column headed with something like 'goods returned', so that a **description of the goods returned** can be entered into the returns day book as well.

2.3 There might be no separate sales returns day book, with returns being entered as **figures in brackets in the sales day book** instead.

3 ENTERING SALES TRANSACTIONS IN THE DAY BOOKS

3.1
- In a **manual system of accounting**, which might be used by a small business, writing up the sales day book will probably involve writing out the details of each invoice - each transaction - by hand. The details of credit notes can similarly be written directly into the sales returns day book.
- In a **computerised sales ledger**, transaction details will probably be entered onto the system using a keyboard and VDU (visual display unit).

Analysing sales

3.2 As well as the kinds of information which we showed in the example from the sales day book shown earlier (the date, the invoice number, the name of the customer, the net total, VAT and the gross total), it is common for the **net value of the sales** made to be analysed into different categories in the day book. This is because it can be helpful for a business to have information about the amount of **sales of different types** which it is making.

3.3 In a manual day book, we can achieve this analysis by adding more columns to the sales day book. For example, the transactions which we used as examples in Paragraphs 1.5 and 2.1 above might be analysed into columns headed 'Boot sales' and 'Shoe sales'.

3.4 Rather than set this out as if an analysed sales day book had been written out in full by hand, we shall look at how an analysis might be prepared using a **computer spreadsheet**.

A spreadsheet model

3.5 You may already be familiar with spreadsheets. The use of spreadsheets is covered in detail at the AAT Intermediate level. Here we illustrate a **simple use of spreadsheets,** and some introductory details are given in case you are unfamiliar with them.

3.6 A spreadsheet is basically a **grid** - like the grid on a large sheet of 'analysis paper' - which is held in the memory of a computer. There are **columns** which are generally headed with the letters of the alphabet and **rows** which are generally given numbers in sequence. The spreadsheet can be used like a large sheet of paper on which information can be written by keying it in through a keyboard to a VDU. Each position on the spreadsheet (given by where a column and a row meet, eg A1, C4, G7) is called a 'cell'.

3.7 EXAMPLE: ANALYSED SALES DAY BOOK USING A SPREADSHEET

Suppose that we wanted to analyse our sales transactions (at sales value excluding VAT) into the following types:

GB	Gents' boots
LB	Ladies' boots
GS	Gents' shoes
LS	Ladies' shoes
A	Shoe polish/accessories

Once we have keyed in the information on each invoice, our sales day book spreadsheet model might look like this. Note that the totals of columns F to J come to the total of column C (the sales net of VAT), not column E.

	A	*B*	*C*	*D*	*E*	*F*	*G*	*H*	*I*	*J*	*K*
1	Boot and Shoe Supplies					Credit sales			Date:	10100	
2	Invoice	Cust	Net	VAT	Gross	GB	LB	GS	LS	A	
3	No	No	£	£	£						
4	20247	J042	172.00	30.10	202.10		95.45		76.55		
5	20248	A009	84.50	14.78	99.28					84.50	
6	20249	C124	292.70	51.22	343.92				292.70		
7	20250	T172	172.00	30.10	202.10			172.00			
8	20251	D249	74.75	13.08	87.83	74.75					
9	20252	M201	272.05	47.60	319.65	94.20		72.42	105.43		
10											
11											
:											
24	Total		1,068.00	186.88	1,254.88	168.95	95.45	244.42	474.68	84.50	

3.8 Although spreadsheets can be very useful, it is important to recognise them for what they are. If a spreadsheet has been **set up incorrectly**, or if data has been **entered incorrectly** without any check being carried out on its accuracy, then the

spreadsheet may contain errors. Just because a spreadsheet has been produced using a computer, it does not follow that it is going to be free of errors.

Sales ledger packages

3.9 As with a manual sales day book, a sales day book spreadsheet can be updated by each individual invoice being entered by somebody. Many businesses operate computerised accounting packages, however, with one part which deals with sales transactions (generally called a 'sales ledger package'). We now look at how this can affect the entering of sales transactions.

3.10 It may be that a computerised sales ledger system involves entering sales transactions in a similar way to that described for the spreadsheet model we looked at above.

Step 1 Sales invoices are typed out.

Step 2 The details on invoices are keyed into the computer using a keyboard and VDU.

Step 3 One of the 'reports' which the computer is able to produce might be a listing of sales invoices and credit notes for a particular day. This listing might be similar to the spreadsheet we looked at earlier.

3.11 Most businesses would want to save themselves the duplicated work of preparing invoices and then keying in the invoice details. This saving can be made by a sales ledger **package which will produce invoices itself**.

Step 1 Certain information will be input, such as the date, the customer number, product codes and quantities.

Step 2 The computer package will use this information to produce invoices.

Step 3 The package will collect the information on the invoices and credit notes needed to create the sales day book.

3.12 In some computer systems, a **system for recording stocks of goods held** is combined (or 'integrated') with **the system for processing sales orders**.

Step 1 The details of goods which a customer orders are keyed in and recorded by the Sales Order Processing (SOP) system, which can then produce an order acknowledgement form to send out to the customer.

Step 2 When the goods are despatched or sent out to the customer, details of this despatch can be keyed in to the computer together with the number of the order which is being satisfied.

Step 3 The computer will then produce a sales invoice, using the information it already has about the order.

Step 4 Reports may be produced of sales and returns made on a particular day or in a particular period to give the information which a 'traditional' sales day book would contain.

4 POSTING THE DAY BOOK TOTALS

4.1 We have seen above how details of sales transactions may be entered in a sales day book. We mentioned at the beginning of the chapter that a business will want, among other things, to make sure that it receives the money due from all of the sales that it makes. It needs records to show when it should ask for the money due to it following a credit sale. Can the sales day book achieve that objective on its own?

Personal accounts for debtors

4.2 The answer is no. A listing of sales transactions in chronological order, such as the sales day book shows, would not meet these needs of a business of any size at all.

- For many businesses, the chronological record of sales transactions might involve very large numbers of invoices per day or per week.
- The same customer might appear in several different places in the sales day book, for purchases he has made on credit at different times. So at any point in time, a customer may owe money on several unpaid invoices.

What we need is a way of showing **who** owes **what** amount to the business and **when**.

4.3 This need is met by maintaining '**personal accounts**'. For sales, there will be personal accounts for each individual debtor maintained in the **sales ledger**.

- Each individual sales transaction is entered in the sales day book(s) and needs to be recorded in the personal sales ledger account of the customer.
- We will see below that day book totals need to be posted to the total debtors and sales accounts in the general ledger.

Personal accounts are sometimes called 'memorandum accounts' to indicate that the recording of transactions in these accounts is **not** part of the double entry. The **general ledger** accounts to which the double entry postings are made are sometimes called 'impersonal accounts'.

Recording the double entry

4.4 The transactions entered in the sales day book need to be recorded in the 'double entry' system of bookkeeping.

4.5 Before we can record the double entry, the sales day book must be **totalled** and **ruled off**, to include all transactions since the book was last ruled off. In our examples in Paragraphs 1.5 and 3.7 the day books have already been ruled off and totalled.

4.6 Remember that a business will have a **cash account** as part of its double entry, posted from the cash book. This is the general ledger account in which receipts and payments of cash are recorded. Clearly no entries can be made in the cash account when a credit transaction first takes place, because initially no cash has been received or paid. Where then are the details of the transaction entered?

4.7 The solution is to use the total debtors' account.

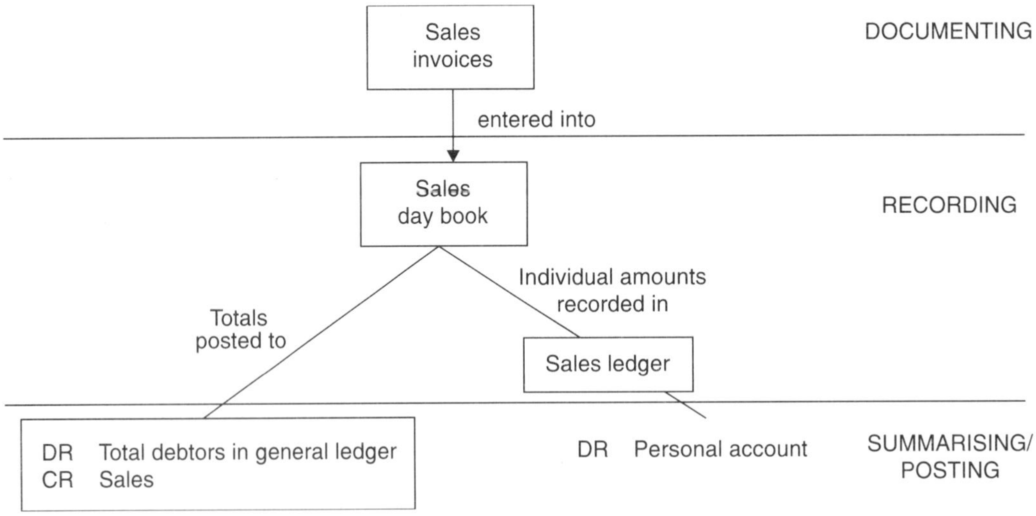

The double entry

4.8 Remembering basic double entry rules, we can see that the sales summarised in the sales day book are transactions having two aspects:

- An increase in our **asset** (debtors)
- An increase in **income** (sales)

> **KEY TERM**
>
> A **total debtors account**, or **'sales ledger control account'**, is maintained in the general ledger to record in total the amounts which are posted to the debtors' individual personal memorandum accounts in the sales ledger.

4.9 For sales made to credit customers the entries made will be:

		£	£
DEBIT	Total debtors account ('control account')	X	
CREDIT	Sales account		X

- The **total debtors account** records an **asset** - the debts owed by the customers.
- The **sales account** records **income** - the amount of sales which the business is making.

4.10 We show the basic double entry as follows.

		£	£
DEBIT	Total debtors account	X	
CREDIT	Sales account		X

4.11 We do not need to record each sales transaction separately in the general ledger. We make use of day book totals to summarise the transactions.

VAT

4.12 Looking back at the transactions in Paragraph 3.7, you can see that value added tax (**VAT**) is charged on the sales. As you know, the business must account to HM Customs & Excise for the output VAT it collects. In order to keep track of the amount it owes to or is owed by Customs and Excise, the business keeps a Value Added Tax Account (perhaps called a VAT Control Account) in the general ledger.

4.13 The VAT which customers owe to the business is included in the overall amount owed (total debtors), but the other side of the entry for the amounts of VAT invoiced to customers is an **increase in the liability of the business to pay over VAT to HM Customs & Excise**. The double entry will have this form (we'll show actual figures a little later).

		£	£
DEBIT	Total debtors account	X	
CREDIT	VAT account		X
	Sales account		X

Sales returns day book

4.14 The double entry arising from posting of totals from a **sales returns day book** will be like a mirror image of the posting of sales which we have just looked at. When goods are returned, we want to 'reverse' the transaction (or part of it) as it was shown in the books when we recorded the sale. The double entry will take the following form.

		£	£
DEBIT	VAT account	X	
	Returns account (or sales account)	X	
CREDIT	Total debtors account		X

Sales analysis

4.15 Earlier we saw how sales can be analysed into different categories in the sales day book. Rather than maintaining a single account in the general ledger for sales, a business may split the sales into a number of general ledger accounts so that it has **a record in the general ledger of the amounts of the different types of sales.**

4.16 EXAMPLE: DOUBLE ENTRY RECORDING OF SALES

Using the example in Paragraph 3.7, the double entry for Boot and Shoe Supplies would look like this:

		£	£
DEBIT	Total debtors account	1,254.88	
CREDIT	VAT control account		186.88
	Sales - gents' boots account		168.95
	Sales - ladies' boots account		95.45
	Sales - gents' shoes account		244.42
	Sales - ladies' shoes account		474.68
	Sales - shoe polish/accessories account		84.50

As ever, the total amount posted to the debit side equals the total amount posted to the credit side (check this).

The posting summary

4.17 How then will we carry out the postings for the sales made by Boot and Shoe Supplies on 10 January 20X7? We can either:

(a) Use a double entry posting summary for the general ledger accounts, and post the sales ledger memorandum accounts straight from the individual invoices in the sales day book

(b) Or use a double entry posting summary for the general ledger, and use it to post the sales ledger too.

4.18 Boot and Shoe Supplies uses a posting summary to deal with the sales ledger postings as well as the general ledger (double entry) postings. Here is the posting summary for the 10 January 20X7 sales day book, and the sales returns day book shown in Paragraph 2.1 (which, you are informed, was of gents' boots).

BOOT AND SHOE SUPPLIES

General ledger posting summary

Account name	Account code	General ledger Dr £	p	Cr £	p
Total debtors	60400	1,254	88	34	54
Sales - GB	01010			168	95
Sales - LB	01020			95	45
Sales - GS	01030			244	42
Sales - LS	01040			474	68
Sales - A	01050			84	50
Returns - GB	01110	29	40		
VAT	70700	5	14	186	88
TOTALS		1,289	42	1,289	42

Posted by C.F .... Date 10/1/X7 ....

4.19 The total of the **debits** posted to the general ledger must equal the total of the **credits** posted to the general ledger. If these two columns do not add to the same figures, whoever is completing the form knows that they must have made some error and will look for the error before going any further.

Note that each general ledger account has an account code to identify the correct account to be posted.

4.20 The **sales ledger postings** to be made from the sales day book are as follows.

Ref	*A/c name*	*A/c code*	*Debit* £	*Credit* £
20248	Abbey Supplies	A009	99.28	
20249	Cook & Co	C124	343.92	
20251	Dinham Shoes	D249	87.83	
20247	S Jones	J042	202.10	
20252	Mentor Ltd	M201	319.65	
C2214	Pediform Ltd	P041		34.54
20250	Texas Ltd	T172	202.10	
			1,254.88	34.54

4.21 Check that you can see where the various figures come from and how they reflect the form of double entry of transactions which we have looked at above. Note also the following points.

- There is an **account code** for each customer, which is what will be used to identify the correct account to which a sales ledger posting should be made.
- The **debit and credit totals** posted to the individual sales ledger accounts are the same as the amounts posted to the total debtors account as shown at the top of the columns of postings to the general ledger in Paragraph 4.18 above.

4.22 Once the general ledger and the sales ledger postings have been keyed in to Boot and Shoe's computerised accounts package, the general posting summary is **filed for future reference**.

Activity 5.2 **Level: Assessment**

Task

Complete the journal entry form below with the double entry required to record the sales on 17 and 18 March 20X7 as detailed in Activity 5.1.

DINERS' SUPPLIES LIMITED			No:
Journal Entry			
Date			
Prepared by			
Authorised by			
Account	Code	DR £ p	CR £ p
Totals			

Further information

The last journal entry form was numbered 120.

The following is a list of account codes, for use in Activities 5.2 and 5.3.

Sales C	2010
Sales G	2020
Sales E	2030
Sales X	2040
Sales returns C	2310
Sales returns G	2320
Sales returns E	2330
Sales returns X	2340
VAT control account	4000
Creditors ledger control account	0310
Debtors ledger control account	0210

Activity 5.3 — Level: Assessment

On 24 March 20X7, the sales returns day book of Diners' Supplies Ltd records the fact that credit notes were issued to Anston Mayne and Major John Design in respect of all the purchases they made on 18 March 20X7 (as recorded in Activity 5.1).

Task

Using the account codes given in Activity 5.2, complete the journal entry form below (to be numbered 132) with the double entry required to record the issue of these credit notes.

DINERS' SUPPLIES LIMITED			No:
Journal Entry			
Date			
Prepared by			
Authorised by			
Account	Code	DR £ p	CR £ p
Totals			

Activity 5.4 — Level: Assessment

(a) The closing balance at the end of an accounting period for Diners' Supplies Ltd's VAT control account is £12,572.50 CR.

(i) This means that £12,572.50 is owed by .... to .... (complete the blanks).

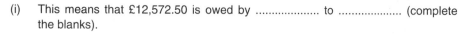

(ii) Does the balance represent an asset or a liability for Diners' Supplies Ltd?

Asset / Liability (circle the correct answer)

(b) The closing balances on the nominal ledger accounts below are credit or debit balances, as indicated. Indicate by circling the correct answer whether the balances represent an asset to the business, a liability of the business, an expense item or revenue earned.

Account	*Credit or debit balance*				
Sales	CREDIT	Asset	Liability	Expense	Revenue
Sales returns	DEBIT	Asset	Liability	Expense	Revenue
Debtors' ledger control account	DEBIT	Asset	Liability	Expense	Revenue
Discounts allowed	DEBIT	Asset	Liability	Expense	Revenue
Cash	CREDIT	Asset	Liability	Expense	Revenue

Cash sales

4.23 Remember that if a cash sale is made, say of ladies' shoes, **this will not pass through the sales ledger** nor the **total debtors account** in the general ledger, and the double entry can be completed in the form:

		£	£
DEBIT	Cash account	X	
CREDIT	VAT account		X
	Sales - ladies' shoes account		X

ASSESSMENT ALERT

You should make sure you understand the material in this chapter especially thoroughly. A substantial task involving posting from the day books is likely to appear in the Devolved Assessment.

Key learning points

- The **sales day book** lists the invoices raised by a business when it supplies goods or services on credit. The **sales returns day book** lists the credit notes raised when goods are returned. The sales day book and the sales returns day book are '**books of prime entry**': transactions are recorded in them before being recorded elsewhere.
- **How transactions are entered in the books of prime entry depends upon the accounting system which is used** by the business. Details will be entered from invoices in some systems. In others, information about which orders have been despatched will be entered and the invoices and primary records of sales will be generated by computer from this information.
- **Sales may be analysed** into different categories, according to the information needs of the business and its system of accounting. A **spreadsheet** could be used as a model to produce an analysed sales day book.
- The day book totals for sales and returns are posted to the **general ledger total debtors account**, the **VAT control account** and the **sales account**. The amounts owed by individual debtors are entered in the **sales ledger personal accounts** (where these are maintained as **memorandum accounts** separate from the nominal ledger).

Quick quiz

1 What is the purpose of the sales day book?

2 What is the purpose of the sales returns day book?

3 Why do businesses maintain personal accounts in the sales ledger?

4 What is another name for the 'total debtors account'?

5 What is the function of this account?

6 A cash sale will be shown in the sales ledger. True or false?

Answers to quick quiz

1 To record credit sales on a daily basis.

2 To record returns of credit sales on a daily basis.

3 To show who owes what to the business at any given time. This information is not in the sales day book or the total debtors account.

4 The debtors control account.

5 To record in total the amounts posted to the debtors' individual memorandum accounts in the sales ledger.

6 False. The sales ledger only records credit sales.

6 The sales ledger

This chapter contains

Learning objectives

On completion of this chapter you will have learned about:

- Relationship between the accounting system and the ledger
- Relevant understanding of the organisation's accounting systems and administrative systems and procedures

Performance criteria

1.1.6	Statements of account are prepared and sent to debtors
1.2.1	Receipts are checked against relevant supporting information
1.2.2	Receipts are entered in appropriate accounting records

Range statement

1.1.4	Ledger: main ledger; subsidiary ledger; integrated ledger
1.1.6	Source documents: aged debtors analysis
1.2.1	Receipts: cash; cheques; automated payments
1.2.2	Accounting records: cash book

Chapter 6 scenario – Steps. This scenario applies to activities 6.1 to 6.3 in this chapter.

You are setting up the sales ledger system for Steps. The firm has a wide variety of customers.

1 PERSONAL ACCOUNTS FOR CREDIT CUSTOMERS

The need for personal accounts

1.1 We have seen how the sales day book provides a chronological record of the invoices and credit notes sent out by a business to credit customers. In addition to keeping a chronological record of invoices, a business needs a record of how much money each individual credit customer owes, and what this total debt consists of. The need for a **personal account** for each customer is thus a practical one.

- A customer might telephone, and ask how much he currently owes; staff must be able to **tell the customer the state of his account.**
- It is a common practice to send out **statements** to credit customers at the end of each month, showing how much they still owe, and itemising new invoices sent out and payments received during the month.
- The managers of the business will want to keep a check on the **credit position of an individual customer**, and to ensure that no customer is exceeding his **credit limit** by purchasing more goods.
- Perhaps most important is the need to **match payments against debts owed**. If a customer makes a payment, the business must be able to set off the payment against the customer's debt and establish how much he still owes on balance and which particular items are left unpaid.

The sales ledger

1.2 **Debtors are people or organisations who owe money to the business.**

KEY TERM

The **sales ledger** contains the individual personal accounts showing what each individual debtor of the business owes. (It is sometimes called the **debtors ledger**.)

1.3 Sales ledger accounts are written up as follows.

DEBIT When invoices are entered in the **sales day book,** they are subsequently also made in the **debit** side of the relevant customer account in the sales ledger.

CREDIT When entries are made in the **cash book** in respect of payments received from customers, or in the **sales returns day book** for goods returned, they are made in the **credit** side of the relevant customer account.

1.4 The entries recorded in a customer's personal account can be represented by a 'T'-account, as follows.

CUSTOMER ACCOUNT CU01

On the debit side	£	*On the credit side*	£
Invoices sent out inc VAT	X	Sales returns (credit notes) inc VAT	X
		Payments received	X
		Discounts allowed	X

1.5 Each customer account is given a reference or code number (CU01 above). This reference (sometimes called the 'sales ledger folio') can be used in the sales day book. In a manual ledger, a page in the sales ledger would normally be allocated for each account in the ledger.

1.6 Here is an example of how a sales ledger account can be laid out.

CHEF & CO — A/c no: C124

Date	*Details*	£	*Date*	*Details*	£
1.1.X7	Balance b/d	250.00			
10.1.X7	Sales - SDB 48				
	(invoice 0249)	343.92	11.1.X7	Balance c/d	593.92
		593.92			593.92
11.1.X7	Balance b/d	593.92			

- The **debit** side of this personal account shows amounts owed by Chef & Co.
- When Chef pays some of the money it owes it will be entered into the cash book (receipts) and subsequently recorded in the **credit** side of the personal account.

For example, if Chef had paid £250 on 10 January 20X7, it would appear as follows.

CHEF & CO — A/c no: C124

Date	*Details*	£	*Date*	*Details*	£
1.1.X7	Balance b/d	250.00			
10.1.X7	Sales - SDB 48		10.1.X7	Cash	250.00
	(invoice 0249)	343.92	11.1.X7	Balance c/d	343.92
		593.92			593.92
11.1.X7	Balance b/d	343.92			

The opening balance owed by Chef & Co on 11 January 20X7 is now £343.92 instead of £593.92, because of the £250 receipt which came in on 10 January 20X7.

Personal accounts as memorandum accounts

1.7 As we have seen, in manual systems of accounting and in **some** computerised accounting systems, the personal accounts of customers **do not form part of the double entry system of bookkeeping**. This is because the personal accounts include details of transactions which have already been summarised in day books and posted to ledger accounts. For example, sales invoices are recorded in sales and total debtors general ledger accounts, and payments received from debtors are recorded in the cash and total debtors accounts. **The personal accounts of customers do not then form part of the double entry system: if they did, transactions would be recorded twice over.**

Integrated sales ledger

1.8 But in some computerised systems, **the sales ledger is 'integrated' with the general ledger**. Instead of being maintained as memorandum accounts reflecting the various customer balances making up the total debtors account in the general ledger, individual customers' accounts effectively do form part of the double entry system, and there is **no separate total debtors account.** This means that the general ledger posting summary and the sales ledger postings that we saw in Chapter 5 Paragraphs 4.18 and 4.20 could effectively be combined as follows.

BOOT AND SHOE SUPPLIES			General ledger posting summary			
Account name	Account code	Ref	General ledger Dr £	p	Cr £	p
Abbey S	A009	20248	99	28		
Cook & Co	C124	20249	343	92		
Dinham	D249	20251	87	83		
S Jones	J042	20247	202	10		
Mentor	M201	20252	319	65		
Pediform	P041	C2214			34	54
Texas Ltd	T172	20250	202	10		
Sales GB	O1010				168	95
Sales LB	O1020				95	45
Sales GS	O1030				244	42
Sales LS	O1040				474	68
Sales A	O1050				84	50
Returns GB	O1110		29	40		
VAT	70700				181	74
TOTALS			1284	28	1284	28
Posted by ....C.F....				Date ....10/1/X7....		

Businesses not needing a sales ledger

1.9 You might think that all but the very smallest businesses will need to maintain a sales ledger. **But even some very large businesses have no credit sales at all.**

- Chains of supermarkets which make all of their sales by cash, cheque or plastic card.
- Other businesses, such as a defence contractor selling only to a government, may not sell to enough different organisations to make it worthwhile to operate a sales ledger.

2 MAINTAINING CUSTOMER RECORDS

2.1 A business will keep a **personal account for each of its regular customers**. Normally, it will be simpler if there is just one account for each customer. But a business with a number of branches may want to keep separate personal accounts for a single customer at each of the branches from which the customer makes purchases.

Opening a new customer account

2.2 What do we do if an order is received from someone who does not hold a credit account with the business? The obvious answer is that we need to open an account in the sales ledger for the new customer. To **account for** the sale, we do indeed need to do this. But before this is done, we must be sure that the new account is **properly authorised**, in accordance with the procedures of the organisation in which we are working.

2.3 Supplying goods and services on credit involves the **risk that the customer may be unable to pay**. Before supplying on credit, we should be confident that supplying the value of goods which the customer wants is an acceptable risk for the business.

2.4 In Chapter 4, we explained how a **credit limit** will be allocated to each customer.

- In the case of a customer which is a **large and well-known public company** (a 'plc'), a business may set a very high credit limit for this customer because it is confident that the risk of the customer being unable to pay is very small.
- A much lower credit limit would be set for a **small business in a declining industry** about which little is known.
- If a prospective customer is known to be in some financial difficulties, it may be decided that **no credit account should be allowed at all for that person or company**. We are then saying that if the prospective customer wants to do business with us, payment must be made **in cash** when the sale is made.

We return to the topic of allocating credit limits in Chapter 10.

How is a sales ledger account opened?

2.5 In a **manual system of bookkeeping**, the necessary customer details may simply be written on to a new page in the sales ledger. Customer details will include the following.

- Customer name and address
- Credit limit
- Customer account number (sales ledger folio)

The terms of business applying to the customer may also need to be specified, if they are different for different customers (such as credit period, sale or return basis and so on).

2.6 In a **computerised sales ledger system**, opening an account will be one of the activities involved in maintaining customer records, which in a menu-driven system will form one of the Sales Ledger Processing menu options.

2.7 For example, option 1 of the Sales Ledger Processing menu might be headed **'Update Account Name/Address'**. Using this option, we can do the following.

- Enter new customer details
- Delete customer accounts which are no longer required
- Amend details of existing customers (eg change of credit limit or change of address)

2.8 The layout of the computer screen when we call up this option might look like the illustration below.

SALES LEDGER SYSTEM: CUSTOMER DETAILS

ACCOUNT CODE:	I 024	CUSTOMER NAME:	Ivory Carpets Ltd
CONTACT NAME:	Frank Ward	CUSTOMER ADDRESS:	23 Switchback Rd Headingly Leeds LS3 4PS
SALES REPRESENTATIVE:	S Morley		
CREDIT LIMIT:	£2,000		
CREDIT PERIOD:	30 days	LAST TRANSACTION DATE:	07.02.X4
		CURRENT BALANCE:	£1,424.67

Account code number

2.9 Each customer's account **code number** is **unique**. To add a new customer record to the file (ie to open a new customer account), you simply enter a new customer account code and then complete the remaining details.

2.10 The **name and address box** should contain the full postal address, as this will serve as the reference in the system for the customer address. If the system is used to produce sales invoices then the full postal address will appear on the invoice. A section of the customer record may be available for the business to record any **extra information** which it wishes to keep on the customer.

Credit limits

2.11 The **credit limit** is entered to show the amount of credit which the business will allow the customer.

- If an invoice is recorded in the sales ledger which will result in the customer exceeding his credit limit, most computerised systems will **warn the operator** of this, giving him or her the option of **cancelling the transaction**.
- If it is not possible to cancel the transaction (for example, goods may already have been supplied to the customer) at least the operator will be alerted to the fact that no further sales should be made until the customer **pays off some of the outstanding balance**.

Existing customer accounts

2.12 Some customers may only make occasional purchases from the business, so that usually they do not owe anything to the business. Once a customer has an account with the business, it will probably make sense to **keep the account open** even if the customer has not made a purchase very recently and owes nothing to the business. If the customer wants to make another purchase, the customer's account can be allowed to become 'active' again.

2.13 If there are **dormant accounts** for which there have been no transactions for some time, it may be that they are unlikely to be used again in the foreseeable future. It may be a good idea to close accounts like this to tidy up the ledger and avoid unnecessary or 'redundant' data being produced.

2.14 A computerised sales ledger package may include an optional facility for the **automatic deletion of zero balances from the sales ledger at the end of a period.**

For deleting zero balances	Against deleting zero balances
This may save time by deleting customers making 'one-off' sales.	If there is a good chance of 'zero' accounts becoming active again, it may be useful to keep them on the ledger. It avoids the need to re-input account details for customers whose accounts become active again. Keeping all previous customers on the ledger may provide a useful customer listing for marketing purposes.

The decision to opt for a facility to delete all zero accounts will depend on the nature of the business.

Dividing the sales ledger

2.15 In the days when the sales ledger was generally maintained in bound ledger books, it made sense for larger businesses to **divide up the sales ledger into sections,** each of which could be kept in a separate book. Keeping all accounts in only one ledger book means that only one person can use the ledger at any one time. The division of the ledger might be along geographical or alphabetical lines; you might see something like the following in a very large organisation.

Sales ledger division		
Geographical	or	*Alphabetical*
Scotland		A - B
N Ireland		C - E
NE England		F - H
NW England		I - K
Midlands		L - M
Wales		N - P
SW England		Q - S
SE England		T - V
London		W - Z

2.16 Even where the sales ledger is **computerised**, dividing up the sales ledger may make good administrative sense. It may also reduce the possibility of fraud.

2.17 It is important to realise that dividing up the ledger in this way has no effect on the way that sales ledger accounts are written up.

Activity 6.1 **Level: Pre-assessment**

You are setting up the sales ledger system for Steps. The firm has a variety of customers.

Draw up a typical proforma record in your sales ledger, showing all the information you are likely to need about a customer.

3 RECORDING TRANSACTIONS IN THE SALES LEDGER

3.1 Let us now look at a more detailed example of how sales ledger accounts are produced from entries in the **sales and sales returns day books** and from details of cash received from the **cash book**.

3.2 In a computerised system, transactions may be input directly to customer accounts in the sales ledger ('**transaction processing**') or alternatively stored as a **transaction file** to form a part of the next updating run.

3.3 EXAMPLE: SALES LEDGER TRANSACTIONS

Marlon & Co started trading at the beginning of April. During April, the sales day book and the sales returns day book of Marlon & Co showed the following transactions.

Sales day book

Date	*Name*	*Invoice ref*	*Net total*	*VAT*	*Gross total*
			£ p	£ p	£ p
2 April	Turing Machinery Ltd	2512	250.00	43.75	293.75
4 April	G Wright	2513	300.00	52.50	352.50
9 April	G Wright	2514	725.00	126.87	851.87
9 April	Turing Machinery Ltd	2515	620.00	108.50	728.50
10 April	Simpsons Ltd	2516	85.00	14.87	99.87
24 April	Simpsons Ltd	2517	1,440.00	252.00	1,692.00
25 April	Simpsons Ltd	2518	242.00	42.35	284.35
25 April	G Wright	2519	1,248.00	218.40	1,466.40
30 April	Totals		4,910.00	859.24	5,769.24

Sales returns day book

Date	*Name*	*Credit note*	*Net total*	*VAT*	*Gross total*
			£ p	£ p	£ p
23 April	G Wright	0084	220.00	38.50	258.50
25 April	Turing Machinery Ltd	0085	250.00	43.75	293.75
30 April	Totals		470.00	82.25	552.25

During May, the following payments for goods sold on credit were received.

Payments received

		£ p
7 May	Turing Machinery Ltd	728.50
14 May	G Wright	352.50
14 May	Simpsons Ltd	99.87

We need to show the entries as they would appear in the sales ledger accounts to reflect the above transactions.

3.4 SOLUTION

Sales ledger

TURING MACHINERY LTD

Date	*Details*	£ p	*Date*	*Details*	£ p
2 April	Invoice 2512	293.75	25 April	Credit note 0085	293.75
9 April	Invoice 2515	728.50	7 May	Cash book	728.50

G WRIGHT

Date	*Details*	£ p	*Date*	*Details*	£ p
4 April	Invoice 2513	352.50	23 April	Credit note 0084	258.50
9 April	Invoice 2514	851.87	14 May	Cash book	352.50
25 April	Invoice 2519	1,466.40			

SIMPSONS LTD

Date	*Details*	£ p	*Date*	*Details*	£ p
10 April	Invoice 2516	99.87	14 May	Cash book	99.87
24 April	Invoice 2517	1,692.00			
25 April	Invoice 2518	284.35			

In this example, we show the sales ledger accounts as **'T'-accounts**, with debits on the left and credits on the right. This is how ledger accounts are usually shown in ledger books in manual accounting systems and the 'T'-account format helps to show the logic of double entry principles.

3.5 Many computerised accounting systems use a **single-column format**, with **debit** items being shown as **negative** and **credit** items being shown as **positive**.

For example, the entries in G Wright's account in the sales ledger might appear as follows in a single-column format.

Sales ledger	*A/c name: G Wright*	*Dr(–)/Cr(+)*
4 April	2513	– 352.50
9 April	2514	– 851.87
23 April	0084	+258.50
25 April	2519	–1,466.40
14 May	Cash book	+352.50

3.6 So far we have recorded Marlon and Co's transactions in the sales ledger memorandum accounts, but not in the double entry system of the general ledger. In this example, we shall assume that the cash book forms a part of the double entry (rather than being a book of prime entry from which a separate cash account is prepared).

3.7 EXAMPLE: POSTING TRANSACTIONS TO THE GENERAL LEDGER

The **payments received** will be posted as debits in the **cash account.**

CASH BOOK/ACCOUNT (IN THE GENERAL LEDGER)

Date	*Details*	£ p		£ p
7 May	Turing Mach. Ltd	728.50		
14 May	G Wright	352.50		
14 May	Simpsons Ltd	99.87		

Sales income excluding VAT will be **credits** in the **sales account.**

SALES ACCOUNT

		£ p	Date	Details	£ p
			30 April	Sales day book	4,910.00

Sales returns excluding VAT will be **debits** in the **sales returns account.**

SALES RETURNS ACCOUNT

Date	Details	£ p			£ p
30 April	Sales returns day book	470.00			

VAT on sales and **sales returns** will be **credits** and **debits** respectively in the **VAT account.**

VAT ACCOUNT

Date	Details	£ p			£ p
30 April	Sales returns day book	82.25	30 April	Sales day book	859.24

To complete the double entry in the general ledger accounts, we need to post the **total amounts owed** and the **payments received** as the result of credit sales transactions in the period to the **debit** and **credit** side respectively of **total debtors account** in the general ledger.

TOTAL DEBTORS ACCOUNT

Date	Details	£ p			£ p
30 April	Sales day book total	5,769.24	30 April	Sales returns day book total	552.25
			7 May	Cash book	728.50
			14 May	Cash book	452.37
			31 May	Balance c/d	4,036.12
		5,769.24			5,769.24
1 June	Balance b/d	4,036.12			

Note that in this case the two amounts of cash received on 14 May have been added together to give the **daily total** posted to the total debtors account.

3.8 Section summary

Ledger	Source	DR		CR	
Sales ledger (memorandum a/c)	SDB	Sales (inc VAT) [1]	117.50		
	SRDB			Sales returns inc VAT [2]	23.50
	CB			Cash received [3]	94.00
General ledger (double entry)	SDB	Total debtors (inc VAT)[1]	117.50		
	SDB			Sales	100.00
	SDB			VAT	17.50
		Invoices			
	SRDB			Total debtors (inc VAT) [2]	23.50
	SRDB	Returns account	20.00		
	SRDB	VAT	3.50		
		Credit notes issued for goods returned			

Ledger	Source	DR		CR	
	CB			Total debtors (inc VAT) [3]	94.00
	CB	Cash account *Cash received*	94.00		

The total entries in the sales ledger memorandum accounts will equal the correspondingly numbered entries in the general ledger shown above.

3.9 You would normally expect to find that the total debtors account has a **debit balance** overall.

3.10 Sometimes it is easier to see how accounting entries are made by looking at a diagram of the process. The chart on the following page illustrates the process of **sales ledger postings** which we have examined above.

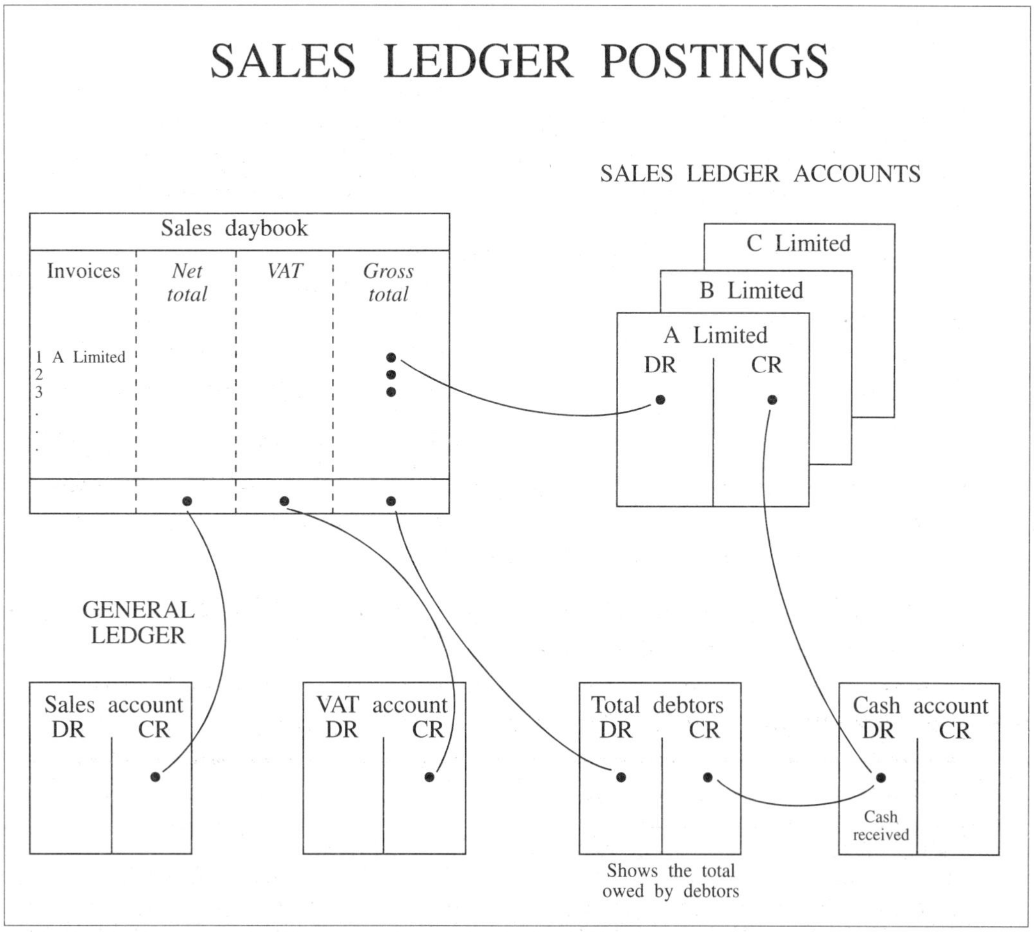

Checking the sales ledger recording: reconciling totals to total debtors account

3.11 Having recorded the sales invoices, credit notes and cash received, we can now check the **accuracy** of the amounts recorded in the sales ledger memorandum account. This can be done by working out the total of the balances on individual sales ledger accounts and comparing this with the total balance on the general ledger total debtors account.

3.12 In the example of Marlon & Co, we have balanced the postings to the total debtors account. The balance is £4,036.12. If this balance does not agree with the total of individual account balances, an **error or errors must have been made**. Check this for yourself by balancing the sales ledger accounts in the example.

(You should find that the balances are: £0 for Turing, £2,059.77 for Wright and £1,976.35 for Simpsons, which come to a total of £4,036.12.)

Activity 6.2 — Level: Assessment

Steps has only recently begun to sell goods on credit in a big way. Up until now, the company has run one set of books: the nominal ledger. Every transaction has been entered in the nominal ledger. This is proving unwieldy - it is becoming difficult to chase individual debtors as all the amounts they owe are jumbled together in one account.

In outline only, show a way of accounting for credit transactions which would get round this problem.

Activity 6.3 — Level: Assessment

You are presented with the following transactions from the sales day book and sales returns day book for 1 January 20X7.

SALES DAY BOOK FOLIO 82

Date	*Customer account*	*Invoice number*	*Goods value*	*VAT (17½%)*	*Total*
			£.00	£.00	£.00
1/1/X7	001	100	72.34	12.66	85.00
1/1/X7	030	101	83.53	14.62	98.15
1/1/X7	001	102	14.46	2.53	16.99
1/1/X7	132	103	17.20	3.01	20.21
1/1/X7	075	104	104.77	18.33	123.10
1/1/X7	099	105	30.40	5.32	35.72
1/1/X7	001	106	64.97	11.37	76.34
Total 1/1/X7			387.67	67.84	455.51

SALES RETURNS DAY BOOK FOLIO 73

Date	*Customer account*	*Credit note*	*Invoice reference*	*Goods value*	*VAT (17½%)*	*Total*
				£.00	£.00	£.00
1/1/X7	099	C44	89	301.03	52.68	353.71

Tasks

(a) Post the transactions to the sales ledger accounts provided below.

(b) Set out the double entry for the transactions shown.

(c) Comment on any unusual items resulting from your work in (a) and itemise any additional procedures which you consider necessary. Is there anything which should be brought to your supervisor's attention?

CUSTOMER NAME: Arturo Aski

ACCOUNT 001

ADDRESS: 94 Old Comedy Street, Vaudeville, 1BR, W. Meds

CREDIT LIMIT: £2,200

Date	Description	Transaction Ref	DR £	DR p	CR £	CR p	Balance £	Balance p
Brought forward 1/1/X7							2,050	37

CUSTOMER NAME: Maye West

ACCOUNT 030

ADDRESS: 1 Vamping Parade, Holywood, Beds, HW1

CREDIT LIMIT: £1,000

Date	Description	Transaction Ref	DR £	DR p	CR £	CR p	Balance £	Balance p
Brought forward 1/1/X7							69	33

CUSTOMER NAME: Naguib Mahfouz

ACCOUNT 075

ADDRESS: 10 Palace Walk, London NE9

CREDIT LIMIT: £1,500

Date	Description	Transaction Ref	DR £	DR p	CR £	CR p	Balance £	Balance p
Brought forward 1/1/X7								

CUSTOMER NAME: Josef Sveik

ACCOUNT 099

ADDRESS: 99 Balkan Row, Aldershot

CREDIT LIMIT: £700

Date	Description	Transaction Ref	DR £	DR p	CR £	CR p	Balance £	Balance p
Brought forward 1/1/X7							353	71

CUSTOMER NAME: Grace Chang							ACCOUNT 132	
ADDRESS: Red Dragon Street, Cardiff, CA4								
CREDIT LIMIT: £1,200								
Date	Description	Transaction Ref	DR		CR		Balance	
			£	p	£	p	£	p
Brought forward 1/1/X7							1,175	80

4 MATCHING CASH RECEIVED

What is the customer's sales ledger balance made up of?

4.1 The sales ledger account for a customer records the **invoices and credit notes issued** to a particular customer and sets against these any **payments received** from the customer. The result of this system of recording will be that the **balance** on the sales ledger account shows **how much that customer owes** at any particular time.

4.2 In the case of a customer who only makes **occasional purchases**, it may be fairly easy to see which invoices have not yet been paid, and therefore what items make up the account balance at any particular time.

4.3 EXAMPLE: SALES LEDGER ACCOUNT

The computer printout below shows all entries in Martlesham Ltd's account in the sales ledger of Domma Ltd, since Martlesham became a customer of Domma in June 20X3.

DOMMA LIMITED		SALES LEDGER SYSTEM
A/C NAME: MARTLESHAM LTD		A/C NO: MO24
		DATE: 22.1.X4
30.6.X3	Invoice 7214	–472.25
28.7. X3	Cash received	+472.25
3.8. X3	Invoice 7298	–282.00
21.8. X3	Invoice 7342	–424.70
7.9. X3	Credit note 0141	+74.50
17.9. X3	Cash received	+632.20
10.12. X3	Invoice 7621	–845.25
24.12. X3	Invoice 7710	–92.24
7.1.X4	Cash received	+845.25
20.1.X4	Invoice 7794	–192.21
	Balance	–284.45

It should be fairly easy for you to work out that the balance at 22 January 20X4 of £284.45 is probably made up of the amounts due on invoices 7710 and 7794 (check if you're not sure).

4.4 A business may have some regular customers to whom hundreds of invoices are issued each year.

- Some invoices may be **queried** by the customer and payment withheld until a credit note is issued.
- Payments received from the customer may be made according to the order in which the invoices are **approved** for payment by the customer, which could be very different from the order in which the invoices are issued.

Clearly, in the case of a customer like this, it is not likely to be so easy to see what the account balance at any time is made up of from a list of **all** the transactions on the account.

4.5 Why do we need to know exactly which items make up a customer's sales ledger balance?

- A business will want to try to get its customers to **stick to their allocated credit terms**, and so will want to chase up any invoices not paid within the period allowed by the terms.
- In order to settle any **disagreement** with the customer about the amounts owed, it will be necessary to have a record of exactly which items have not been paid rather than simply a record of the total balance owed.

4.6 There are two ways of keeping track of the customer's account.

Method	Technique
Open item	Keeps track of individual items (invoices and credit notes) in a sales ledger account which remain unpaid or become paid.
Balance forward	Any payment received is simply allocated to the oldest items or part items which remain unpaid.

How these different methods work will become clearer in what follows.

Matching cash received with invoices and credit notes: open item

KEY TERM

The **'open item' method** involves the matching of cash received with the invoices and credit notes to which it relates.

4.7 The first step in this process takes place when the customer **sends the payment** with a **remittance advice.**

- A remittance advice **totals** the value of all of the invoices which are being paid, less the value of any credit notes for which credit is being 'taken' with the payment.
- **The resulting net figure will then be the amount of the payment sent**.

4.8 The member of staff who records the receipt should compare it with the remittance advice as follows.

Step 1	Check that the amounts shown or marked off on the remittance advice **add up** to the total or **add up** the total of the items marked off yourself.
Step 2	Compare the **total** with the amount of the **cheque**.
Step 3	If there is a disagreement between the two amounts, mark on the remittance advice the amount received and calculate the **difference**.
Step 4	Send the cheque to be **banked** and record the receipt.
Step 5	Send the marked up remittance advice to the **sales ledger department**.

4.9 EXAMPLE: MATCHING CASH RECEIVED IN OPEN ITEM SYSTEMS

Continuing the above example, Martlesham Ltd sent with their payment of 17 September 20X3 a remittance advice as shown below.

Remittance advice

Domma Ltd
The Green
Menton PR2 4NR

Martlesham Ltd
24 Heath Road
Menton PR7 4XJ

17 September 19X3

Date	Details	Amount/£
3.08.X3	Invoice 7298	+282.00
21.08.X3	Invoice 7342	+424.70
07.09.X3	Credit note 0141	-74.50
	PAYMENT ENCLOSED	632.20

When the sales ledger clerk at Domma Ltd, Bill Feeny, posted the cash receipt of £632.20 in the sales ledger system, the system asked him to indicate which items the receipt was to be matched with.

Because of this process of matching, the sales ledger system was able to record which items were paid, so that the printout of transactions illustrated earlier appeared as follows (* denotes a cash receipt which has been matched).

DOMMA LIMITED — SALES LEDGER SYSTEM
A/C NAME: MARTLESHAM LTD — A/C NO: MO24
DATE: 22.1.X4

30.6.X3	Invoice 7214	–472.25	PAID
28.7.X3	Cash received	+472.25	*
3.8.X3	Invoice 7298	–282.00	PAID
21.8.X3	Invoice 7342	–424.70	PAID
7.9.X3	Credit note 0141	+74.50	PAID
17.9.X3	Cash received	+632.20	*
10.12.X3	Invoice 7621	–845.25	PAID
24.12.X3	Invoice 7710	–92.24	
7.1.X4	Cash received	+845.25	*
20.1.X4	Invoice 7794	–192.21	
	Balance	–284.45	

To find out the make-up of a customer's balance, it will be cumbersome and unnecessary to keep printing out details of all transactions even after they have been paid. A computer report may be produced showing only those items which remain unpaid (open items). In the case of Martlesham Ltd, this appears as follows on 22 January 20X4.

DOMMA LIMITED — SALES LEDGER SYSTEM
A/C NAME: MARTLESHAM LTD — A/C NO: MO24
DATE: 22.1.X4

24.12.X3	Invoice 7710	–92.24
20.1.X4	Invoice 7794	–192.21
	Balance	–284.45

However, to settle some queries, a listing of all transactions may be useful and records of all transactions need to be retained for control and audit purposes.

Unmatched cash in an open item system

4.10 If whoever posts cash received does not match the receipt or matches the receipt with items which do not total the amount received, then an amount of **unmatched cash** will be shown.

4.11 EXAMPLE: UNMATCHED CASH IN AN OPEN ITEM SYSTEM

Suppose that Bill Feeny had omitted to match the cash received on 7 January 20X4 with items on the account. The following printout of the account is then produced on 22 January 20X4.

DOMMA LIMITED		SALES LEDGER SYSTEM
A/C NAME: MARTLESHAM LTD		A/C NO: MO24
		DATE: 22.1.X4
10.12.X3	Invoice 7621	–845.25
24.12.X3	Invoice 7710	–92.24
7.1.X4	Unmatched cash	+845.25
20.1.X4	Invoice 7794	–192.21
	Balance	–284.45

4.12 There are different reasons why an amount of cash may remain unmatched.

- The clerk may **omit to match the cash in error**.
- There may be an **error on the customer's remittance advice** which means that the cash cannot be fully matched.
- The payment may have been **sent without a remittance advice**.
- The customer may have sent a '**round sum**' **amount** or payment on account (eg exactly £1,000, or 25% of balance) to pay off part of their balance without specifying to which items the amounts relate.

4.13 If a customer is making round sum payments or payments on account, this may be because of a **schedule of payments** which has been agreed with the customer. Such an agreement is sometimes made if the customer is in **financial difficulties**. In such a case, it may make sense for cash received to be matched with the oldest part of the debt by the '**balance forward**' method rather than just leaving it all as 'unmatched cash'.

4.14 However, if round sum payments are being made, this will almost always result in an amount of cash **remaining unmatched** because it is insufficient to match with the next invoice on the ledger.

4.15 EXAMPLE: ROUND SUM PAYMENTS OR PAYMENTS ON ACCOUNT

Domma Ltd has a customer Hampstead Ltd (Account number H002) with which it has agreed a schedule of payments whereby Hampstead Ltd pays £1,000 at the beginning of each month to clear its remaining debt. £1,000 was paid under this agreement on 2 January 20X4.

At 31 January 20X4, the items remaining unpaid by Hampstead Ltd were shown in Domma Ltd's sales ledger as shown below.

DOMMA LIMITED		SALES LEDGER SYSTEM
A/C NAME: HAMPSTEAD LTD		A/C NO: H002
		DATE: 31.1.X8
10.9.X3	Invoice 7468	–649.45
24.9.X3	Invoice 7513	–424.91
14.10. X3	Invoice 7581	–342.72
15.11. X3	Invoice 7604	–724.24
2.1.X4	Unmatched cash	+322.90
	Balance	–1,818.42

We need to show how £1,000 cash received from Hampstead Ltd on 1 February 20X4 will be recorded in the ledger.

4.16 SOLUTION

The cash available for matching, and the items with which it is matched, are shown below.

	£	£
2.1.X4 payment - unmatched part		322.90
1.2.X4 payment		1,000.00
Cash to be matched		1,322.90
Items to be matched		
Invoice 7468	649.45	
Invoice 7513	424.91	
		(1,074.36)
Cash remaining unmatched		248.54

The remainder of the January payment has now been matched, as has part of the February payment. The balance remaining after invoices 7468 and 7513 have been matched is £248.54, which is not sufficient to match fully with invoice number 7581 for £342.72.

After matching the cash received on 1 February, the ledger shows the account balance as follows.

DOMMA LIMITED		SALES LEDGER SYSTEM
A/C NAME: HAMPSTEAD LTD		A/C NO: H002
		DATE: 2.2.X4
14.10.X3	Invoice 7581	–342.72
15.11.X3	Invoice 7604	–724.24
1.2.X4	Unmatched cash	+248.54
	Balance	–818.42

4.17 In Domma Ltd's sales ledger system, only the **full value** of an invoice may be matched with a payment. Some sales ledger systems may allow an invoice to be shown as 'part-paid'. In this case, it should be made clear whether an invoice amount shown on a listing is a **part-paid** amount or whether it is instead the full amount of the invoice. You should be able to see that this is how a **'balance forward' system,** as opposed to the open item system, would work.

Activity 6.4 — Level: Assessment

A long-established customer of the firm where you work, Coldcut Ltd, is called Mr Ranjit Singh, of 19 Amber Road, St Mary Cray. His account number is 1124.

Mr Singh's business is a seasonal one but he still requires a steady supply of your product throughout the year.

Mr Singh pays you in two different ways. Some invoices he pays off in full. At other times he sends in a payment 'on account' to cover amounts outstanding, but these are not allocated directly to any particular invoice. They are deemed to apply to the earliest uncleared invoices outstanding, unless there is a dispute, or the invoice has had a specific payment made to it.

A computer virus has wreaked irrecoverable damage to your computer system.

Task

You have to 'reconstruct' the sales ledger for the past few months to discover what Mr Singh owes you, as he has requested a statement.

You unearth the following transactions.

Cash receipts (from cash book)

Date	*Cash book reference*	£	
15/2/X7	004	1,066.05	(Note)
25/3/X7	006	500.00	
15/4/X7	007	500.00	
15/5/X7	031	500.00	
20/5/X7	038	500.00	
20/6/X7	039	500.00	
22/6/X7	042	923.91	
Total receipts		4,489.96	

Note. This covers invoices 236 and 315.

Invoices	*Date*	*Value (inc VAT)* £
236	1 January 20X7	405.33
315	2 February 20X7	660.72
317	3 February 20X7	13.90
320	5 February 20X7	17.15
379	21 February 20X7	872.93
443	31 March 20X7	213.50
502	1 May 20X7	624.30
514	15 May 20X7	494.65
521	19 May 20X7	923.91
538	22 May 20X7	110.00
618	1 July 20X7	312.17
619	2 July 20X7	560.73
Total		5,209.29

Credit notes

C32 (against invoice 538)	8 July 20X7	110.00

Tasks

(a) Post all the transactions to a reconstructed sales ledger. Assume that there was a nil balance at the beginning of the year. Head up the columns: *Date; Transaction reference; Debit; Credit;* and *Balance.*

(b) Give a breakdown of Mr Singh's balances, stating which invoices are still outstanding.

5 THE AGE ANALYSIS OF DEBTORS AND OTHER REPORTS

The age analysis of debtors

5.1 It is important for a business to know what customer sales ledger balances are made up of so that **disagreements** with the customer and other queries can be resolved quickly. There also needs to be a way of knowing whether some of the invoices are **long overdue** so that those invoices can be followed up with the customer.

5.2 If a sales ledger consists of a large number of accounts, it would be a laborious and time-consuming process going through the details of each account to look for items which ought to be followed up. A lot of time can be saved by summarising the 'age' of the items in the various sales ledger accounts in a single schedule. This is achieved by what is called an **age analysis of debtors**.

KEY TERM

An **age analysis of debtors** breaks down the debtor balances on the sales ledger into different periods of outstanding debt.

What does the age analysis look like?

5.3 An age analysis of debtors will look very like the schedule illustrated below. The analysis splits up the total balance on the account of each customer across different columns according to the **dates of the transactions** which make up the total balance. Thus, the amount of an invoice which was raised 14 days ago will form part of the figure in the column headed 'up to 30 days', while an invoice which was raised 36 days ago will form part of the figure in the column headed 'up to 60 days'. (In the schedule below, 'up to 60 days' is used as shorthand for 'more than 30 days but less than 60 days'.)

DOMMA LIMITED

AGE ANALYSIS OF DEBTORS AS AT 31.1.X4

Account number	*Customer name*	*Balance*	*Up to 30 days*	*Up to 60 days*	*Up to 90 days*	*Over 90 days*
B004	Brilliant Ltd	804.95	649.90	121.00	0.00	34.05
E008	Easimat Ltd	272.10	192.90	72.40	6.80	0.00
H002	Hampstead Ltd	1,818.42	0.00	0.00	724.24	1,094.18
M024	Martlesham Ltd	284.45	192.21	92.24	0.00	0.00
N030	Nyfen Ltd	1,217.54	1,008.24	124.50	0.00	84.80
T002	Todmorden College	914.50	842.00	0.00	72.50	0.00
T004	Tricorn Ltd	94.80	0.00	0.00	0.00	94.80
V010	Volux Ltd	997.06	413.66	342.15	241.25	0.00
Y020	Yardsley Smith & Co	341.77	321.17	20.60	0.00	0.00
Totals		6,745.59	3,620.08	772.89	1,044.79	1,307.83
Percentage		100%	53.7%	11.4%	15.5%	19.4%

5.4 An age analysis of debtors can be prepared manually or by computer. **Computerisation does make the job a lot easier.** You should be able to see how the schedule is prepared by looking at the analysis of the balances of Martlesham Ltd and Hampstead Ltd which we looked at earlier.

- For Martlesham Ltd, at 31 January 20X4, Invoice No. 7794 for £192.21 is less than 30 days 'old', and Invoice No. 7710 for £92.24 is between 30 and 60 days old. The total balance owed at 31 January 20X4 by Martlesham Ltd to Domma Ltd is £284.45.
- The unmatched cash of £322.90 shown on Hampstead's account as at 31 January 20X4 has been deducted from the oldest part of the balance in compiling the age analysis.

How is the age analysis used?

5.5 As already suggested, the age analysis of debtors may be used to **help decide what action to take about older debts**. Going down each column in turn starting from the column furthest to the right and working across, we can see that there are some rather old debts which ought to be investigated.

- **Correspondence** may already exist in relation to some of these items.
- Perhaps some older invoices are still **in dispute**.
- Maybe some debtors are known to be in **financial difficulties**. (If there are newer invoices also for customers who could be in financial difficulties, we should perhaps be asking whether we ought to be continuing to supply goods to these customers.)

5.6 We can see from the above age analysis of Domma Ltd's debtors that the relatively high proportion of debts over 90 days (19.4%) is largely due to the debts of Hampstead Ltd. Other customers with debts of this age are Brilliant Ltd, Nyfen Ltd and Tricorn Ltd.

5.7 As well as providing information on the state of individual debtors' accounts, the age analysis of debtors may be used to give us a broader picture of the total debtors of the business. If there seems to be a high percentage of debts which are older than the usual payment terms allowed by the business, we may question whether the **credit control department**, one of whose jobs is to chase up slow payers, is performing its role properly.

5.8 Sometimes, a **column listing customer credit limits** will appear on the age analysis of debtors. This will make it easy to see which customers (if any) have exceeded or are close to exceeding their current credit limit.

Other computerised reports

5.9 **Computerisation of sales ledger processing** also allows a number of other reports to be printed out from the information held on the ledger, such as those outlined in the remainder of this section below. Access to sales ledger reports will probably be restricted, so that reports can only be obtained by authorised staff members whose password will allow them access.

Sales day book

5.10 **Sales day book listings** provide a way of keeping track of all of the items entered in the sales ledger. Typically, the information listed will include the following.

- The date of the item
- The account reference

- A transaction reference (eg invoice number)
- Type of transaction (eg invoice, credit note or adjustment)
- Net total before VAT
- VAT
- Gross total

If the sales ledger is not integrated with the general ledger then the sales day book listings can be used as a **posting summary** to the general ledger.

Statements of account

5.11 **Statements of account** are sent to customers at the end of each month to tell them how much they owe the organisation, with details of the transactions involved. These are discussed in Chapter 10.

5.12 At any time in the month, it will be possible to obtain for internal use a printout of the same details as are included in a **statement of account**. This may be needed from time to time to check details of transactions.

VAT analysis

5.13 If the rates of VAT (or other purchase taxes, in other countries) applying to the goods and/or services which a firm sells vary, then this report will show how much **output tax** has been invoiced at each of the different rates which apply. Even if different rates do not apply, in the European Union regulations require that statistics are submitted in **EU Intrastat** to show how much VAT-able supplies were made to other EU countries.

Sales analysis

5.14 Sales analysis reports allow the organisation to **analyse sales** in any way that it wants. The types of analysis required must be provided for when the system is set up for use by the organisation. (This is called the **configuration of the system**.) Among the more useful types of analysis could be those by product type, by area, by customer, or by sales representative.

5.15 EXAMPLE: SALES ANALYSIS

Purestream Water Filters Ltd produces water filters for domestic and industrial applications. When it bought a computerised sales ledger package two years ago, it configured the system so that transaction codes take the form product type/ product number/sales representative/invoice number. Thus, DOM/220/RKP/33141 refers to a transaction for the sale of a domestic water filter, model number 220, sold by the sales representative with initials RKP on invoice number 33141.

Purestream can now easily get a printout run off of sales by product type, by product number or by sales representative. Other distinctions might be reflected in the account number. For example, if accounts for all sales in Scotland are prefixed with an 'S', it will be a straightforward matter for the computer to summarise all sales made in Scotland in any period.

An analysis of **sales by sales representative** might look like the illustration below.

Purestream Water Filters Ltd - Sales ledger	
Sales ledger analysis	
08-MAR-X0	Page 1
SALES REP	£
AB	463.80
KL	1,314.55
AMM	454.60
RN	1,123.65
RKP	881.70
Total	4,238.30

List of customer accounts

5.16 A **list of customer accounts** summarises all debtors' accounts on the ledger. It will usually be possible to select for analysis all the accounts which have exceeded their credit limit. Lists such as this present **more selectively** information which is included in the full age analysis of debtors which was discussed earlier.

Customer mailing lists

5.17 The list of customer names and addresses held on the sales ledger is likely to be a **powerful marketing tool**, and may well be more up-to-date than mailing lists maintained on separate database packages for marketing purposes. If the firm wants to send a mailshot to all customers, or more selectively to all customers with turnover above say £20,000 per year, then the appropriate name/address labels can easily be printed out.

Key learning points

- The **sales ledger contains the personal accounts** of credit customers of the business. An account must be kept for each customer so that the business always has a full record of how much each customer owes and what items the debt is made up of.
- A **customer's account** in the sales ledger will **normally show a debit balance**: the customer owes money to the business and is therefore a debtor of the business.
- It is common for **customers' personal accounts** to be maintained separately from the nominal (or 'impersonal') ledger, as **'memorandum' accounts**. Sales ledger postings then do not form part of the double entry in the system of bookkeeping being used. Instead, a **total debtors' or sales ledger control account** is maintained in the nominal ledger to **keep track of the total of the amounts** which make up the entries in the individual personal accounts.
- Opening a **new sales ledger account** requires **authorisation** by a senior official. The amount of credit allowed to each individual customer should be kept **within acceptable limits of risk.**
- To make it clear exactly what a sales ledger customer's balance is made up of (which invoices remain unpaid), cash received from the customer is matched with the items for which it has been sent as the customer's payment. The customer indicates on the **remittance advice** which items are being paid.
- The **age analysis of debts** is useful to a credit controller wishing to decide on which debts to chase up. It also provides a general guide as to whether the debts of

a business are being collected quickly enough. Various other useful reports may be printed out from a **computerised sales ledger package**.

- Some debts may need to be written off as '**bad debts**' because there is no real prospect of them being paid. Alternatively or additionally, a **provision for doubtful debts** may be created.
- Rather than affecting individual customer balances, a provision for doubtful debts recognises the fact that ordinarily a certain **proportion** of all debts are unlikely to be collected. It is therefore prudent to make such a general 'provision' when calculating the overall profit or loss of the business.

Quick quiz

1. What does the sales ledger contain?
2. In manual accounting systems the personal accounts of customers do not form part of the double entry system. True or false?
3. What factors determine the credit limit allocated to a particular customer?
4. Why might the sales ledger be divided up?
5. How might you check the accuracy of the amounts recorded in the sales ledger?
6. What is the 'open item' method of keeping track of a customer's account?
7. What is the 'balance forward' method?
8. What is the function of an age analysis of debtors?
9. What accounting entries in the VAT account should be made when the provision for doubtful debts is set up?

Answers to quick quiz

1. The personal accounts of customers.
2. True.
3. (i) The trading record of the customer
   (ii) The industry in which he operates
   (iii) The size of the customer
4. For administrative convenience and to reduce the risk of fraud.
5. Work out the total of the balances on the individual sales ledger accounts and compare this with the total balance on the total debtors account.
6. A method which keeps track of individual items which remain unpaid or get paid.
7. Any payment received is simply allocated to the oldest items or part items which remain unpaid.
8. It breaks down the debtor balances on the sales ledger into different periods of outstanding debt.
9. None: it is a general provision and does not affect VAT.

Part C

Accounting for receipts

7 Receiving and checking money

This chapter contains

Learning objectives

On completion of this chapter you will have learned about:

- Organisational procedures for filing source information
- Cheques, including crossings and endorsements
- Methods of handling and storing money, including the security aspects
- The use of banking documentation
- Credit and debit cards
- Credit card procedures
- Automated payments: CHAPS, BACS, Direct debits, Standing orders

Performance criteria

1.2.1 Receipts are checked against relevant supporting information

1.2.4 Unusual features are identified and either resolved or referred to the appropriate person

Range statement

1.2.1 Receipts: cash; cheques; automated payments

1.2.3 Unusual features: wrongly completed cheques; out of date cheques, credit and debit cards; limits exceeded; disagreement with supporting documentation; under payments; over payments; cheques returned to sender

1 CONTROL OVER RECEIPTS

1.1 In any business, whatever its size, good **control over cash flow** is of great importance.

(a) The company must remain **solvent** (paying its debts as they fall due)

(b) Funds need to be available for **larger purchases** when necessary, such as the machines used to make the goods which the business sells.

1.2 A business cannot make any payments unless it has received money first, so controls over cash **receipts** are required if the company is to keep a healthy cash position. **Control over cash receipts** will concentrate on three main areas.

(a) Receipts must be **banked promptly**.

(b) The **record of receipts must be complete** and this is generally checked by comparing the receipt with supporting documentation (usually a **remittance advice**, which is described in Section 2 of this chapter).

(c) The loss of receipts through **theft or accident** must be prevented.

The difference between these three controls can be demonstrated with an example.

1.3 EXAMPLE: CONTROL OVER CASH RECEIPTS

Your company sells goods for £10,000 during the month of April to XYZ & Co. You receive a payment of £10,000 by cheque along with a remittance advice which shows exactly which invoices the cheque covers.

(a) You examine the cheque to ensure it is valid and completed correctly and you pay it in to the company account within 24 hours as company policy dictates (**banked promptly**).

(b) A colleague records the cheque details and compares the amount of the cheque to the remittance advice (**checking for completeness**). Usually the payment would also be checked against the total amount owed by the customer as part of the completeness check.

(c) The segregation of duties between the person who banks the money and the person who records it is considered to be a very good control to prevent **theft and accidental loss**; we will look at **segregation of duties** again later. Some businesses, when a cheque is received, will immediately **cross** the cheque in favour of the business which helps to protect against **theft**. We will look at **cheque crossing** later.

2 REMITTANCE ADVICES

2.1 Documents which are used to record transactions in the books of account of the company are called **source documents**. Source documents were covered in detail in Chapter 3 of this text. You should make sure you understand the form and content of these documents in particular.

- Invoice
- Credit note
- Purchase order
- Sales order

2.2 When a **cheque** arrives from a trade (ie business) customer it is usually accompanied by a **remittance advice**.

KEY TERM

A **remittance advice** shows which invoices a payment covers.

STATEMENT

Las Ninjos & Co
Belton Estate
Peterborough

TO: ABC & Co
4 The Mews
Middlesborough

A/C REF: 12379
DATE: 0104X7
PAGE: 1

DATE	DETAILS		DEBIT	CREDIT
0202X7	Invoice	017220	96.27	
0502X7	Invoice	017496	113.44	
1102X7	Invoice	017649	84.95	
2102X7	C/note	024173		22.00
0103X7	Cash received	C100		272.66
1203X7	Invoice	017780	212.11 ✓	
1503X7	Invoice	017821	106.07 ✓	
2903X7	Invoice	017944	78.90 ✓	
3003X7	C/note	025327		23.48 ✓

CURRENT	30 DAY	60 DAY	90 DAY	120+ DAY
373.60	0	0	0	0

AMOUNT DUE
£373.60

REMITTANCE ADVICE

Las Ninjos & Co
Belton Estate
Peterborough

FROM: ABC & Co
4 The Mews
Middlesborough

A/C REF: 12379
DATE: 0104X7
PAGE: 1

DATE	DETAILS		DEBIT	CREDIT
0202X7	Invoice	017220	96.27	
0502X7	Invoice	017496	113.44	
1102X7	Invoice	017649	84.95	
2102X7	C/note	024173		22.00
0103X7	Cash received	C100		272.66
1203X7	Invoice	011780	212.11 ✓	
1503X7	Invoice	017821	106.07 ✓	
2903X7	Invoice	017944	78.90 ✓	
3003X7	C/note	025327		23.48 ✓

OUR TERMS 30 DAYS. YOUR PROMPT SETTLEMENT WOULD BE APPRECIATED. THANK YOU.

AMOUNT DUE
£373.60

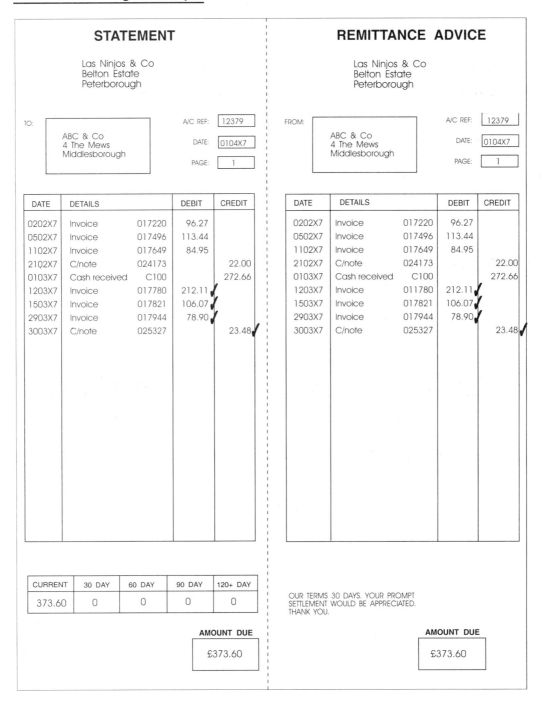

2.3 The paying company may send out its own remittance advices with its payment; however, it is common for the **receiving** company to send a statement which has a **detachable remittance advice** as shown here. The paying business or individual will mark off those invoices which are covered by the particular payment; this tear-off advice will then be returned by the paying company, although it may send its own remittance advice as well.

Procedures to compare receipt with remittance advice

2.4 The member of staff who records the receipt should compare it with the remittance advice sent by the paying company, using the following procedures.

Step 1 Check that the amounts shown on the **remittance advice add up** to the total.

Step 2 **Compare** the **total** with the amount of the **receipt** (usually a **cheque**).

Step 3 If there is a **disagreement** between the two amounts, mark on the remittance advice the amount received and calculate the **difference.**

Step 4 Send the cheque to be **banked** and then **record the receipt** (we will discuss **banking receipts** in Chapter 8 of this text and **recording receipts** in Chapter 9).

Step 5 Send the marked up remittance advice to the **sales ledger department** (where amounts which are owed to the business by individual customers are dealt with).

2.5 The discrepancies which have arisen (if any) will be dealt with by the **sales ledger department** (the department that deals with customers who buy on credit). They will contact the customer, usually by telephone, to discuss the problem and, if necessary, to request a further payment.

REMITTANCE ADVICE

ABC & Co
4 The Mews
Middlesborough

TO: Las Ninjos & Co
Belton Estate
Peterborough

Account Ref: 01NIN | Date: 0504X7 | Page: 1

DATE	DETAILS		INVOICES	CREDIT NOTES	PAYMENT AMOUNT
12.3.X7	Invoice	017780	212.11		212.11
15.3.X7	Invoice	017821	106.07		106.07
29.3.X7	Invoice	017944	78.90		78.90
30.3.X7	Credit note	025327		23.48	- 23.48
			397.08	23.48	373.60

2.6 On the statement shown in Paragraph 2.2 the customer has marked off a total of £373.60 (remember to deduct the credit notes). The example above shows the remittance advice ABC & Co would prepare itself.

Other forms of supporting documentation for a receipt

2.7 A remittance advice is the most likely documentation to accompany a receipt from a credit customer. In the course of business **other kinds of receipt** may occur, which will have different kinds of documentation to support them.

Completion statement

2.8 Suppose your company owns a building. It is not being used and so a decision is made to sell it. When it is sold a cheque is received from the solicitor who has dealt with the sale (it is quite normal practice for the buyer to pay the solicitor and then for the solicitor to pay the seller). The cheque is received with a **completion statement**.

MESSRS R DRY & CO
SOLICITORS

To: ABC & Co
Completion Statement for sale of 3 Orchard Road to XYZ & Co

	£	£
Sale price agreed		530,000.00
Less disbursements		
Stamp duty @ 2%	10,600.00	
Agent's fees @ 1½% (invoice attached)	7,950.00	
Solicitors' fees (invoice attached)	892.45	
		19,442.45
Remittance enclosed		510,557.55

2.9 This has the same effect and purpose as a remittance advice. Very few businesses will receive completion statements, unless they **buy and sell property all the time** as part of their trade as, perhaps, property developers. The sale of other assets, such as motor vehicles used by staff, will be more frequent and normal documentation will be given for such sales.

Retail receipts

2.10 Payments (using cash, cheques and card vouchers) by **shop or retail customers** are not accompanied by any supporting documentation written by the customer. The business selling the goods creates its own 'remittance advice' by recording the receipt on a cash register's till receipt or on a manually written receipt voucher (these are described in the next section).

3 RECEIPTS GIVEN TO CUSTOMERS

KEY TERM

A **receipt** is a document given by the seller to the buyer when goods change hands in exchange for payment. It may be a till receipt, a written receipt or some other form of receipt.

Till receipts

3.1 **Cash registers** or '**tills**' are used mainly in retail shops where the money is handed over directly by the customer when the transaction takes place, in the form of cash, cheques and card vouchers (discussed later in this chapter). Most shops have electronic cash registers, often registering the details of items sold using bar code readers, which operate as follows.

- Store full price information on all stocks
- Record the value of the sale of each item
- Calculate the total value of the sale if more than one item is sold
- Calculate the required change to give to a customer once the operator has keyed in how much money has been handed over
- Issue a till receipt showing the entire transaction
- Sum up the transactions of the day at closing time

3.2 The cash register is acting as part of the **control over calculating and giving change** to customers. There are a number of potential errors in giving change, each of which will affect the customer directly and the business indirectly.

Potential error in giving change	Effect	Controlled by
Calculating and giving **too little change**	Customer annoyance - loss of goodwill	Cash register
Calculating and giving **too much change**	Loss of money by business	Cash register
Physically taking **incorrect amount** from till	Either of the above	Making sure staff are careful, well trained and have reasonable mathematical ability

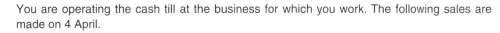

Activity 7.1 — Level: Pre-assessment

You are operating the cash till at the business for which you work. The following sales are made on 4 April.

Customer	*Amount of sale* £	*Notes and/or coin tendered*
1	7.42	£10 note
2	29.21	Three £10 notes
3	7.98	£10 note
4	44.44	Two £20 notes and five £1 coins
5	39.25	Four £10 notes
6	57.20	Five £10 notes, £5 note, four 50p coins and four 5p coins
7	9.46	£10 note, two 20p coins and three 2p coins
8	10.17	£10 note and 50p coin
9	59.62	Three £20 notes, 10p coin and 2p coin
10	12.93	£20 note

Task

Assuming that, at the start of the day, there are all the notes and coins which will be needed:

(a) State the amount of change which is due to each customer.

(b) State the notes and/or coin which will be given to each customer, using the minimum possible number of notes and/or coin.

Do not use a calculator for this activity - it is a good test of mental arithmetic.

3.3 Here is an example of a till receipt from a restaurant.

YOUR RECEIPT
THANK YOU
*** ARNIE'S (a) ***
VAT NO 423 4895 26 (g)
15-08-X7 (b) (h) K. SMITH 123456
12:19 (i) 33

TABLE NO	(c)	123
ROAST CHICKEN	(c)	£9.50
SOUP	(c)	£3.25
SALAD	(c)	£3.00
ORANGE	(c)	£3.75
COFFEE	(c)	£1.20
5N8		
TOTAL	(d)	£20.70
CASH	(e)	£25.00
CHANGE	(f)	£4.30

Each till **receipt** will show some or all of the following (marked on the receipt above).

(a) The name of the selling company or business
(b) The date/tax point (and possibly the time) of the transaction
(c) The price of each of the goods purchased
(d) The total value of goods purchased
(e) The amount tendered (given) by the customer
(f) The amount of change given to the customer
(g) The VAT number (if applicable) of the selling company or business
(h) The name of the assistant and/or cashier
(i) The till number

The first four items are those which normally **must** be shown in order to give sufficient information; the others are optional, but most businesses find that the more information on each receipt, the easier it is to sort out queries. The VAT number will often be shown because it is useful for customers who are VAT-registered; for normal retail customers it is irrelevant.

The legal standing of a till receipt

3.4 A till receipt is **not conclusive evidence of a payment**, although *prima facie* (at first sight) it is. Although the payment can be proved by other means when a till receipt is lost, it is modern practice for many retail shops to refuse to exchange goods or refund money unless the original till receipt is produced. This does not apply to all shops; it depends on whether the goods are easy to recognise as their own brand, or the ease with which the shops themselves can return the goods to the manufacturer. To be safe, it is wise for customers to keep till receipts until they are sure the goods are satisfactory.

Written receipts

3.5 Where a cash register is not used then a **written or typed receipt** may be required. The same information should appear as that which appears on the till receipt, although it is often easier to enter more detailed information about the goods sold on a written receipt.

3.6 Some goods sold have a **unique registration or code number** to make them identifiable. Unique code numbers are often assigned to goods which are sold under guarantee (the supplier will repair or replace the goods for free within the time period specified in the guarantee). The code number is used by the supplier to make sure that the correct goods are being repaired or replaced, and not something that was bought elsewhere. Examples of such goods are electrical goods and cameras. The shop will usually keep a copy of the receipt by using carbon paper to write through onto another piece of paper.

Clarence's Cameras Ltd 14 The View Brighton VAT no 721 9903 47	Date/tax point: List Price	17.7.X7 VAT rate	**No. 78** Total
1 x Pencos 38 SL Camera ref: 34782938	372.00	17½%	372.00
1 x 35mm lens Pencos ref: 4983297	89.00	17½%	89.00
	461.00		461.00
VAT @ 17½%			80.67
Total			£ 541.67

Evidence of payment other than in cash

3.7 When a customer pays by some means other than cash, he may obtain some evidence of payment which is **not** a receipt. We will discuss each of these methods of payment in more detail later on in this chapter; here they are listed only briefly.

Method of payment	Evidence of payment
Credit card	The customer will receive a copy of the **signed credit card voucher** and there will be a record of the transaction on the **customer's monthly credit card statement** (which is important when a credit card has been used to buy things over the telephone).
Debit card	As with credit cards, the customer receives a copy of the signed **debit card voucher** and a record will appear on the **customer's bank statement**.
Cheque	The payment will appear on the **customer's bank statement**. The customer may have his **cheques returned** to him after they have cleared through the banking system (although this is rare).
Banker's draft, postal orders etc	The **issuing bank** or post office will hold records of the items issued.

Use of receipts in business trading

3.8 When businesses trade with each other on a **credit basis** (goods are ordered and received before being paid for), **it is very unusual to issue a receipt.** For instance, ABC & Co have an account with XYZ. ABC buys £1,000 in goods in June 20X4. The terms of the trading agreement are to pay for the goods within 30 days of the end of the month in which the goods were sent; in this case payment is due on 30 July 20X4. ABC & Co pay the bill on time, sending a remittance advice. They get no receipt for their cheque for £1,000. The only acknowledgement of the payment is that the next statement of their account will show the cash receipt deducted from the balance outstanding.

3.9 We will look in more detail at cash registers in Chapter 9.

4 TIMING AND TYPES OF MONEY RECEIVED FROM CUSTOMERS

Types of receipt from customers

4.1 In the last section, when we mentioned a 'receipt', we were referring to the document given **to the purchaser by the seller** when goods changed hands. In this section we use the term receipt in a different sense.

> **KEY TERM**
>
> A **receipt** refers to the act of the **seller accepting payment** and to **the payment** itself once it has been accepted.

In this chapter we will look at the most common forms of receipt.

- Cash
- Cheque
- Plastic cards

4.2 Generally, the way a company receives money will depend on the type of business it is in. There are other less usual forms of receipt (depending on the type of business).

- Standing order
- Direct debit
- Mail transfer and telegraphic transfer
- BACS

Timing of money received from customers

4.3 The **timing of the receipts of a business** will depend on a variety of factors.

- The type of business (see Paragraph 4.4 below)
- The type of sales (credit/cash or both - see Paragraphs 4.5 and 4.6 below)
- Seasonal and economic trends (see Paragraphs 4.7 to 4.11 below)

Type of business

4.4 Different kinds of business tend to generate **different patterns of cash receipts**. We can use a simple example to demonstrate. Let us look at three different kinds of business and the receipts they would expect on an average day.

Newsagent	Building contractor
500 receipts at an average of £1 each	3 receipts at an average of £150,000 each
Total = £500	Total = £450,000

Clothes shop
20 receipts at an average of £200 each
Total = £4,000

Compare a newsagent's shop on a street corner with a large building firm; it is not just in **total receipts** that there is a difference between the two.

- The **newsagent** will receive a large number of very small amounts of money, mainly in **cash**.
- The **contractor** will receive a relatively small number of very big payments for the buildings it finishes, mainly by **BACS, cheque or banker's draft**. (We will discuss these forms of receipt later in this chapter.)
- The **clothes shop** falls somewhere between the newsagent and the contractor; the takings will be in a **combination of forms**, namely **cash, cheques** and **plastic cards**.

Credit/cash sales

4.5 Some kinds of business make the bulk of their sales to customers on **credit** (they invoice customers); others deal only with **cash sales**, in the sense that customers must pay for the goods on taking them, although the actual payment might be by cheque or card. The easiest way of distinguishing between these two types of business is as follows.

Type of sale	Typical business	Typical customer	Examples
Cash sale	Retailers	General public face-to-face as final consumer	Supermarkets Newsagents Chemists
Credit sale	Trading businesses	Other trading or retail businesses, who *ultimately* sell to general public as final consumer	Manufacturers of steel, gas, plumbing equipment, providers of training

4.6 Ignoring seasonal trends it can be seen that the pattern of receipts experienced by these two types of business will be completely different.

- A **retail business** will get a fairly **steady flow of receipts** with perhaps more on Saturdays and late night shopping days
- A **trading business** will get the bulk of its receipts on the date credit customers are due to pay. This is often the **end of the month**, although customers may be given different dates to pay to spread receipts more evenly over time.

Seasonal trends

4.7 The effect of the seasons on various types of business is fairly obvious. These are some examples, but you should be able to think of many more.

- Sales receipts will increase dramatically for many **retail shops** and **manufacturers of consumer goods** in the period up to **Christmas**.
- **Easter egg manufacturers** will have very low sales receipts during most of the year but will get nearly all their receipts in the few months around **Easter**.
- Makers of **swimming costumes** will get far more in sales receipts in **summer** than in winter.

4.8 It is worth remembering that manufacturers, and to some extent shops, will **diversify** what they produce and sell (make and sell lots of different things) in order to get a **more even cash flow during the year**.

Economic trends

4.9 When the economy of the country is doing well (a time of **boom**), then many businesses will increase their sales volume and therefore the money they receive for sales.

4.10 When the economy is doing badly (a time of **recession**) then **total sales volume will often fall**, producing a lower level of receipts. Receipts from sales will also be affected if a **customer goes bankrupt** before he has paid his bill; this can happen quite often in a recession.

4.11 Cash flow becomes very important in a recession because, if a company cannot pay the money it owes people when it is due, then it is said that it has become **insolvent**. When a company becomes insolvent, the law says that it must stop trading and close down. It is against the law for the directors to let their company carry on trading when they know it is insolvent.

5 CASH: PHYSICAL SECURITY

5.1 We all know what **money** looks like but what is it?

> **KEY TERM**
>
> **Cash** is the notes and coin which make up the legal tender of a country.

5.2 The Coinage Acts specify what must be accepted as **legal tender** in the UK.

Form	**Made of**	**Denomination**	**Maximum tendered**	**Comments**
Coins	Bronze	1p, 2p	20p	Known as copper
Coins	Cupro-nickel	5p, 10p	£5	
Coins	Cupro-nickel	20p, 25p (commemora-tive crowns), 50p	£10	Known as silver
Coins	Cupro-nickel	£1, £2	Any amount	
Bank of England notes	Paper	£5, £10, £20, £50	Any amount	Bank of Scotland notes are legal tender in Scotland, *not* in England, Wales and N Ireland, though they are generally accepted

5.3 We will spend most of the rest of this section looking at the problems of **security** (mainly forgery, theft and accidental loss) which trouble organisations dealing with large amounts of cash, mostly retailers (including banks) and charities who deal with the general public and final consumer. When a business mainly has cash transactions, it exposes itself to various dangers; **cash is the most insecure form of receipt**. There are many aspects to security and some will only apply to businesses of a certain size.

Forgery

5.4 There are frequent cases of **forgery** of larger denomination notes (£50, £20 and £10). It is advisable to examine all notes carefully before they are accepted; the metal thread incorporated into all these notes is difficult to duplicate. Even **small denomination notes and coins are forged**. London Underground Ltd was at one time forced to stop accepting 50 pence coins in ticket machines as some people were using 10 pence pieces wrapped in foil to fool the machines. Special marker pens and ultra-violet light detection equipment can now be used to check **bank notes**.

Theft

5.5 **Theft by staff** is a risk which many businesses have to take. This risk can be reduced by being careful about the people the business employs; their references should be checked properly and they should be monitored closely for their first few months of work.

Larger companies might decide to take out **fidelity insurance** to cover staff who deal with cash and other forms of money. The company can reclaim stolen money from the insurer when a member of their staff has been proved to be dishonest. Some of the security precautions discussed below are helpful in preventing staff theft as much as customer theft.

Cash register security

5.6 The **cash register should be secure**, with keys needed to operate it. Staff should be trained to make them aware of the importance of keeping their keys safe and of not leaving the cash register open. Cash registers which are activated by different keys unique to each member of staff can give a **breakdown of sales by staff member**. This is another aid to preventing staff theft because it will indicate staff who are not entering sales and pocketing the customer's money.

Activity 7.2 **Level: Pre-assessment**

Suppose that the cash held in the till at the start of business on 4 April in Activity 7.1 is £36.40.

Calculate the amount of money which you would expect to find in the till at the end of the day.

Present your answer in the following form.

	£
Cash float at start of the day	
Sales in the day	
Cash held at the end of the day	

Safes

5.7 If possible, cash should be removed from the till regularly (so that there is only a relatively small amount of cash in the till) and stored in a safer place. Obviously, the ideal place would be a **safe**. Safes come in several varieties.

- Stand-alone safes
- Wall safes
- Floor safes

Whatever kind of safe is used it should be in a place out of view of the customer. Floor safes are often the best hidden. For convenience a chute may be incorporated into the safe, to allow money to be put into the safe in a container without opening the safe door. The number of **safe keys** should be kept to a minimum and access to the keys should be restricted.

Protective glass

5.8 Some businesses use **protective glass** (called a 'bandit screen') between the customer and the cashier to protect against theft *and* to ensure the safety of the cashiers. This measure is used in banks and building society branches, and also at petrol stations and many off licences after dark.

Strong box

5.9 Many retail outlets use a **strong box** at each cash register. When the cashier receives a large bank note, he or she will not place it in the cash register, but will put it down a chute or slot which leads to a strong box. The strong box will be built in to the counter under the cash register. The cashier can put money in but cannot take any out and of course customers cannot get into it. The money in the strong box can be removed at the end of the day when all the customers have gone home. This also helps to remove cash from the tills on a regular basis.

Security guards and collections

5.10 Larger organisations will employ their own **in-house security staff**. As well as watching cashiers to check for theft, these security guards will accompany the staff who remove cash from the tills regularly during the day to take it to a safer location.

5.11 **External security firms** may be employed to collect money from the business premises and take it directly to the bank. This kind of firm uses trained staff and secured transport and is liable for the goods or money it carries.

Night safes

5.12 Where a business finds it impossible to bank money during normal banking hours, most banks will provide a key to their **night safe**. This is, in effect, a hole in the wall of the bank. When it is unlocked and the lid is opened it exposes only a small space in which the cash is deposited. Once the lid is closed the cash drops into a larger storage area within the bank. The bank issues boxes or wallets in which to put money and a press to mark the tags which close the boxes. Each press has a unique number on it which is allocated to one customer. In this way each box can be identified by the bank before it is opened and customers' deposits cannot be mixed up.

Frequent banking

5.13 In general, cash should be taken to the bank on a **regular and fairly frequent basis**; this minimises the amount of money on the business premises. This may be particularly important if the amount of money the business can hold is limited under its insurance policy.

It is not a good idea to let the same person go to the bank every day at the same time; for security reasons it is better to **vary the member of staff** who takes the money to the bank and the **time of day it is taken**.

Accidental loss

5.14 **Cash should never be sent by post**; if it is lost or stolen there is no way to trace or recover it.

Security of other receipts

5.15 **Cheques** and **card vouchers** are less valuable by far to a thief but they are as important to a business as the cash it receives. Consequently, the same security procedures should be maintained for cheques and card vouchers as for cash (where applicable). A cheque may be sent through the post, although it should be properly prepared (as discussed later). A cheque which is blank *except for the signature* should not be sent through the post.

5.16 Other forms of receipt are rarer in nature and are likely to be banked immediately (for instance, a bankers' draft). Alternatively, there are the types of receipt (standing orders, direct debits, BACS transfers and so on) which will be **transferred automatically** into the business's bank account and physical security procedures are therefore unnecessary.

6 CHEQUES: LEGAL CONSIDERATIONS

6.1 **Cheques** are the most common receipt most businesses deal with and retail businesses will receive a high proportion of their revenue from the general public in the form of personal cheques (although these are gradually being replaced by card transactions - see below).

ASSESSMENT ALERT

Legal considerations surrounding cheques are likely to come up frequently. Read through this section very carefully, and more than once if you can.

Legal aspects of cheques

6.2 It is useful at this stage to consider the legal aspects of cheques and how they can affect us in practice.

KEY TERM

A **cheque** is 'an unconditional order in writing addressed by a person to a bank, signed by the person giving it, requiring the bank to pay on demand a sum certain in money to or to the order of a specified person or bearer'.

6.3 This formal definition can be explained more easily if we look at a specimen cheque.

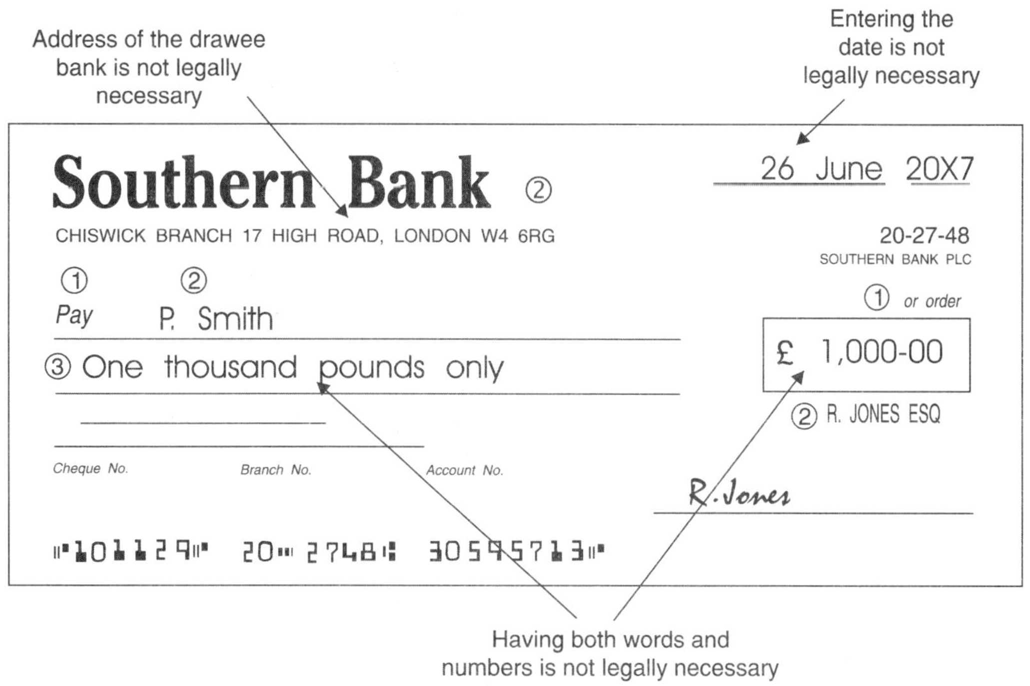

6.4 Any additional particulars may be added to the cheque unless they infringe the legal definition, but the important parts of the cheque, numbered (1) to (3) here, are explained below.

An unconditional order in writing (1)

6.5 (a) This means that the cheque must be payable to '**bearer**', *or* the cheque must be payable 'to or to the order of' a **specified person**. The 'to the order' part means that the person you write the cheque payable to can **endorse the cheque to someone else.** Endorsement is explained in Paragraphs 6.9 to 6.11.

(b) The cheque may be **written** on anything, though paper is most convenient. The kind of preprinted form used by banks (shown above) is just for convenience. It is worth noting that the numbers at the bottom of the cheque are metallic-based which enables them to be read automatically by special machines at the bank.

(c) It must be **unconditional**. This means that you cannot, for instance, say that you want payment to be made out of the funds received from selling your BT shares, as you are making payment *conditional* on certain events (that the sale will take place and will realise sufficient funds).

6.6 Under the Cheques Act 1992, it is permitted to substitute 'only' for 'or order' and this is what most preprinted bank cheques now do. (If the drawer crosses out the words 'or order' and writes in 'only', then he or she should initial the change.) This is sufficient on its own to stop the cheque being endorsed (see Paragraphs 6.9 to 6.11 below).

Three parties (2)

6.7 **Three parties are *always* required for a cheque to be valid.**

(a) **The drawer:** the customer who issues the cheque and whose signature is an essential part of it (R Jones)

(b) **The drawee:** the bank on which the cheque is drawn; the *order* to pay is addressed to that bank (Southern Bank)

(c) **The payee:** the person to whom payment is ordered to be made (P Smith). If the cheque is **payable to 'bearer' then anyone who possesses it can demand payment on it**

A **holder** of a cheque is a person who is in possession of a cheque which is **either** payable to him **or** is payable to bearer (which means he can obtain payment of it).

Sum certain in money (3)

6.8 The whole point of writing a cheque in someone's favour is that **you wish to give them some money**. It follows that the cheque must show the amount of money you wish to pay.

The amount does not have to be stated in both words and numbers but, if it is, and they do not agree, then **the amount in words will be assumed to be the correct sum.**

Endorsement

6.9 It is not normally necessary for the **payee** to sign a cheque but if he wishes to transfer the rights in the cheque to someone else, he must **sign the back of the cheque to endorse it.**

Using the cheque shown above, if the payee P Smith wanted to give the cheque to ABC & Co to settle a debt, then he would sign the reverse of the cheque and send it to ABC & Co. Once the cheque has been received, ABC & Co might then put its own name and account number on the reverse of the cheque, so that the bank will know for certain that it now belongs to ABC & Co and to ensure that it will be paid into the correct account.

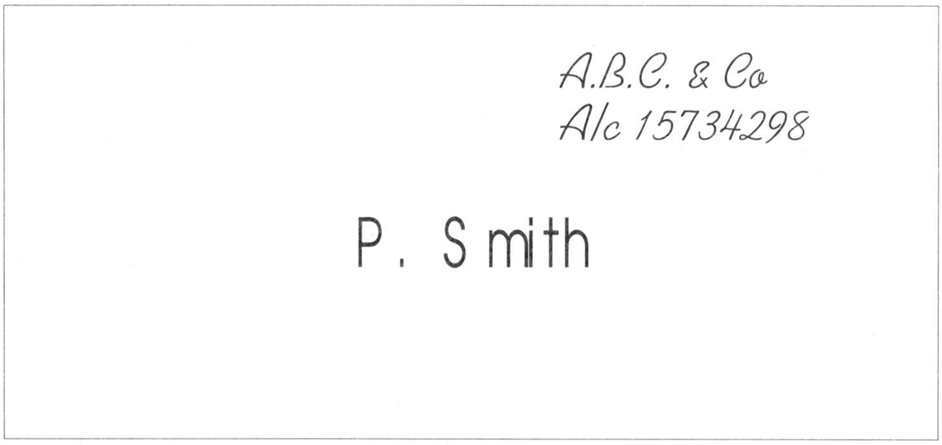

6.10 P Smith has made an **endorsement in blank** which converts the cheque from an **order cheque** (payable to a specific person) to a **bearer cheque** (payable to the holder). The cheque now belongs to ABC & Co because P Smith has endorsed it *and* delivered it to the company. But if it had been intercepted by another person that person could in theory obtain payment of the cheque as it is payable to the holder (the person in possession of it).

Because of the rights of endorsement in blank, P. Smith would have been better advised to make a **special endorsement** by writing 'Pay ABC & Co' and signing the back of the cheque. This would mean that the cheque would still be an order cheque.

6.11 The practice of endorsing cheques is much rarer now that it is increasingly common for banks to issue cheques with '**only**' printed on them (see paragraph 6.8 above) and/or with an '**account payee**' **crossing** printed on them (see below).

Crossing cheques

6.12 Crossings on cheques are used to **restrict the use** that can be made of the cheque.

- When a cheque is **uncrossed** (R Jones's cheque to P Smith is uncrossed), then the payee may **cash** the cheque at the bank without having to pay the money into another bank account.
- A cheque is **crossed** when two parallel lines are pre-printed on or added to a cheque, as shown below. Banks will issue uncrossed cheques on request; usually they preprint crossings. There are four types of crossing, each of which has a different effect.
  - **General** (just two lines). This tells the paying bank to make payment *only* to another bank (on behalf of its customer).

  - **Special** (two lines with receiving bank's name). This tells the paying bank to make payment only to the bank shown by the special crossing.

  - **Not negotiable**. This means that whoever has the cheque cannot have a better claim to it than the person who gave the cheque to him.

  - **A/c (account) payee**. This tells the bank to pay only to another bank for the account of the **original** payee: Cheques Act 1992.

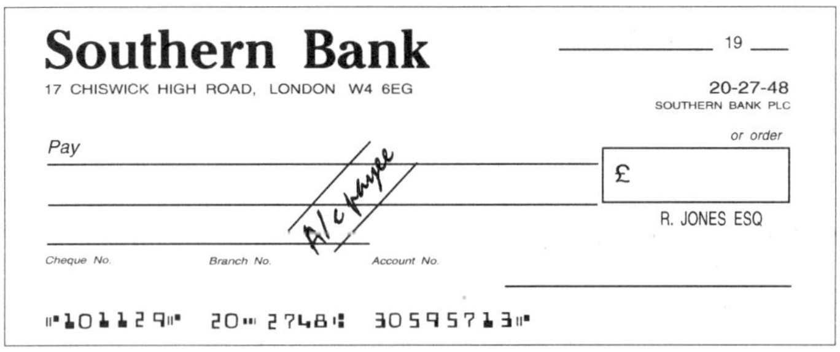

6.13 Most banks now issue cheques which already have 'only' instead of 'or order' *and/or* an 'account payee' crossing pre-printed on the cheques. **This effectively outlaws the practice of endorsing cheques**. The old type of cheque is still available, but the banks are keen to do away with endorsing as they suffer a higher incidence of fraud with so-called 'third party' cheques.

Forgery

6.14 If the **drawer's signature is forged** then the cheque is invalid and worthless. If the bank does not realise in time that the signature is a forgery, then it cannot (normally) take the money out of the drawer's account.

6.15 If an **endorsement is forged**, the previous holder (whose endorsing signature was forged) can recover the cheque, or its value, from the person in possession of it.

Fictitious or non-existent payee

6.16 If the named payee is **fictitious** or **non-existent** (say, Mickey Mouse) the cheque is not invalid, but it has become a **bearer cheque**. Bearer cheques can be transferred without an endorsement so, even if an endorsement is forged, the cheque can still be cashed by the person who is in possession of it.

More than one payee

6.17 Cheques may be made **payable to more than one payee**, either jointly (P Smith *and* R Harris) or alternatively (P Smith *or* R Harris).

Signatories

6.18 A person may sign a cheque under a **business name** which he uses or even under an assumed name. If he does so he is liable as if he had signed in his personal or real name.

6.19 An **agent** who signs a cheque should also state 'for' or 'on behalf of' his **principal,** otherwise he might be liable for the cheque.

6.20 A cheque may be signed in the name of a **partnership** and it is usual for partnership cheques to be signed this way; it is equivalent to all the signatures of all the individual partners. Hence a firm such as KPMG would have cheques signed 'KPMG'.

6.21 A **director** who signs his own name on a cheque for a **company** in accordance with the **mandate** is signing as the **company's representative**, and the company is liable on it. The company name must appear clearly on the cheque and the name

must be correct (although 'Co' instead of 'Company' is acceptable). If the company name does not appear, or it appears wrongly, **the director is personally liable if the company does not pay.**

Incomplete and altered cheques

6.22 Cheques may be issued with the signature of the drawer but they are **incomplete without the name of the payee** or the **amount**, and the holder can enter these details as long as it is done as the drawer wished and is done within a reasonable time. If there is no **date** on the cheque then the holder can enter a date.

6.23 Unless all parties to a cheque agree to it, if a cheque has been **altered** then it makes the cheque invalid except against anyone who sanctioned the alteration and any person who endorses it after the alteration was made.

Stale and out-of-date cheques

6.24 Banks consider that the drawer's authority to pay his cheque expires, and that cheques have become 'stale', **six months after the date of issue**. After six months the bank would return the cheque marked 'stale cheque' or 'out of date'.

Post-dated cheques

6.25 **Post-dated cheques** can be issued, meaning that the date on the cheque is later than the date the cheque was drawn. If the cheque is presented before the date on the cheque then the bank **should** refuse to pay it. Unfortunately banks, usually by oversight, may pay such cheques early.

Dishonoured cheques

6.26 If a cheque is presented for payment at the proper place and is not paid, it is then **dishonoured for payment**. When this happens the holder of the cheque must tell the drawer (and any endorser) within a reasonable time (normally 24 hours). The holder can recover the amount of the cheque plus interest from any liable party. We shall look in more detail at dishonoured cheques in Chapter 8.

Cheque guarantee cards

6.27 When receiving a cheque which is *not* a company or business cheque, it is usual to accept the cheque only when it is supported by a **personal cheque guarantee card**. This card has on it a specimen of the account holder's signature and it will guarantee that a cheque written by the card holder will be **honoured** (cashed) by the bank **up to the amount** stated on the guarantee card. This is usually £50 although it is possible to obtain £100 and even £250 cheque guarantee cards.

6.28 If the cheque is written for an amount **greater** than that on the guarantee card then **the bank is not bound to honour it** although the cheque will normally be honoured if there are sufficient funds in the account and if the cheque is otherwise in order.

6.29 A typical cheque guarantee card looks like this.

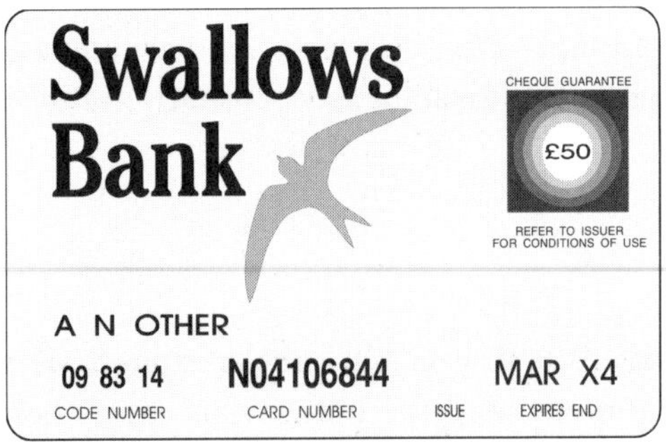

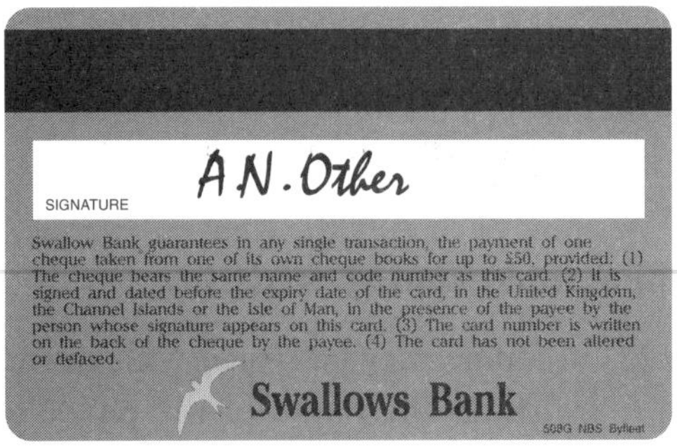

It shows many details that are on a cheque: sort code, account number and name, but it also has a **unique card number**. When the card is used to support a cheque this number will be written on the back of the cheque to prove to the bank that the cheque was guaranteed by a card.

7 RECEIPT OF CHEQUE PAYMENTS

7.1 It is best practice to follow these procedures when an individual customer pays by cheque supported by a cheque guarantee card.

Step 1 Examine the face of the cheque to ensure all the **details are correct,** namely:

- **Date** (including the year)
- **Payee** name
- **Amount** in both words and figures

Step 2 Make sure that the cheque is **signed** by the drawer.

Step 3 **Compare the signature** on the cheque with that on the cheque guarantee card. It is unlikely that the match will be exact but it should be sufficiently close to avoid any doubt.

Step 4 **Check the details on the cheque guarantee card,** namely:

- **'Expires end' date** (has the card expired?)
- **Amount of the guarantee** (does it exceed the cheque amount?)
- **Name** agrees with that on the cheque
- **Other details** agree with the cheque (account number, sort code).

Step 5 **Copy details** from the cheque guarantee card on to the back of the cheque:

- **Card number**
- **Guarantee limit**
- **Expiry date**

7.2 Note that **only one guaranteed cheque can be used in one transaction;** a large number of cheques, each for an amount within the limit on the guarantee card, cannot be issued to make up one large aggregate amount.

7.3 Some businesses help their staff to make sure that all these checks are performed by using a **stamp** to list them on the back of the cheque. The cashier has to sign off or tick each check as it is performed.

7.4 Cheques received by a business through the **post,** from credit customers or individuals, will not be supported by cheque guarantee cards. Only Steps 1 and 2 above need be performed.

Cheques: security procedures

7.5 **Banks** recommend and carry out various security precautions with regard to cheques.

(a) Customers are asked to keep **cheque books and cards separate,** although this is not always easy or convenient, especially for women carrying handbags.

(b) The **number of cheques** in a book is kept to a minimum.

(c) Cheque cards tend to be sent by **registered post** so that customers must sign for their receipt.

(d) The **card remains the property of the bank** and it can be withdrawn if it is being improperly used. New customers are often not issued with a cheque card until they have proved their reliability.

Activity 7.3 — Level: Assessment

You work for Finney's Ltd, a hardware retailer. The firm has only one store, and accepts the following methods of payment.

(a) Cash

(b) Cheque, if supported by a cheque guarantee card

(c) Credit cards (Visa and Mastercard). A floor limit of £100 applies, above which an authorisation code must be obtained.

Staff working on the tills sometimes need to ask for your guidance on procedures for receiving payments.

A new member of staff, Barry, has started work at the store. He is required to obtain your authorisation for all transactions by cheque and credit card, although it is his responsibility to check that the amount paid agrees with the till roll record.

On 7 August 20X7, Barry presents the documentation as detailed below on three different transactions by cheque (a), (b) and (c) for your authorisation.

Task

In each case, consider whether you would authorise the transaction. State clearly the steps, if any, which need to be taken before your authorisation can be given. You may assume that the signature has been correctly checked by Barry and that he has entered the number of the cheque card on the back of the cheque. You may also assume that the name on the cheque guarantee card agrees with that printed on the cheque.

(a)

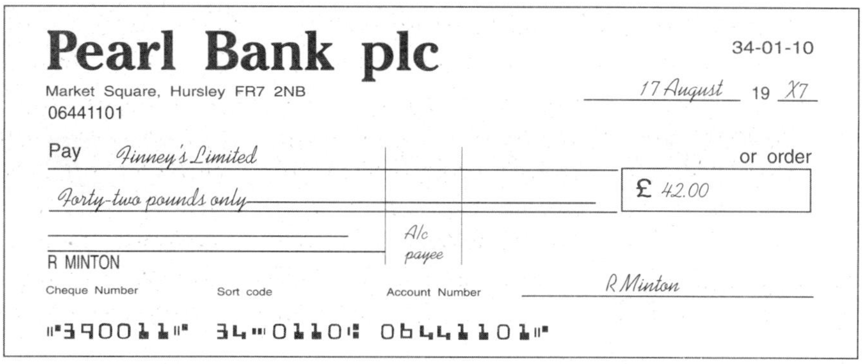
Pearl Bank plc
34-01-10
Market Square, Hursley FR7 2NB
06441101
17 August 19 X7
Pay Finney's Limited or order
Forty-two pounds only
£ 42.00
A/c payee
R MINTON
R Minton
Cheque Number Sort code Account Number
⑈390011⑈ 34⑆0110⑆ 06441101⑈

Cheque guarantee card (£100 limit): code number 33 04 40; card number E03131042; expires end 03/X9

(b)

Cheque guarantee card (£50 limit): code number 79 21 49; card number 20572358; valid from 08/X6; expires end 07/X7

(c)

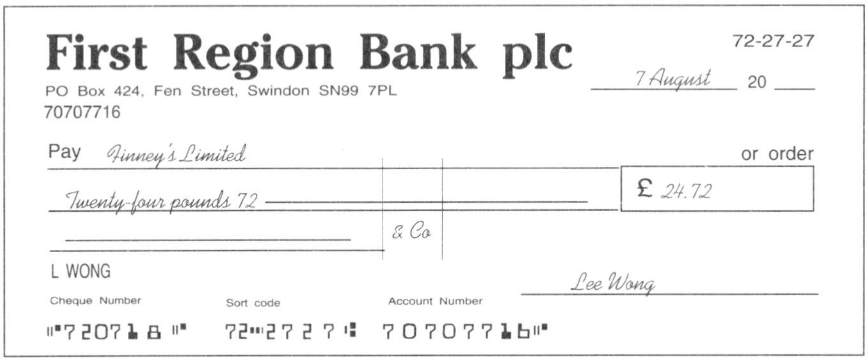

First Region Bank plc
72-27-27
7 August 20
PO Box 424, Fen Street, Swindon SN99 7PL
70707716
Pay Finney's Limited
or order
Twenty-four pounds 72
£ 24.72
& Co
L WONG
Lee Wong
Cheque Number
Sort code
Account Number
720718 72 2727 70707716

Cheque guarantee card (£50 limit): code number 72 27 27; card number 1306749265; valid from 09/X7; expires end 08/X9

8 RECEIPT OF CARD PAYMENTS

8.1 **Plastic card payments** have become progressively more popular as methods of payment over the last few years. They are used **primarily by individuals**, rather than by companies (although companies do own credit cards which are generally allocated to members of staff for their use to pay business expenses). Most retail outlets which accept credit and charge cards now use EFTPOS (Electronic Funds Transfer at Point of Sale). However, some small shops and restaurants still use manual processing which is described in this section. We will examine EFTPOS procedures in Section 9.

Plastic cards

8.2 A typical plastic card will consist of a piece of plastic approximately 8½cm × 5½cm upon which various pieces of information are imprinted, etched or moulded. A typical card would look like this and the letters (a) to (j) are explained below.

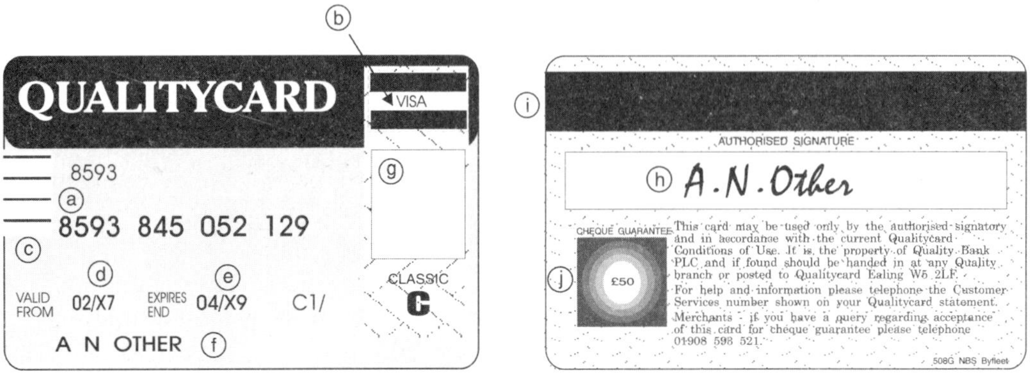

Feature		Explanation
(a)	*Card number*	Each card issued has a unique number allocated to it.
(b)	*VISA*	This is the type of credit card (which could be VISA or MasterCard).
(c)	*Qualitycard*	This is the issuing company. There are many different issuing companies (mainly banks and building societies).
(d)	*02/X7*	This is the date from which the card can be used, in this case 1 February 20X7.
(e)	*04/X9*	This is the date on which the card expires, so the last date it can be used is 30 April 20X9.
(f)	*A N Other*	The name of the card holder.
(g)	*Hologram*	This is a special security device which seeks to prevent forgery of the card. A hologram (a 3-dimensional image) can only be reproduced by sophisticated machinery and its requirement deters casual forgers. Some cards now have photos of their owners.
(h)	*Signature strip*	This holds the specimen signature of the card holder.
(i)	*Magnetic strip*	This black strip holds all the information on the card (except the signature) in code enabling a computer to read it.
(j)	*£50*	This is a cheque guarantee limit. Some cards double up as cheque guarantee cards.

The card number, the 'valid from' and 'expires end' dates, and the card holder name are all **raised lettering** so that when the card is imprinted onto a transaction voucher these details will appear on the voucher (see below).

8.3 It is worth splitting the types of card which can be obtained into four categories.

- Credit cards
- Charge cards
- In-house store cards
- Debit cards

We shall look at each of them in turn.

Credit cards

8.4 A **credit card payment** involves three transactions and three parties (see below). Whilst credit is involved, for a supplier receiving payment in this way, credit card payments are treated as cash.

Transaction	Comments
Purchase of goods from a supplier by card holder	On producing his card to a **supplier** for goods and/or services, the **card holder** can obtain what he requires without paying for it immediately
Payment of supplier by card issuer	The **supplier** recovers from the **card issuer** the price of goods or services less a commission which is the card issuer's profit margin.
Payment of card issuer by card holder	At monthly intervals the **card issuer** sends to the **card holder** a statement. The card holder may either settle interest-free within 28 days or he may pay interest on the balance owing after 28 days. He is required to pay a minimum of 5% or £5, whichever is the greater.

8.5 Card issuers often charge a flat yearly **membership fee** as well as charging **interest.**

8.6 The credit cards issued in the UK include **Visa** and **MasterCard** (Access). Most banks, building societies and finance houses issue either Visa or MasterCard credit cards; some issue both. American Express issues its own credit card (Optima).

8.7 Suppliers are allowed to charge more for goods purchased by credit card than the same goods purchased by cash or cheque. This reflects the **cost to the supplier** of accepting the credit card as payment. The card issuers charge the supplier a percentage of the supplier's credit card receipts (perhaps between ½% and 4%, depending on volume) for processing. **Differential pricing** of credit card purchases has not so far become widespread as it deters customers who wish to buy on credit.

8.8 Many card issuers issue special charity cards called **affinity cards** which are connected to a specific charity or cause. When a customer applies for and receives such a card, the issuer will donate, say £5, to the charity. Each time the card is used a small percentage of the purchase price of the item bought (say 0.25%) is also donated to the charity.

ASSESSMENT ALERT

The possible disadvantages of a retailer accepting credit card payments may come up.

Accepting a credit card receipt

8.9 Credit card transactions can be accepted over the telephone or in person over the counter. If goods are ordered by credit card over the **telephone** then either:

(a) The goods must be sent to the address of the cardholder

(b) The goods must be collected in person by the cardholder (for example, theatre tickets)

8.10 EXAMPLE: HOW TO ACCEPT A CREDIT CARD RECEIPT IN PERSON

Let us follow the procedure using an example where EFTPOS (which is the most common means of acceptance now, and is covered in Section 9 below) is *not* in use.

You are gaining some experience on the retail side of the DIY business you work for as an accounting technician. You are currently working on one of the tills. You have processed the goods a customer wishes to buy and he now gives you the credit card with which he wishes to pay. The total amount payable is £157.85. How do you proceed?

8.11 SOLUTION

You will begin by filling in a **credit card voucher** for the transaction. The voucher is in four parts: the original or top copy and three copies underneath. There is carbon paper between the pages to allow details to be passed to all three copies. The top copy is given to the customer and the bottom three are retained when the transaction has been processed.

Here is an example of all the parts of a blank voucher.

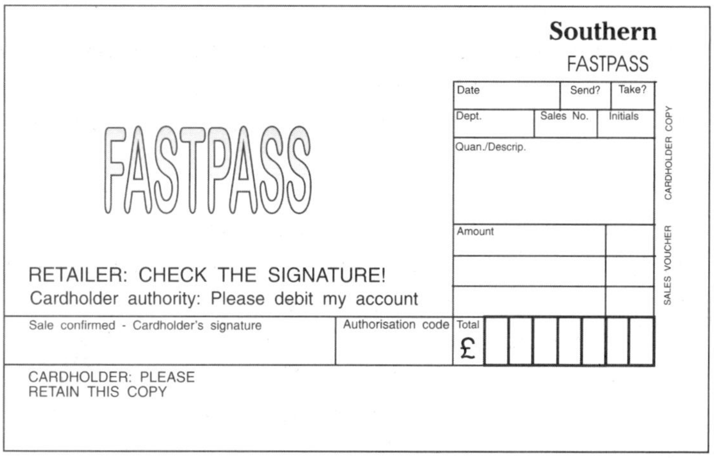

Southern
FASTPASS
Date | Send? | Take?
Dept. | Sales No. | Initials
Quan./Descrip.
Amount
FASTPASS
RETAILER: CHECK THE SIGNATURE!
Cardholder authority: Please debit my account
Sale confirmed - Cardholder's signature | Authorisation code | Total £
CARDHOLDER: PLEASE RETAIN THIS COPY
SALES VOUCHER CARDHOLDER COPY

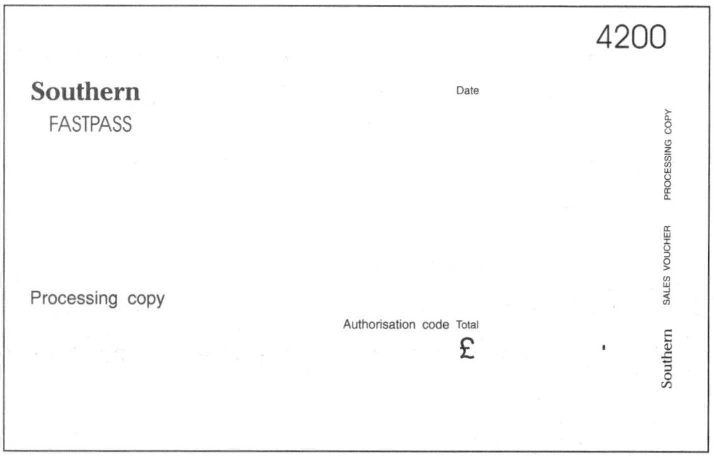

4200
Southern
FASTPASS
Date
Processing copy
Authorisation code | Total £
Southern SALES VOUCHER PROCESSING COPY

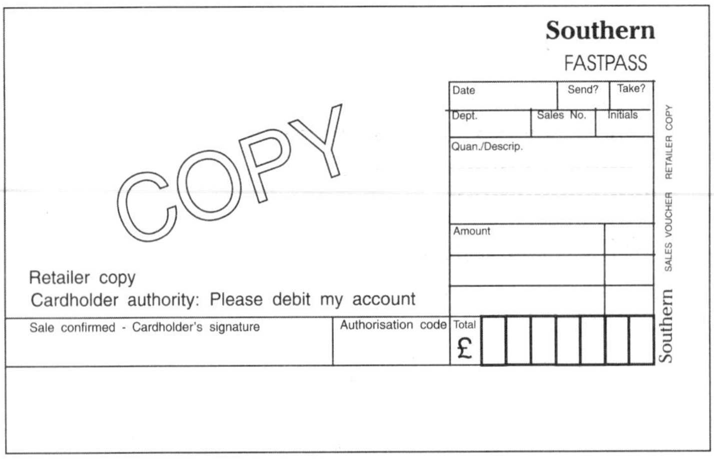

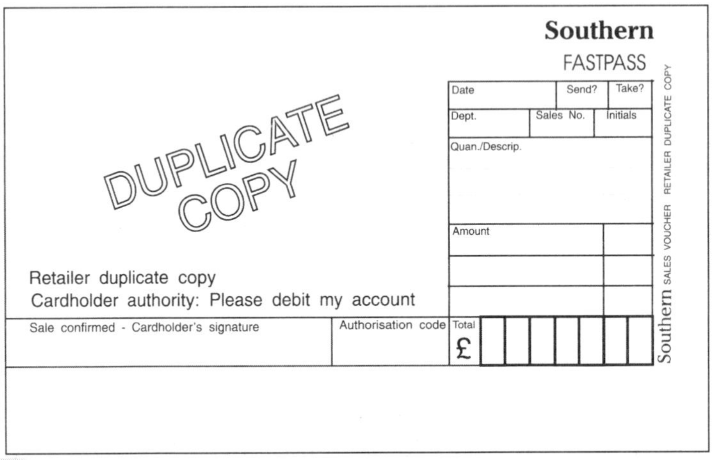

Step 1 You should fill in the details of the transaction on the voucher as follows.

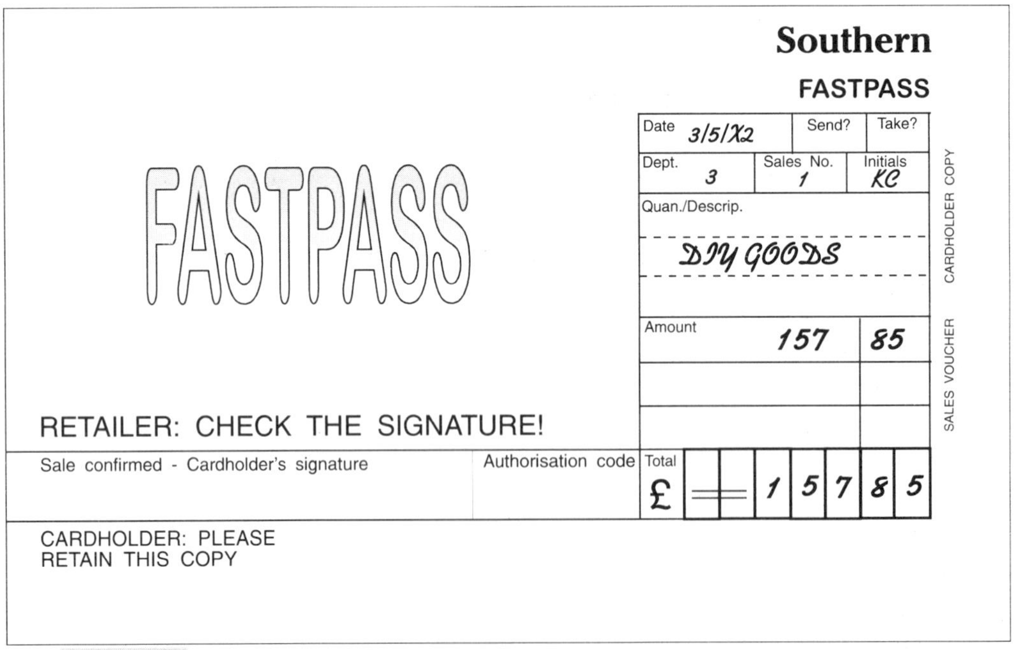

Step 2 **The details on the card need to be** imprinted on the voucher. **At the same time as this happens, details about the place of purchase will appear. This is done using a very basic machine.**

- **A plate is fixed to the machine which holds the information about the place of purchase.**

- **The credit card is slotted into a place on the machine face up.**
- **The voucher is placed on top of both and a roller is pushed over the top of the voucher causing the plate and the card to be imprinted onto the voucher.**

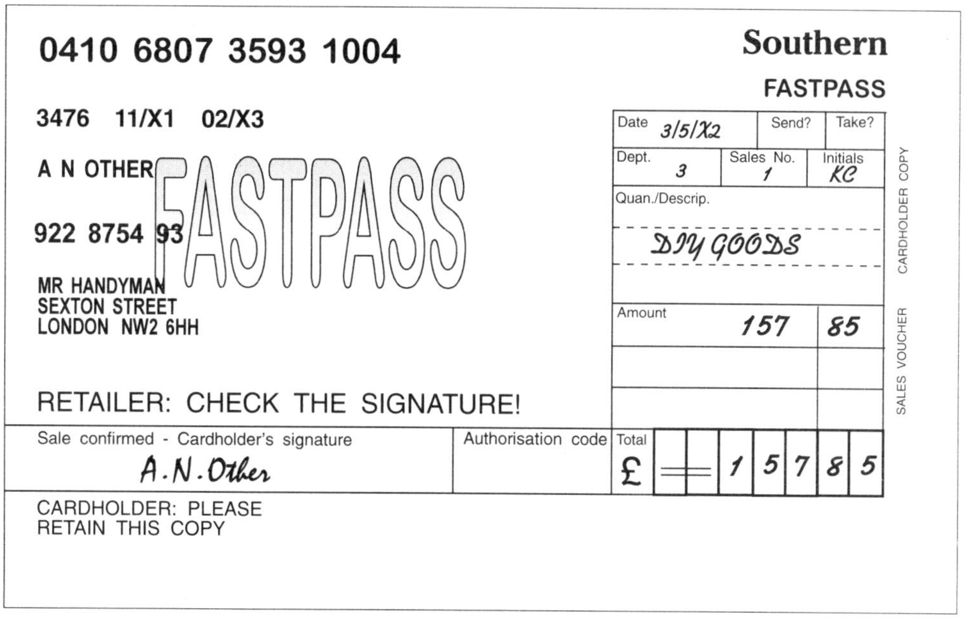

0410 6807 3593 1004

Southern
FASTPASS

3476 11/X1 02/X3

A N OTHER

922 8754 93

FASTPASS

MR HANDYMAN
SEXTON STREET
LONDON NW2 6HH

Date 3/5/X2		Send?	Take?
Dept. 3	Sales No. 1	Initials KC	
Quan./Descrip. DIY GOODS			
Amount		157	85

CARDHOLDER COPY
SALES VOUCHER

RETAILER: CHECK THE SIGNATURE!

Sale confirmed - Cardholder's signature	Authorisation code	Total
A.N.Other		£ = = 1 5 7 8 5

CARDHOLDER: PLEASE
RETAIN THIS COPY

Step 3 **You now ask the customer to** sign the voucher **where indicated. Hold the card while the customer signs. You should be suspicious of hesitancy and printed signatures.**

Step 4 **The transaction is nearly complete, but there are certain** security checks **that you must make before you can accept the credit card as payment.**

Security check	Comments
Rub your thumb over the **signature panel**	It should be flush with the card, not raised (if it is not flush with the card then it may have been tampered with).
Compare the customer signature on the card with that on the voucher	They will not normally match exactly but the likeness should be close enough to leave no doubt.
Check whether the card is stolen against the warning lists regularly issued by the card issuing companies	These lists should be kept up to date and close to all tills where credit cards are accepted. Remember that there is currently a £50 reward for recovering a stolen credit card!
Check that the card is valid by the date	If the current date is past the expiry date, or if it is before the 'valid from' date, then the credit card is not valid. Also, if the 'valid from' date is the current month you should be wary as much fraud occurs on newly issued cards.

Security check	Comments
Check that the transaction does not exceed the business **floor limit**	When a credit card company allows a business to accept its cards as payment it will set a **floor limit** for the shop or business. Up to this limit the business can process all credit card transactions without any authority. The floor limit might be £100. If you want to accept a credit card for a purchase above that amount then you must ring the credit card company up to ask for **authorisation**. If there is no problem then the credit card company will give you an authorisation code which you need to enter in the relevant box.
Final checks	**These are all worth checking, even for the second time.** • Customer signature • Figures are correct • All details imprinted • Floor limit/authorisation code • Dated correctly

The telephone check system does not only exist for when a transaction is over the floor limit. A retailer can ring up if he is suspicious of the validity of the card and use a code to warn the credit card company that he is worried. The credit card company staff can then double check their records and they may also ask questions of the retailer and/or the customer to prove the identity of the customer.

Step 5 **The last procedure in the transaction is to tear off the** top copy of the voucher **and give it to the customer along with the credit card. The carbon paper between the copies should be removed and discarded. The other copies will be put in the till together. They are usually not separated out until they are banked (see Chapter 8).**

0410 6807 3593 1004

3476 11/X1 02/X3

A N OTHER

922 8754 93

MR HANDYMAN
SEXTON STREET
LONDON NW2 6HH

Southern
FASTPASS

FASTPASS

Date 3/5/X2	Send?	Take?
Dept. 3	Sales No. 1	Initials KC

Quan./Descrip.
DIY GOODS

Amount 157 85

CARDHOLDER COPY

SALES VOUCHER

RETAILER: CHECK THE SIGNATURE!

Sale confirmed - Cardholder's signature A.N.Other

Authorisation code 3859

Total £ 157 85

CARDHOLDER: PLEASE
RETAIN THIS COPY

Charge cards

8.12 The term **charge card** covers cards such as American Express and Diners Club. As a means of payment, they are very similar to credit cards. However, they do differ in a number of respects.

Feature	Credit card	Charge card
Cost	Issued free or with an annual 'membership' fee Interest charged on outstanding balance	Enrolment fee, plus annual 'membership' fee. No interest charged.
Payment	Monthly or by instalments. Credit period may be up to six weeks.	Full balance must be cleared monthly. No credit period allowed after date of account.
Credit limit	Set individually, according to customer's circumstances.	No limit (in theory).

8.13 Charge cards are popular for paying **business expenses**. The main advantage is that they overcome the problem of the limit on cheque guarantee cards (usually £50) for someone who does not wish to have credit (which he would obtain with a credit card).

8.14 The five-step procedure for accepting payment by charge card is the same as for credit cards, except that the **authorisation process is unnecessary**.

In-house store cards

8.15 **In-house store cards** are issued and operated by large retail chains such as Marks & Spencer and the John Lewis Partnership. These chains will often, but not always, refuse to accept other credit or charge cards. The cards operate in the same way as a credit card but they tend to be more expensive for the customer (higher interest rates). Again, the same five-step procedure for accepting them as payment applies, although it would be rare for a charge card to be processed manually; normally EFTPOS would be used (see Section 9 of this chapter).

Debit cards

8.16 **Debit cards** are designed for customers who like paying by plastic card but who do not always want credit.

(a) The customer **signs a voucher** at the point of sale

(b) This is then either **processed** through the credit card system (for example Barclays Connect card is a Visa card) and/or through an EFTPOS system (see below).

(c) The amount of the transaction is **deducted directly from the customer's bank account.**

8.17 If the debit card is accepted for a purchase where the transaction has to be processed manually then the voucher used is very similar to the vouchers used for credit card transactions.

9 EFTPOS

> **KEY TERM**
>
> **EFTPOS (Electronic Funds Transfer at Point of Sale)** makes possible the automatic transfer of funds from a customer's bank account to a retail organisation at the point in time when the customer purchases goods (or services) from it. It is also used simply for automatic processing of credit card, charge card and store card transactions.

9.1 EFTPOS is an established system of payment for goods and services, in almost universal use throughout the UK. The effect has been to reduce the number of cheques written, as transactions are settled more and more frequently by plastic.

The EFTPOS terminal

9.2 Most types of **credit card, charge card, store card** and **debit card** can be processed through the EFTPOS terminal which sits on or by the retailer's counter. The terminal can read the magnetic strips on the backs of cards automatically.

9.3 The terminal allows businesses to capture card transactions **electronically,** which has many **advantages** over the manual system outlined above.

(a) They do not **physically** have to take vouchers to the bank to get paid.

(b) When a retailer carries out a transaction on the terminal it will automatically telephone the appropriate card company and seek **authorisation**, eliminating the need to ring them for approval of transactions above the floor limit.

(c) At the same time the transaction will also be **accepted** by the card company for processing and subsequent payment to the retailer's account.

9.4 The terminal prints a **two part receipt** for the customer to sign that is used in place of the manual vouchers we discussed above. The **details of the card,** the **transaction amount** and the **supplier details** are all printed on the receipt. The customer receives the top copy of this receipt and the retailer keeps the bottom part for his records.

9.5 The terminal will look something like this (although remember that larger organisations have these built into the tills and thereby connected to a central computer system, for example in supermarkets).

The keys on the keyboard, as numbered on the diagram, are used as follows.

1 The 'ENTER' key is used to say 'YES' and accept entries. It is represented by an 'E' on the terminal display.

2 The 'DEL' key is used to delete numbers entered incorrectly or to enter the 'TOTALS' feature.

3 The 'CAN/CLR' key is used to delete incorrectly entered numbers.

4 The 'SPACE' key is used to insert spaces when keying in information or to enter the 'TOTALS' feature.

5 The 'FEED' key is used to feed the paper through the terminal.

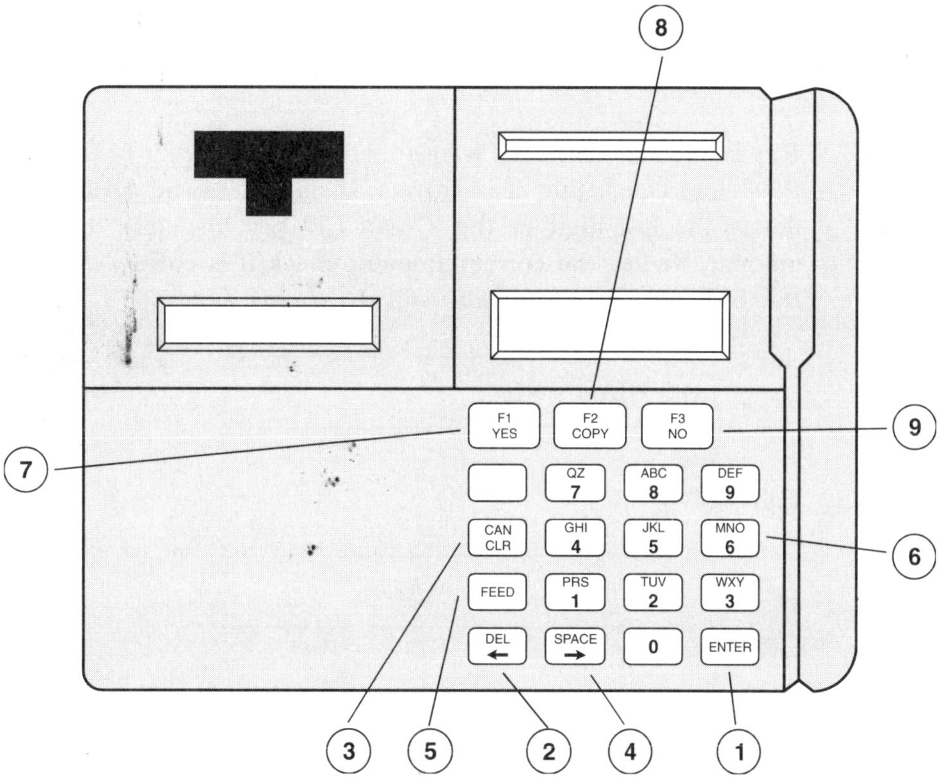

6 The number keys are used for keying in card numbers, transaction amounts and authorisation codes. If an authorisation code is given which contains letters, the letters on the numeric keys are used.

7 The 'F1' key is used to access the sale function and to say 'YES' to a question asked by the terminal.

8 The 'F2' key is used to obtain duplicate transaction receipts.

9 The 'F3' key is used to access the Refund facility and to say 'NO' to a question asked by the terminal.

Transactions using EFTPOS

9.6 The most frequent transaction using an EFTPOS terminal will be a **sale**. We will look at an example of how this would be carried out.

Step 1 **The transaction can only be processed when the main menu appears on the screen.**

SALE	RETURN

Step 2 **Press the 'F1' key. The display will change to:**

WIPE CARD

Step 3 **Wipe the customer's card through the card reader from top to bottom with the magnetic stripe pointing downwards and facing to the right. The display will change to:**

ENTER AMOUNT

Step 4 **Key in the amount of the transaction in pence, eg for £25.00, press '2500' and check that it is correct. If not, press the 'DEL' key to delete the last digit or the 'CAN/CLR' key to delete the whole amount. Re-key the correct amount, check it is correct and press the 'ENTER' key. The display will change to:**

DIALLING

Followed by:

CONNECTION MADE

Step 5 **The terminal has connected with the Authorisation Centre. The display will usually change to:**

AUTH CODE	12345

Step 6 **The transaction is authorised. The display will change to:**

SIGNATURE OK?

Step 7 **Tear off the receipt and ask the customer to sign it. Check the signature matches with that on the card and that the card number printed on the receipt matches with the number embossed on the card.**

Step 8 **The transaction is nearly complete, but you need to check the signature panel and compare the signatures as for manual card processing before you can accept the card as payment.**

Step 9 **If you are satisfied with the signature and card press the 'F1' key. The display will change to:**

COMPLETED	E

The transaction is now completed. Press the 'ENTER' key.

9.7 The voucher produced by an EFTPOS sales transaction will look like this:

Retailer name and address	A MERCHANT HIGH STREET ANYTOWN		
Card issuer name	VISA		
Account number	4929000000014321		
Expiry date (mm/yy)	08X9		
	Sale	£25.25	Amount
	PLEASE KEEP THIS FOR YOUR RECORDS SIGNATURE		
	M. Stephens		
Authorisation code	AUTH CODE	12345	
Retailer message	THANKYOU		
Merchant number	M1234567		
Terminal ID	T06500015	R0019	Transaction number
Date	DATE 06/07/X7	07:25	Time

No VAT number appears on this voucher. It depends on the retailer as to whether a till receipt is also issued; if it is (as in this case) the VAT number appears on the till receipt.

9.8 Note that, even though the terminal carries out most checks for you, you should still consider carrying out all the **checks in Step 4** of Paragraph 8.11 as computers have been known to get it wrong!

9.9 There are a variety of further procedures, particularly for where the transaction is **not authorised** (the terminal can tell you to retain the card). Other types of transactions can also be processed, including **mail order** sales (where the card number is keyed in manually), **reversals** (ie returns) and the machine can also issue **duplicate receipts**.

9.10 The terminal will come with a **training card** for staff training and a **supervisor's card**, which has to be used in order to carry out certain transactions (for control purposes). Such transactions include refunds and report requests. These cards look like credit cards and they are 'wiped' through the terminal as normal credit cards are.

Reports

9.11 The reports which can be requested will usually include:

(a) Transactions processed through the terminal for **each card issuer** since the last report.

(b) **'End of day' procedures**, which we will discuss in Chapter 9.

10 OTHER RECEIPTS

10.1 We have examined the types of receipts which are dealt with by most businesses. There are some more **specialised kinds of receipts** which are used by certain businesses. They use these methods because it suits their particular business.

Banker's draft

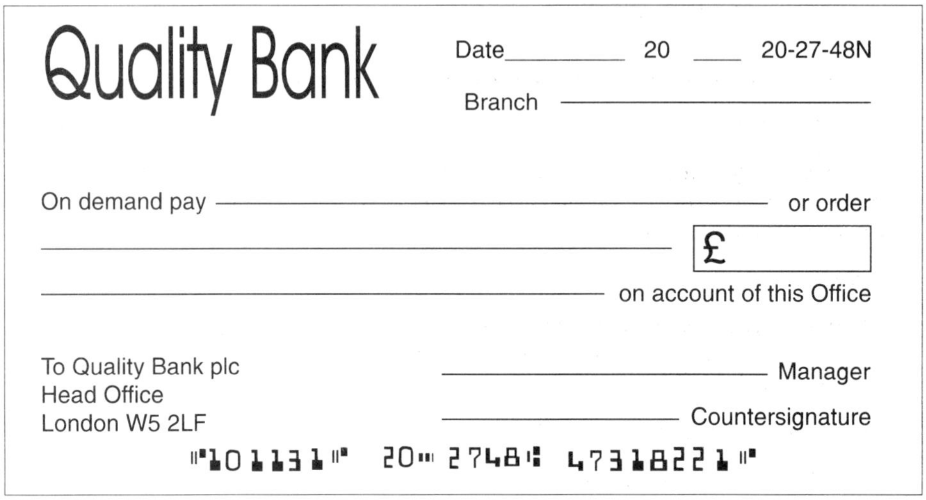
Quality Bank

Date__________ 20 ____ 20-27-48N

Branch ____________________

On demand pay ____________________ or order

____________________ £

____________________ on account of this Office

To Quality Bank plc
Head Office
London W5 2LF

____________________ Manager

____________________ Countersignature

101131 20 2748 47318221

10.2 This is a method of payment which is available from banks on request (and on payment of a fee) to customers who need to eliminate the risk of a cheque being 'bounced'. Paying by **banker's draft** is common when a customer is buying property and needs a guarantee that the payment **cannot be dishonoured** in order to complete the purchase. The customer must have sufficient cleared funds to cover the debit made by the bank to his account in return for the issue of the draft, which is effectively a cheque drawn on the bank by itself, payable to a person specified by the customer. This is a *fast* way of getting money to someone.

10.3 The alternative to a banker's draft is a **building society cheque**. This is *not* a personal cheque issued by an individual on his building society account. Instead it is where a customer withdraws money from his building society account and asks for the money as a cheque. He may specify to whom the cheque is made payable. **The cheque cannot be stopped.**

Standing orders and direct debits

10.4 These types of payment are **regular payments** (usually monthly). The amount of a standing order can only be changed by the payer, but the amount of a direct debit can be changed by the receiver as well. Only certain kinds of businesses will receive money by this means.

- Banks and building societies: mortgage and other loan repayments
- Insurance companies: insurance and personal pension premiums
- Local authorities: rates and community charge instalments
- Credit card companies: minimum amounts due to credit card issuers
- Large clubs/associations: subscriptions

- Utilities (gas, electricity, telephone): especially when customers are paying a fixed monthly amount reviewed annually
- Hire companies: equipment rental and maintenance

10.5 Normally only quite large organisations use **direct debits** and **standing orders**. Where there are a large number of relatively small amounts to be collected and processed, it is better to use standing orders or direct debits as the bank will process them automatically.

Activity 7.4 **Level: Pre-assessment**

Imagine that you are employed in various different businesses, as detailed below. In each case, a customer or potential customer telephones you with a query about how a payment or payments may be made.

Task

State what you would say in response to the customer, making any assumptions about the policies of the businesses which you consider appropriate. You should explain your reasons as part of your response.

The customers' queries are as follows.

(a) *Business: electricity company*

'I am a domestic customer, and receive a bill from you each quarter. I want to continue to pay quarterly, but I don't want to go the trouble of writing out a cheque or making a special trip (for example to a bank or your office) to pay the bill. However, I do need to know how much the bill is going to be before I am due to pay it. What method of payment would you suggest?'

(b) *Business: house builder*

'If I buy one of your houses, I'll be getting a mortgage, and so some of the funds will be coming from my building society. However, some will be due from me when the sale is completed. How will that need to be paid?'

(c) *Business: mail order company*

'I want to place an order with you. I don't have a bank account, building society account or a credit card, so I suppose that I'll need to send you the amount due by cash through the post. Is that OK?'

(d) *Business: DIY retailer*

'I want to call in to your store to buy something costing £34 for a friend. I understand that you accept cheques supported by a cheque guarantee card. My friend has made out and signed the cheque and given me her cheque guarantee card. I'd like to bring the cheque and card in when I collect the goods.'

Key learning points

- Receipts have to be well **controlled** to ensure a good cash flow. There are three key features of control.
  - **Banking** (performed promptly and correctly)
  - **Security** (avoiding loss or theft)
  - **Documentation** (remittance advice)
- Trade customers usually send a *remittance advice* with their payment.
- **Till receipts** or **written receipts** are *prima facie* proof of purchase and they must contain certain information.

- There are various ways a company can **receive money**. The main ones are:
  - Cash
  - Cheque
  - Credit, debit or charge card
- The **timing and types of receipt** a business experiences will depend on:
  - The type of business
  - The type of sale
  - Seasonal and economic trends
- **Holding cash** creates problems and careful security procedures are required.
- A **cheque** is: 'an unconditional order in writing addressed by a person to a bank, signed by the person giving it, requiring the bank to pay on demand a sum certain in money to or to the order of a specified person or to bearer'.
- **Cheque guarantee cards** are issued to guarantee personal cheques up to a certain limit. Strict procedures should be followed when accepting a personal cheque as payment.
- **Strict procedures** should also be followed when accepting credit, debit or charge cards as payment.
- **EFTPOS** is a means of allowing a transaction to be recorded immediately on customer bank accounts or credit card statements, while at the same time authorising the transaction.

Quick quiz

1. Control over cash receipts will concentrate on which three key areas?
2. What is the function of a remittance advice?
3. Why is it important to give the correct change to customers?
4. Is a till-receipt conclusive evidence of a payment?
5. What has happened when a business becomes insolvent?
6. What is fidelity insurance?
7. Which three parties are always required for a cheque to be valid?
8. What is the effect of an 'endorsement in blank'?
9. What are the four possible types of cheque crossing?
10. When is a cheque 'stale'?
11. How many guaranteed cheques can be used in one transaction?
12. A retailer can use differential pricing for credit card purchases. True or false?
13. What does EFTPOS stand for?
14. A banker's draft cannot be dishonoured. True or false?

Answers to quick quiz

1. Receipts should be banked promptly, correctly recorded and loss or theft should be prevented.
2. A remittance advice shows which invoices a payment covers.
3. Giving correct change prevents customer annoyance and loss of money by the business.
4. No, although *prima facie* it is.

5 When a business is insolvent it is no longer able to pay the money it owes people when it is due.

6 Fidelity insurance allows businesses to reclaim stolen money from an insurer when a member of the business's staff has been dishonest.

7 A cheque must name: a drawer; a drawee; and a payee.

8 An endorsement in blank converts a cheque from an order cheque to a bearer cheque.

9 The four types of crossing are: general; special; not negotiable; and a/c payee.

10 A cheque is stale six months after the date of issue.

11 Only one cheque can be used per transaction.

12 True, although the practice of differential pricing is not widespread.

13 EFTPOS = Electronic Funds Transfer at Point of Sale.

14 True.

8 Banking monies received

This chapter contains

1 The banking system
2 The banker/customer relationship
3 Procedures for banking cash
4 Procedures for banking cheques
5 Procedures for banking plastic card transactions
6 Banking and EFTPOS
7 Banking other receipts

Learning objectives

On completion of this chapter you will have learned about:

- Organisational procedures for filing source information
- Types of business transactions and documents involved
- Automated payments: CHAPS, BACS, Direct Debits, Standing Orders
- Identify general bank services and understand the operation of the clearing bank system
- The use of banking documentation
- Credit and debit cards
- Basic law relating to contract law, Sale of Goods Act and document retention policies
- Banking and personal security procedures
- Methods of handling and storing money, including the security aspects

Performance criteria

1.2.3 Paying in documents are correctly prepared and reconciled to relevant records

1.2.4 Unusual features are identified and either resolved or referred to the appropriate person

Range statement

1.2.1 Receipts: cash; cheques; automated payments

1.2.3 Unusual features: wrongly completed cheques; out of date cheques, credit and debit cards; limits exceeded; disagreement with supporting documentation; under payments; over payments; cheques returned to sender

1 THE BANKING SYSTEM

1.1 This chapter covers the **practical aspects of banking** the payments received by a business. Before dealing with these aspects, however, it would be useful to understand some background details about two areas:

(a) The **clearing bank system** and how it operates.

(b) The **legal relationship between the customer and the banker** (see Section 2 of this chapter).

ASSESSMENT ALERT

It is helpful to know something about these matters, to be able to feel confident when talking to the bank about a query, particularly when you think the bank may have made a mistake. This type of problem may come up in the Devolved Assessment.

The banking system

1.2 The banking system in the UK consists of the following components.

- The **Bank of England** is the British **central bank** which controls or polices the banking industry in this country. It is controlled by the state. Among many other functions, the Bank of England acts as banker to the other banks.
- **Clearing** or **retail banks**. There are four major high street banks.
  - Barclays
  - Lloyds
  - HSBC
  - NatWest
- **Smaller retail banks**
  - Co-operative Bank
  - Yorkshire Bank
  - Abbey National

  Various former building societies have taken advantage of legislation and have turned themselves into banks (as Abbey National did).

The clearing system

KEY TERM

Clearing is the mechanism for obtaining payment for cheques.

1.3 Banks settle cheques and credits through the **clearing system**. Once the values of cheques passed between the banks at the end of a particular day's clearing have been determined, the resulting debts arising between the banks need to be settled.

For example, Lloyds may be asking for settlement of £20m worth of cheques drawn on Barclays bank paid in by its customers into their accounts at Lloyds branches. In turn, Barclays may have £25m worth of Lloyds cheques paid into branches of Barclays.

	£m
Lloyds owes Barclays	25
Barclays owes Lloyds	20
Net debt: Lloyds owes Barclays	5

In short, at the end of a day's banking, **banks owe money to other banks, and are owed money in return**. These debts are settled through accounts which the banks maintain at the Bank of England. The balances on these accounts are termed **operational balances** at the Bank of England.

1.4 The diagram on page 193 explains how the cheque clearing system operates.

1.5 The **cheque clearing system** is complicated in its detailed procedure but simple to understand in principle.

Step 1 The receiving bank branches **stamp their names and addresses** in addition to

Day 1 the crossings on the cheques, and **sort the cheques** paid in by its customers into bundles of cheques drawn on each of the other banks which participate in the cheque clearing system. (The 'non-clearing' banks and building societies participate by using one of the clearing banks as their agent.)

Step 2 The bundles of cheques from each receiving bank branch are sent in, by special overnight delivery, to the **head office** of the bank to which the branch belongs.

Step 3 The head office delivers to the **Bankers Clearing House** the bundles of

Day 2 cheques (with covering lists) drawn on each of the other banks, or on non-clearing banks which they represent.

Step 4 The Bankers Clearing House distributes these cheques to the head offices of the relevant **paying banks.**

Step 5 The paying banks' head offices **process the cheques** using computers and

Day 3 distribute the cheques to the various branches of the banks on which the cheques are drawn.

The sequence of delivery to the Bankers Clearing House, exchange between bank head offices, and re-distribution down the chain to individual branches should be completed, as regards each cheque, within **three working days**.

1.6 If the paying bank **dishonours a cheque** (refuses to pay it, usually because the paying bank's customer has insufficient funds) delivered to the branch through the clearing system, it marks on the cheque the **reason for its refusal to pay** and returns it by post **direct** to the receiving bank branch from which it came.

The amount of the cheque will have been included in the total value of cheques passing from the receiving bank to the paying bank at the central clearing. The transaction between the receiving and paying banks is **cancelled** by the receiving bank branch sending in an **unpaid claim** for processing through the clearing system.

1.7 Since the total value of cheques payable by and receivable by each bank with regard to the other banks each day will not be equal, the banks' head offices **adjust the position between them by credits and debits in their respective accounts at the Bank of England.**

The clearing system

Alpha, a customer of Barclays Bank, Penzance, writes a cheque to Beta. Beta is a customer of Lloyds Bank, Stoke and pays the cheque into his branch at Stoke on Monday.

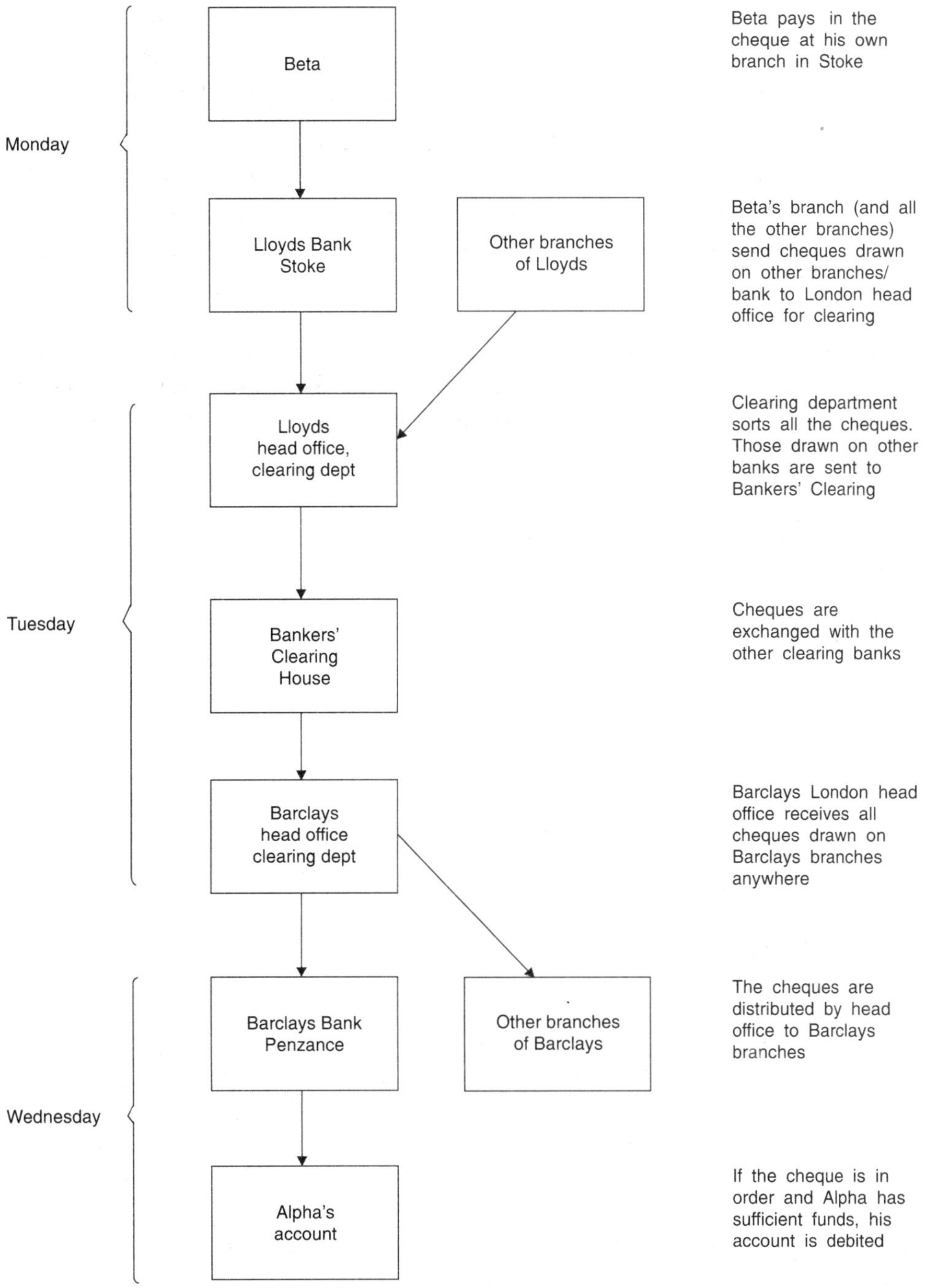
Monday
Tuesday
Wednesday
Beta
Lloyds Bank Stoke
Other branches of Lloyds
Lloyds head office, clearing dept
Bankers' Clearing House
Barclays head office clearing dept
Barclays Bank Penzance
Other branches of Barclays
Alpha's account
Beta pays in the cheque at his own branch in Stoke
Beta's branch (and all the other branches) send cheques drawn on other branches/ bank to London head office for clearing
Clearing department sorts all the cheques. Those drawn on other banks are sent to Bankers' Clearing
Cheques are exchanged with the other clearing banks
Barclays London head office receives all cheques drawn on Barclays branches anywhere
The cheques are distributed by head office to Barclays branches
If the cheque is in order and Alpha has sufficient funds, his account is debited

Activity 8.1 — Level: Assessment

You work in the Yarm branch of Dosh Bank. You receive a telephone call from Mrs Skint, who maintains a current account at your branch. She has the following query.

'I don't usually pay cheques into my current account as normally the only money going in is my pension which is paid by bank transfer. But two days ago I received a cheque for £100 made out to me by my son and I paid it into the bank on that day. Before paying in the cheque, my account balance was £9.62. When I called into the bank yesterday to draw out the £100 from my son, the cashier said I couldn't as I could only draw cleared funds. I asked a friend about this but he couldn't explain, so I'm calling you now to get some explanation. What is this "clearing" business? My son is a very reputable person so I don't think there should be any reason for you to doubt his creditworthiness. I was wondering if the fact that he had written "not negotiable" across the cheque had created some problem.'

Task

Write down what you would say in reply to Mrs Skint, including in your answer an explanation of the term 'cleared funds' and of the effect of the words 'not negotiable' on the cheque.

2 THE BANKER/CUSTOMER RELATIONSHIP

What is a banker?

2.1 The definition of a 'banker' has been decided by a combination of statute (laws passed by Parliament) and case law (results of situations where one person or company takes another person or company to court for the court to resolve a disagreement between the two parties).

KEY TERM

A **banker** is someone who will:

- Put money and cheques **received** on a customer's behalf into his account.
- Take out all cheques and orders **paid out** from the customer's account by the customer.
- **Keep accounts**, such as current accounts, which can be used for paying in or taking out on the customer's behalf.

What is a customer?

2.2 The term 'customer' or 'customer of a bank' is not defined in statute. However, case law has established the following definition.

KEY TERM

A person becomes a **customer** in respect of cheque transactions as soon as the bank opens an account for him in his name.

In any other situation, for example when investment advice is given, a person becomes a **customer** as soon as the bank accepts his instructions and undertakes to provide a service.

2.3 It is important to know if a person is a customer because banks owe many **legal duties** to customers and can be **sued** if they do not carry out these duties adequately. There is also protection in law for a bank doing certain things for customers which would not apply if it did them for non-customers. For example, a bank might advance cash to a person presenting a credit card, who would not by virtue of this transaction alone become a customer.

The contractual relationships

2.4 The relationship between bank and customer arises from legal **contracts** between them which it is necessary to understand. There are **four** main types of contractual relationship which may exist between a banker and a customer.

- Debtor/creditor (see Paragraph 2.5)
- Bailor/bailee (see Paragraph 2.6)
- Principal/agent (see Paragraphs 2.7 and 2.8)
- Mortgagor/mortgagee (see Paragraph 2.9)

ASSESSMENT ALERT

Most of these relationships could come up in the Devolved Assessments.

Creditor/debtor relationship

2.5 If you lend a friend, Wendy, some money, then you are Wendy's **creditor**. Wendy owes you money and therefore she is your **debtor**.

(a) This relationship applies when a bank lends money to a customer: the **customer is a debtor** who must at some stage repay the **bank, who is the creditor**.

(b) Similarly when a customer deposits money in a bank, at some point the bank will have to pay back the money to the customer, so the **customer is a creditor of the bank** whilst the **bank is the debtor of the customer.** The bank **does not hold the client's money in trust**; this would mean that they would have to give any profit made using the money to the client. Banks don't do this, over and above paying any agreed rate of interest to the customer.

The bailor/bailee relationship

2.6 This relationship exists where a bank offers a **safe deposit service** to customers, which allows use of the bank's strong room or safe. When it accepts the customer's property, the bank has an obligation:

- To take '**reasonable**' **care to safeguard** it against damage and loss.
- To **redeliver** it to the customer or some other person authorised by him and not to deliver it to any other person. In law this type of arrangement is known as a **bailment**.

The customer is the bailor, the bank is the bailee.

Principal/agent relationship

> **KEY TERM**
>
> An **agency** relationship is one where one person (the **agent**) acts for another (the **principal**), usually for the purpose of doing business between the principal and a third party.

2.7 The use of an agent is often necessary as the principal does not have sufficient **specialist knowledge** to deal with the third party himself. An example of this is where an accountant deals with the Inland Revenue on behalf of a client, or where an employment agency finds a new employee or a temp for an employer.

2.8 The bank may act as **agent for its customers**; it may also employ agents (for example stockbrokers) to handle certain business, or it may have dealings with agents of its customers. A fairly common example of how the bank can act as agent is when the bank arranges insurance for the customer; the bank is acting as an insurance broker and is the agent of its customer.

Mortgagor/mortgagee relationship

2.9 This relationship arises when a customer asks a bank to give a loan secured by a charge or **mortgage** over the customer's assets such as property. The **customer**, or **mortgagor**, grants the **bank**, or **mortgagee**, a mortgage. **At the same time** the customer is the debtor, and the bank is the creditor for the amount of the loan. If the customer does not pay back the loan the bank can sell the asset or assets to recover its money.

2.10 Section summary

Contractual relationship	Transaction	Customer	Bank
Creditor/debtor	Customer deposits cash at bank	Creditor	Debtor
Debtor/creditor	Bank gives customer money on overdraft	Debtor	Creditor
Bailor/bailee	Customer stores property in bank's safest deposit facilities	Bailor	Bailee
Principal/agent	Bank arranges insurance for customer	Principal	Agent
Mortgagor/mortgagee	Bank lends money to customer with a mortgage on customer's property as its security	Mortgagor (Debtor)	Mortgagee (Creditor)

The fiduciary relationship

2.11 This type of relationship is **not contractual**. In a normal relationship between a bank and a customer, the bank can be in a position of exerting **undue influence** on the customer, perhaps forcing him to do something he does not really wish to do. The law recognises this and therefore expects the 'superior' party, in this case the bank, to act in good faith. This is said to be a **fiduciary** (or **special**) **relationship.**

The rights and duties of bankers and customers

The rights of bankers

2.12 Bankers' rights accrue on the basis of accepted legal or moral justice.

Rights of bankers	Comments
Making charges or commissions	If they are **reasonable** (this is apart from charging interest on overdrafts).
Using customers' money	As noted before, the money deposited is *not* held by the bank on trust and the bank can use it to **earn interest**.
Demanding repayment of overdrawn balances	All overdrafts are **repayable on demand**, unless separate terms state or imply otherwise.
Possessing a lien over securities	A **lien** is a right to retain possession of another's property to discharge a debt. This would *not* apply to items held in safe custody such as jewellery, but would apply to deposits of property as informal security for a loan.

The duties of customers

2.13 On the basis of legal or moral justice, the following duties are owed to the bank by the customer.

Duties of customers	Comment
Ensuring that **fraud** is not facilitated when drawing cheques	Customers must be careful with their cheques in the sense that they should not do things like sign a blank cheque and then send it through the post. They must also tell the bank of any known forgeries.
Indemnifying the bank when it acts on the customer's behalf	'Indemnify' means 'secure against possible loss or damage'. The most common example of this is when the customer uses a cheque guarantee card to indemnify the bank against the possibility that the cheque he writes takes his account into overdraft. The customer is then obliged to repay the overdraft created on demand.

The duties of bankers = rights of customers

KEY TERM

A **duty** is a task or action which a person is bound to perform for moral or legal reasons.

2.14 The duties of a banker fall in the categories listed below. These duties may be said to represent the rights of customers as well as the duties of bankers. Customers' rights are supported by the **Banking Code** and the **Banking Ombudsman** schemes.

Duties of bankers	Comments
Honour a customer's **cheque**	The cheque must be correctly made out, there must be sufficient funds in the account and there must be no legal reason why the cheque cannot be paid (for instance, insolvency of the customer would bar payment of funds from his account).
Receipt of customer's funds	The funds must be credited to the customer's account.
Repayment on demand	There must be a written request for repayment from a customer, during normal bank opening hours and at the customer's branch or another agreed bank or branch.
Comply with customer's **instructions**	When there are sufficient funds, the bank must do as the customer requests.
Provide a **statement**	The banker must provide a statement showing transactions on a customer's account in a 'reasonable time' and also details of the balance of the account on request.
Confidentiality	As a general principle, a bank should keep in confidence what it knows about a customer's affairs. There are four recognised exceptions to this rule. (i) Disclosure may be **required by law**, for instance under the Drug Trafficking Offences Act 1986 and the Criminal Justice Act 1993. (ii) There may be a **public duty to disclose**, as when a customer trades with the enemy during a war. (iii) The **interest of the bank** may require disclosure, as when the bank sues the customer to recover what it is owed. (iv) The customer may have given **express or implied consent** (where, for instance, the customer asks a third party to obtain a 'bankers reference' from the bank).
Advise of **forgery**	The bank must tell the customer when it becomes apparent that cheques bearing a forgery of the customer's signature are being drawn on his account.
Care and skill	Bankers are expected to use care and skill, partly for professional reasons but also to ensure the banks' statutory protection under some legislation.
Closure of accounts	Bankers have a duty to provide reasonable notice to a customer when the bank wishes to close the account. The period of notice should allow the customer to make other arrangements.

2.15 There is **no duty for the customer** to ensure that he keeps records of the account and he has **no duty to check the statements he gets from the bank**.

This means that the responsibility is very much on the bank to ensure transactions are correctly applied to a customer's account. If it gives too much money to the account the customer *may* not have to return it (provided he acted in good faith); if it takes too much money away from the account, then the customer's reputation may be damaged (by the bank's 'libel') if cheques he has drawn are not honoured by the bank. The bank may then have to compensate him for the damage, particularly if he is a business customer with a valuable credit standing.

The Banking Code

2.16 The Banking Code was drawn up jointly by the British Bankers Association, the Building Societies Association and APACS (Association for Payment Clearing Services). The Code shown below came into effect on 31 March 1999.

2.17 The Code is written to promote good banking practice and is in five parts, plus a 'help section'. It is a voluntary code followed by banks and building societies in their relations with **personal customers** in the UK. It covers the following areas:

1 *Key commitments* (see Paragraph 2.18 below)

2 *Information*

Information available - Helping you to choose savings and investment accounts - Terms and conditions - Keeping you informed of changes - Marketing of services - Helping you to choose a mortgage

3 *Account operations*

Running your account - Cards and PINs - Lending - Foreign exchange services

4 *Protection*

Confidentiality - Protecting your account

5 *Difficulties*

Financial difficulties - Complaints - Monitoring and competence

2.18 These are the **key commitments to personal customers** (note - not business customers) undertaken by the Code's subscribers (nearly all UK banks and building societies):

- To act fairly and reasonably in all dealings with customers
- To ensure that all services and products comply with the Code, even if they have their own terms and conditions
- To give information on services and products in plain language, and offer help if there is any aspect which customers do not understand
- To help customers to choose a service or product to fit their needs
- To help customers understand the financial implications of:
  - A mortgage
  - Other borrowing
  - Savings and investment products
  - Card products
- To help customers to understand how their accounts work

- To have safe, secure and reliable banking and payment systems
- To ensure that the procedures followed by staff reflect the commitments set out in the Code
- To correct errors and handle complaints speedily
- To consider cases of financial difficulty and mortgage arrears sympathetically and positively
- To ensure that all services and products comply with relevant laws and regulations

The Ombudsman Scheme

2.19 The main object of the office of the **Banking Ombudsman** is to receive unresolved complaints about the provision of banking services, and to 'facilitate the satisfaction, settlement or withdrawal of such complaints'. The service is provided free and the scheme is financed by the member banks.

2.20 The scheme applies to small companies as well as individuals, sole traders and partnerships. A 'small company' is defined, for these purposes, as having a turnover of less than £1 million in its last financial year prior to a complaint being made.

3 PROCEDURES FOR BANKING CASH

The paying-in slip

3.1 When a business or an individual wants to pay money into the bank, then normally a **paying-in slip** must be used. The bank treats this as a kind of summary document which 'totals up' the cash (or other forms of money) which is being banked.

3.2 A paying-in slip will look similar to the one shown here.

Date
A/c
Notes £50
£20
£10
£5
Coins £1
50p
20p
Silver
Bronze
Cash £
Cheques
£

Date
Cashier's stamp and initials
Fee
No of Cheques

bank giro credit
Paid in by/Customer's Reference
6 83048231 92057419
Quality Bank
EALING BROADWAY BRANCH
ABC & CO
A/C no. 47318221
Please do not write or mark below this line

Notes £50
£20
£10
£5
Coins £1
50p
20p
Silver
Bronze
Cash £
Cheques
£

101131 ⑈101131⑈ 20⑆2748⑆ 47318221⑈

This is a preprinted paying-in slip; the details of the company which is paying in money (ABC & Co) have already been entered. Banks also hold completely **blank forms** for customers to use.

3.3 As you can see, the slip is laid out in such a way that, for cash, all you have to do is to **fill in the amounts of each denomination and add them up** (we will discuss cheques in Section 4 of this chapter).

Counting the cash

3.4 Notes should be paid in with the **Queen's head uppermost and to the right**. This is because in most banks there are special adding machines which count bundles of notes automatically. This is a great help to the banks, but for the machine to be able to work all the notes have to be of the same denomination (for instance, all £20 notes) and they all have to be the same way up. This means that it can take quite a long time for a business to prepare the cash for banking.

Care should be taken to check that the **totals counted are correct** and notes should be put into **bundles** of £100 or £500, where possible.

3.5 Coins should be counted and inserted into the plastic paying-in bags supplied by banks.

3.6 Remember that you may need to leave a **float** in the till for the next day's trading. This should be taken into account; not all the cash should be counted and paid into the bank.

KEY TERM

A **float** is the money kept in the till at the end of the day so that the next day there is some cash available to give change to customers.

Procedures for preparing a paying-in slip

3.7 The following procedures are good practice to follow when preparing money for banking.

Step 1	**Count the cash** as described above.
Step 2	**Add up,** on a separate piece of paper, how much cash you are banking.
Step 3	Compare the **calculated total** to the total according to the **cash register** (as we will discuss in Chapter 9 of this text).
Step 4	**Calculate any discrepancy** between the cash counted and the cash register total. If it is large then it should be investigated, but if it is small then it may be ignored, depending on company policy.
Step 5	Enter the **total for each denomination of note** in the appropriate place on the paying in slip.
Step 6	Add up the numbers again to check the total and **enter the total in the 'total cash' box.**

3.8 EXAMPLE: BANKING CASH

You are preparing the day's takings for banking. When you have sorted and counted the notes you find you have the following.

(a) Five £50 notes
(b) 110 £20 notes
(c) 560 £10 notes
(d) 40 £5 notes
(e) Six bags each containing 20 £1 coins
(f) Two bags each containing 10 50p coins
(g) Ten bags each containing 50 20p coins
(h) Other silver worth £32.20
(i) Bronze worth 93p

The **float** left in the till was £34.90 at the end of yesterday and £43.62 at the end of today. The till summary states that £8,517.41 was received today.

Prepare the paying in slip (use the blank one in Paragraph 3.2) and reconcile cash banked to the till records.

3.9 SOLUTION

The amounts of money to be banked are worked out on a separate piece of paper.

	£
5 × £50	250.00
110 × £20	2,200.00
560 × £10	5,600.00
40 × £5	200.00
6 × 20 × £1	120.00
2 × 10 × £0.50	10.00
10 × 50 × £0.20	100.00
Other silver	32.20
Bronze	0.93
Total	8,513.13

The change in the **float** must be taken into account. If it had stayed the same then we would not need to make any adjustment. Here it has changed by £8.72 (£43.62 – £34.90). If we had not increased the float by that amount then we would have been able to put that money in the bank. So we should add it on to the money we are banking to compare it with what the till says we have taken.

	£
Money to be banked	8,513.13
Add increase in the float	8.72
	8,521.85
Receipts according to the till	8,517.41
Difference	4.44

This difference is very small and would be ignored (or **written off**). The business should set a limit, for instance £5, over which investigations are made. We will now complete the paying-in slip.

Date 23/6/X5

A/c

Notes £50	250	00
£20	2,200	00
£10	5,600	00
£5	200	00
Coins £1	120	00
50p	10	00
20p	100	00
Silver	32	20
Bronze		93
Cash £		
Cheques		
£	8,513	13

Date 23/6/X5

Cashier's stamp and initials

Fee

No of Cheques

bank giro credit

Paid in by/Customer's Reference

6 83048231 92057419

Quality Bank

EALING BROADWAY BRANCH

ABC & CO A/c no 47318221

Please do not write or mark below this line

Notes £50	250	00
£20	2,200	00
£10	5,600	00
£5	200	00
Coins £1	120	00
50p	10	00
20p	100	00
Silver	32	20
Bronze		93
Cash £		
Cheques		
£	8,513	13

101131 ⑈101131⑈ 20⑆ 2748⑆ 47318221⑈

The paying-in slip is now ready to be taken to the bank with the money.

Security procedures when banking cash

3.10 Generally, the **security procedures** below should be considered and implemented where possible.

(a) **Vary the time** of the visit to the bank and **vary which member of staff** takes the money there.

(b) If possible, **send more than one person**. This is particularly important when using the night safe; the banks advise that one person should drive and then watch over the other person who carries the money and puts it into the night safe.

(c) If very large amounts of cash are banked regularly then the business should consider employing a **security firm** to collect the money and deliver it to the bank.

(d) It is always wise to fill in the part of the paying-in slip which is retained by the customer of the bank (on the left hand side) so you have a **record** of paying the money into the bank. You can record the information elsewhere if you wish.

4 PROCEDURES FOR BANKING CHEQUES

4.1 The same paying-in slip is used for cheques as for cash, but this time we also need to look at the **back of the paying-in slip**.

Details of Cheques, etc.			Sub-Total brought forward				
Carried Forward £			Total Carried over £				

In view of the risk of loss in course of clearing, customers are advised to keep an independent record of the drawers of cheques

Please do not write or mark below this line

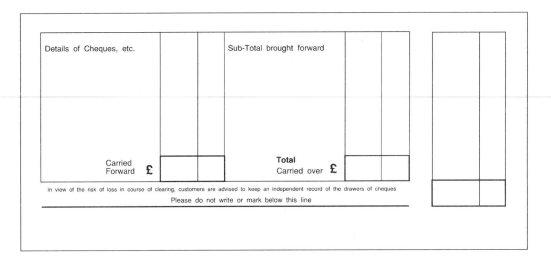

4.2 The bank has to have a **list of the cheques** which you are paying in. The details required are usually only:

- The **drawer** (the person who signs the cheque)
- The **amount**.

If the payee of the cheque is **someone else**, not your business, then it must have been **endorsed** by the payee (see Chapter 7). In this case, the name of the **endorser** is put on the list. Remember that many banks have stopped accepting these 'third party' cheques, as the incidence of fraud is high.

4.3 Many of the procedures for banking cheques are the same as for cash. Let us use an example to work out how to fill in the paying-in slip.

4.4 EXAMPLE: BANKING CHEQUES

At the end of a business day, you are asked to bank the cheques which have been received that day by the business you work for, ABC & Co. Here are just two of the cheques you must bank.

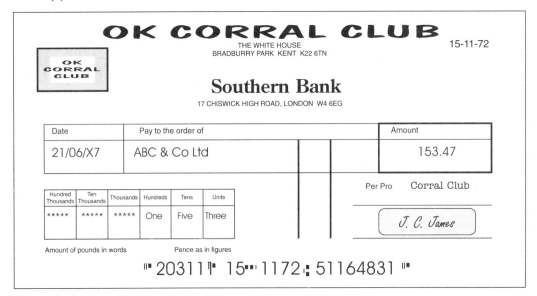

(a)

OK CORRAL CLUB

THE WHITE HOUSE
BRADBURRY PARK KENT K22 6TN

15-11-72

OK CORRAL CLUB

Southern Bank

17 CHISWICK HIGH ROAD, LONDON W4 6EG

Date	Pay to the order of	Amount
21/06/X7	ABC & Co Ltd	153.47

Hundred Thousands	Ten Thousands	Thousands	Hundreds	Tens	Units
*****	*****	*****	One	Five	Three

Amount of pounds in words   Pence as in figures

Per Pro Corral Club

J. C. James

⑈203111⑈ 15⑆1172⑉ 51164831 ⑈

(b)

Southern Bank

22 June 20 X7

CHISWICK BRANCH 17 HIGH ROAD, LONDON W4 6RG

15-11-72
SOUTHERN BANK PLC

Pay M. R. Jones or order

Forty-eight pounds and seventy-three pence

£ 48-73

MR R. U. BENT

Cheque No. Branch No. Account No.

R. U. Bent

⑈102172⑈ 15⑆1172⑆ 30595713⑈

On the reverse of the cheque made out to M R Jones, it says 'Pay to the order of ABC & Co' and it is signed M R Jones.

4.5 SOLUTION

Step 1 **The back of the slip is filled in as shown below with the** details of the cheques. **Note that a postal order is banked in the same way as a cheque.**

Details of Cheques, etc.			Sub-Total brought forward	717	19
Corral Club	153	47			
M. R. Jones	48	73	L. M. Star	11	00
XYZ & Co	379	20	P. Brook	24	92
A. Allen	22	40	S. Cope	15	37
P. Turner	13	45	Postal order	15	00
A. R. Sears	57	82			
J. J. Rook	42	12			
Carried Forward £	717	19	Total Carried over £	783	48

In view of the risk of loss in course of clearing, customers are advised to keep an independent record of the drawers of cheques

Please do not write or mark below this line

153	47
48	73
379	20
22	40
13	45
57	82
42	12
11	00
24	92
15	37
15	00
783	48

Step 2 It is advisable (as noted on this slip) to keep a record of all the drawers of the cheques banked. The easiest way may be to **photocopy** the rear of the paying-in slip, if no carbon copy is taken.

Step 3 Now the **total** is transferred to the front of the slip. The number of cheques is entered in the appropriate box on the slip (11 in this example).

Date 23/6/X5
A/c

Notes £50		
£20		
£10		
£5		
Coins £1		
50p		
20p		
Silver		
Bronze		
Cash £		
Cheques	783	48
£	783	48

Date 23/6/X5
Cashier's stamp and initials

Fee
No of Cheques 11

bank giro credit
Paid in by/Customer's Reference

6 83048231 92057419

Quality Bank
EALING BROADWAY BRANCH

ABC & CO
A/C no 47318221

Please do not write or mark below this line

Notes £50		
£20		
£10		
£5		
Coins £1		
50p		
20p		
Silver		
Bronze		
Cash £		
Cheques	783	48
£	783	48

101131 ⑈101131⑈ 20⑆ 2748⑆ 47318221⑈

Step 4 The cheques and the paying-in slip can be taken to the bank, as for cash.

4.6 The back of the paying-in slip is only capable of holding a certain number of cheques. It is acceptable to list a **larger number of cheques** on a separate piece of paper if necessary, as long as the correct details are written down.

Activity 8.2 — Level: Assessment

You are employed by Easter & Co and have the following amounts to pay in to the bank.

	£	*Cash*
B Wyman	940.00	2 × £50 notes
Pacific Ltd	1,721.50	5 × £20 notes
S McManus	94.26	97 × £10 notes
A Singh	19.29	42 × £5 notes
P L Ferguson	57.37	804 × £1 coins
Dex Ltd	42.91	80 × 50p coins
M Green	12.50	120 × 20p coins
		£34.85 silver (10p/5p)
		£9.28 bronze (2p/1p)
Postal order from		
S R Sykes	15.00	

Task

Complete the paying-in slip and counterfoil below for presentation to the bank on 10 June 20X7.

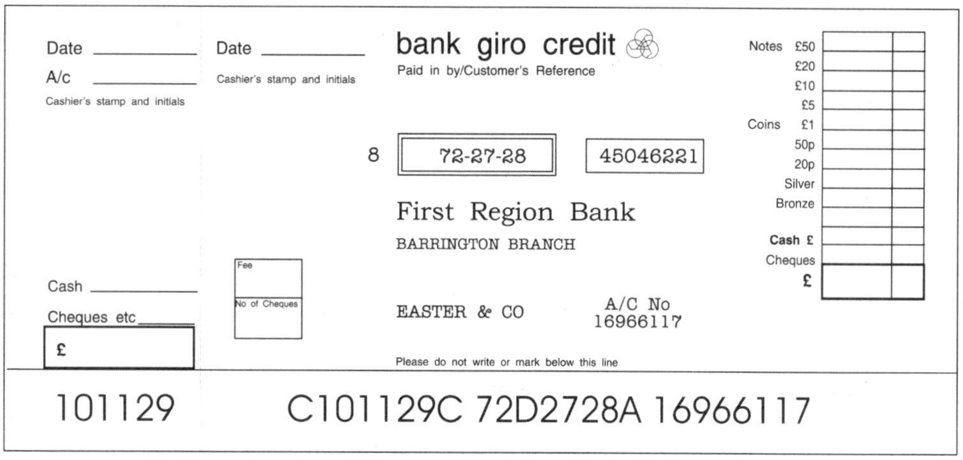

Date ______ A/c ______ Cashier's stamp and initials

Date ______ Cashier's stamp and initials

bank giro credit

Paid in by/Customer's Reference

8 72-27-28 45046221

First Region Bank

BARRINGTON BRANCH

Fee

No of Cheques

EASTER & CO

A/C No 16966117

Cash ______

Cheques etc ______

£

Please do not write or mark below this line

Notes £50 £20 £10 £5

Coins £1 50p 20p Silver Bronze

Cash £

Cheques

£

101129 C101129C 72D2728A 16966117

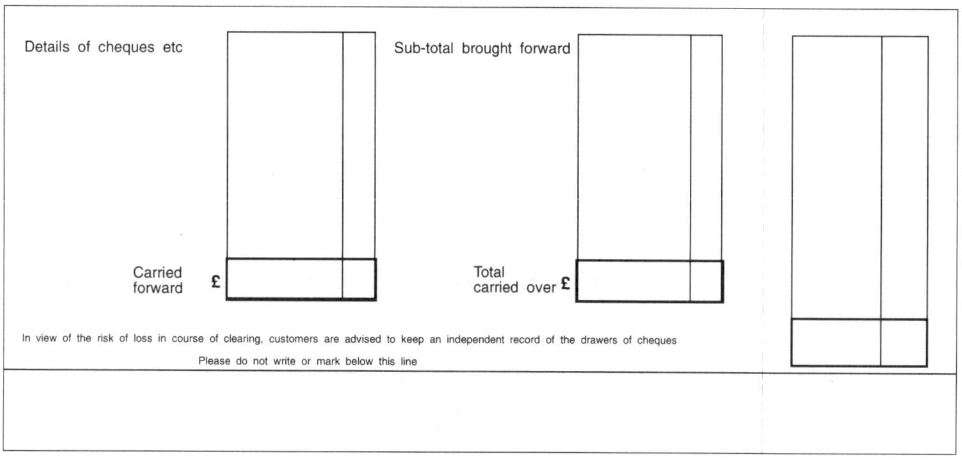

Details of cheques etc

Carried forward £

Sub-total brought forward

Total carried over £

In view of the risk of loss in course of clearing, customers are advised to keep an independent record of the drawers of cheques

Please do not write or mark below this line

Returned/dishonoured cheques

4.7 After a cheque has been received and banked, the bank may find it necessary for a variety of reasons to return the cheque to you and to remove its amount from your bank account. This is because the cheque has been **dishonoured for payment**. You may incur some bank charges when this happens. Below is a list of reasons the bank may give for dishonouring the payment. We shall look in detail at the two main ones - insufficient funds and stolen cheques.

- Insufficient funds
- Stolen cheque/cheque guarantee card
- Refer to drawer
- Refer to drawer, please represent
- Refer to drawer, trustee in bankruptcy appointed
- Drawer's signature required
- No account
- Out of date
- Signature requires drawer's confirmation
- Signature differs

- Orders not to pay
- Telephone orders not to pay
- Drawer deceased
- Mutilated cheque

Insufficient funds

4.8 There may **not be enough money in the customer's account to cover the cheque.** Normally the banks **will** honour a cheque in these circumstances *if:*

(a) The cheque is for an amount **lower than the cheque guarantee card limit** *and*

(b) There is evidence that a **check** was made between the cheque and the guarantee card (card number written on the back of the cheque)

4.9 When a cheque is dishonoured in this way, your bank will attempt to **represent** the cheque twice. 'Represent' means that your bank will go back to the customer's bank twice more to see if money has become available to pay the cheque. If the cheque is still not paid, then the cheque will be returned to you marked 'refer to drawer' and it is up to you to find your customer (the drawer) and obtain the money from him in some other way.

4.10 Banks are very careful about saying whether there are insufficient funds in an account. This is because, if sufficient funds were or should have been in the account and the bank is at fault, then it may have made a 'libel' against its customer (damaging his reputation). They will probably only say 'refer to drawer' although this too can be taken as libellous as it is commonly taken to mean 'insufficient funds'.

Stolen cheques and cheque guarantee cards

4.11 If a cheque is accepted where the cheque is stolen and the signature of the drawer is **forged**, then **the cheque is invalid and worthless** (see Chapter 7). Even if a cheque is accepted with a cheque guarantee card and all details appear to agree, a stolen and forged cheque is still worthless and it will be returned with 'cheque book and cheque guarantee card reported stolen, signatures differ', or something of a similar nature, marked on it. The person who accepted the cheque (any shop, business or individual) appears to have no recourse to the bank; he must pursue the person who actually owes him the money (the person who forged the cheque).

Bulk banking

4.12 Consider the large volume of (relatively) small receipts large supermarkets have to **bulk bank**. For the large chains of supermarkets the problems are multiplied by the number of stores they own across the country. What do they do?

(a) Use a **central bank and cash centre** where all their cash is sorted.

(b) **Bank locally**, using whichever of the major banks is most convenient in each location. Banking is done **daily**.

(c) **Cheques** are not usually presented in a detailed listing by drawer; just an add-list from an adding machine is given. **Notes** are banked by denomination as usual.

(d) Most retailers **do not bank their change** (coins) as this is always needed for the tills.

(e) Money is **removed from the tills** regularly (often in a chute into strong boxes) but is kept segregated on a till-by-till basis in the strong boxes or a secure room. At the end of the day a printout from each till showing all the takings will be matched with the money removed.

(f) **Security carriers** are used to move cash from the premises.

Activity 8.3 **Level: Assessment**

(a) Your firm, Steve, Beppe & Co, provides professional services and bills its clients on completion of the work. The firm has had returned by its bank unpaid three of its customers' cheques which had been paid in to the bank on different dates. The following had been written on the three cheques respectively.

First cheque:	'Drawer's signature required'
Second cheque:	'Re-present on due date'
Third cheque:	'Refer to drawer'

Your colleague is unclear as to what these various words mean.

Task

Explain to your colleague what is meant by the words on the three cheques and advise her what action should be taken, if any.

(b) The bank has made a charge for dealing with each of the three returned cheques. The General Manager of your firm has noted this charge on the bank statement and has asked you to recommend how, in the light of each of these three items, your firm might reduce the number of returned cheques and therefore reduce the likelihood of future such charges being levied.

Task

Prepare a memorandum to the General Manager on this matter.

---

5 PROCEDURES FOR BANKING PLASTIC CARD TRANSACTIONS

5.1 Card vouchers (for credit, debit, charge and store cards) are **processed through the banking system**. Where the retailer processes transactions manually, he pays the vouchers into his bank account and his bank will present the vouchers to the card issuers for payment (so the card issuer pays the bank and the bank pays the retailer). We will consider the more straightforward situation with EFTPOS in Section 6.

5.2 Once again, the **same paying-in slip** is used to bank the card transactions, but other documents must be prepared first.

Card summaries

5.3 The card issuers require the business receiver of card transactions to **summarise all transactions on a summary voucher**. The summary voucher consists of an original or 'top copy' and two copies with carbon paper in between. The bottom copy is the **processing copy**; on the back of it is a place to list the vouchers.

Top copy summary voucher

HAVE YOU IMPRINTED THE SUMMARY
WITH YOUR RETAILER'S CARD?

BANK Processing (White) copy of Summary with your Vouchers in correct order:
1. SUMMARY
2. SALES VOUCHERS
3. REFUND VOUCHERS

KEEP Retailer's copies (Blue & Yellow)
NO MORE THAN 200 Vouchers to each Summary
DO NOT USE Staples, Pins, Paper Clips

	ITEMS	AMOUNT	
SALES VOUCHERS (LISTED OVERLEAF)			
LESS REFUND VOUCHERS			
DATE	TOTAL £		

SUMMARY - RETAILER'S COPY

Southern Bank
FASTPASS

BANKING
SUMMARY

RETAILER'S SIGNATURE

COMPLETE THIS SUMMARY FOR EVERY DEPOSIT OF SALES VOUCHERS AND ENTER THE TOTAL ON YOUR NORMAL CURRENT ACCOUNT PAYING-IN SLIP

Bottom (processing copy) summary voucher: front

3200

	ITEMS	AMOUNT	
SALES VOUCHERS (LISTED OVERLEAF)			
LESS REFUND VOUCHERS			
DATE	TOTAL £		

SOUTHERN BANKING SUMMARY - PROCESSING COPY

RETAILER'S SIGNATURE

Bottom (processing copy) summary voucher: back

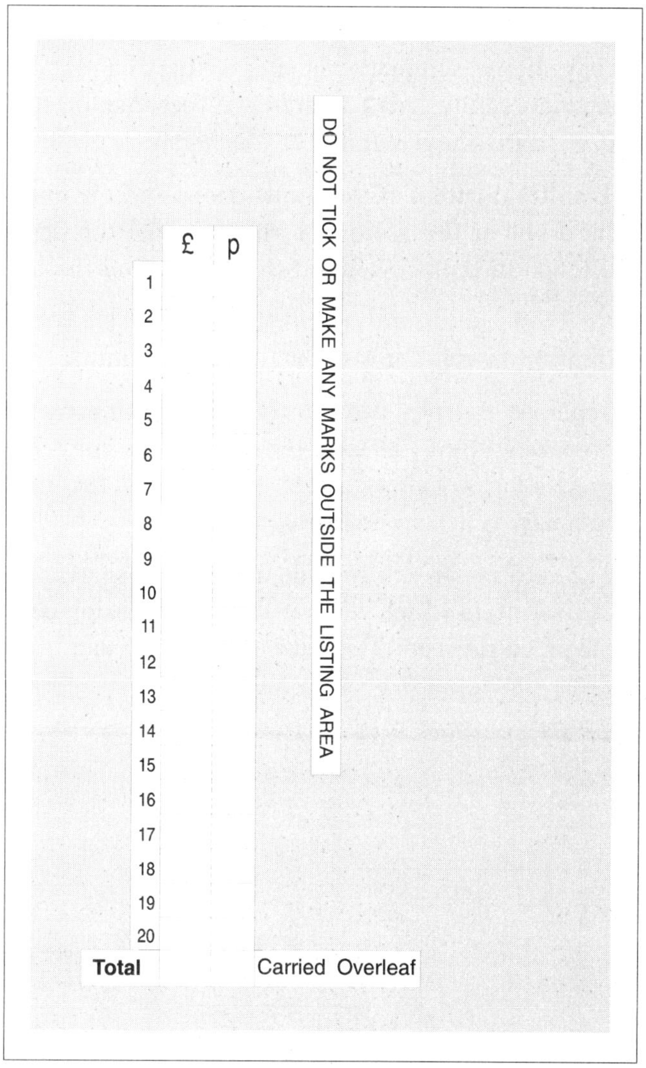
DO NOT TICK OR MAKE ANY MARKS OUTSIDE THE LISTING AREA

	£	p
1		
2		
3		
4		
5		
6		
7		
8		
9		
10		
11		
12		
13		
14		
15		
16		
17		
18		
19		
20		
Total		Carried Overleaf

5.4 The **summary voucher** has to be imprinted with the retailer's plastic card. It contains all the relevant information about the business, including an account number. The summary voucher is imprinted from the card using the same machine as that used to imprint from customer cards.

5.5 Unlike cheques, **only the amount of the card transaction** needs to be entered on the back of the processing copy of the summary voucher - names are not needed.

5.6 EXAMPLE: BANKING CARD VOUCHERS

You are asked to bank all card transactions at the end of a working day. You receive all the card vouchers for the day and you obtain a summary voucher. The transaction vouchers are as follows.

	£		£
Sale	26.41	Sale	12.95
Sale	32.99	Sale	14.48
Sale	32.99	Sale	136.48
Sale	100.40	Sale	12.95
Sale	22.00	Sale	112.95
Sale	46.99	Sale	11.80
Sale	37.80	Sale	56.71
Sale	12.95	Refund	22.00

5.7 SOLUTION

Step 1 Enter the **amount of each transaction** on the back of the processing copy of the summary voucher. (Note that the transaction voucher amounts can be listed separately rather than on the summary voucher if there are a large number of vouchers.)

Step 2 Transfer the **total of the transactions** and the **number of vouchers** to the **front of the summary voucher** (the top copy, which will copy through to the two copies below, including the top of the processing copy).

Step 3 Imprint the **retailer card** details on the summary voucher.

Step 4 **Separate** the top two copies of the summary vouchers from the processing copy. Detach the processing copy from the individual transaction vouchers; these are sent to the card issuer with the summary voucher processing copy.

Step 5 The card issuer will provide a small transparent plastic wallet, or its equivalent, in which you put all the **processing copies.** Note that **only** the processing copies are sent to the card issuer.

Back of processing copy

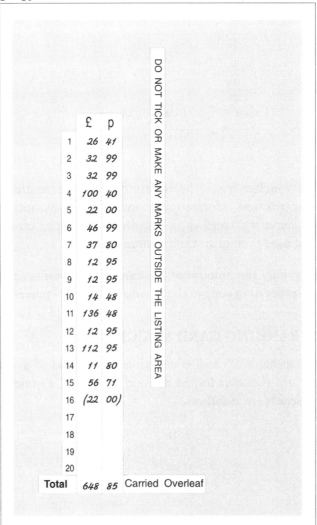

	£	p
1	26	41
2	32	99
3	32	99
4	100	40
5	22	00
6	46	99
7	37	80
8	12	95
9	12	95
10	14	48
11	136	48
12	12	95
13	112	95
14	11	80
15	56	71
16	(22	00)
17		
18		
19		
20		
Total	648	85 Carried Overleaf

DO NOT TICK OR MAKE ANY MARKS OUTSIDE THE LISTING AREA

Front of processing copy

3200

7849 950 1725 05

ABC & CO
LONDON W12

950 1725 05

ABC & CO
LONDON W12

	ITEMS	AMOUNT	
SALES VOUCHERS (LISTED OVERLEAF)	15	670	85
LESS REFUND VOUCHERS	1	22	00
DATE 26/6/X6	TOTAL £	648	85

A. N. Other
RETAILER'S SIGNATURE

SOUTHERN BANKING SUMMARY - PROCESSING COPY

Top copy

HAVE YOU IMPRINTED THE SUMMARY
WITH YOUR RETAILER'S CARD?

7849 950 1725 05

BANK Processing (White) copy of Summary with your Vouchers in correct order:
1. SUMMARY
2. SALES VOUCHERS
3. REFUND VOUCHERS
KEEP Retailer's copies (Blue & Yellow)
NO MORE THAN 200 Vouchers to each Summary
DO NOT USE Staples, Pins, Paper Clips

ABC & CO
LONDON W12

950 1725 05

ABC & CO
LONDON W12

	ITEMS	AMOUNT	
SALES VOUCHERS (LISTED OVERLEAF)	15	670	85
LESS REFUND VOUCHERS	1	22	00
DATE 26/6/X6	TOTAL £	648	85

Southern Bank **BANKING SUMMARY**
FASTPASS

A. N. Other
RETAILER'S SIGNATURE

SUMMARY - RETAILER'S COPY

COMPLETE THIS SUMMARY FOR EVERY DEPOSIT OF SALES VOUCHERS AND ENTER THE TOTAL ON YOUR NORMAL CURRENT ACCOUNT PAYING-IN SLIP

Step 6 Enter the total of the summary voucher on to a **normal paying-in slip.** The paying-in slip and the top copy of the summary voucher (which will be retained by the bank), along with the wallet containing the summary and transaction processing vouchers, can now be taken to the bank.

Details of Cheques, etc.			Sub-Total brought forward	648	85		648	85
Swallows Credit Card Co.	648	85						
Carried Forward £	648	85	Total Carried over £	648	85		648	85

In view of the risk of loss in course of clearing, customers are advised to keep an independent record of the drawers of cheques

Please do not write or mark below this line

Date 26/6/X6

A/c 30595713

Notes £50		
£20		
£10		
£5		
Coins £1		
50p		
20p		
Silver		
Bronze		
Cash £		
Cheques	648	85
£	648	85

Date 26/6/X6

Cashier's stamp and initials

Fee

No of Cheques 1

bank giro credit

Paid in by/Customer's Reference

6 83048231 92057419

Quality Bank

EALING BROADWAY BRANCH

ABC & CO

A/C no 473181221

Please do not write or mark below this line

Notes £50		
£20		
£10		
£5		
Coins £1		
50p		
20p		
Silver		
Bronze		
Cash £		
Cheques	648	85
£	648	85

101129 ⑈101129⑈ 20⑆2748⑉ 47318221⑈

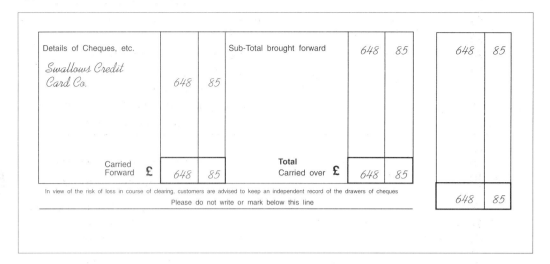

Step 7 The second copies of the summary voucher and the transaction vouchers you have retained should be **filed together** in a way which makes an individual voucher easy to find. This is important as queries will arise from time to time.

Queries arising from card transactions

5.8 The most common types of problem which arise with card receipts are as follows.

Problem with card receipts	Action
Stolen cards	As a general rule it seems that, where a retailer has followed all proper security procedures (as discussed in Chapter 7) the card issuer will honour the transaction even if the card is stolen.
Transactions taking place **above the shop's floor limit**	The card issuer may refuse to honour the transaction as the retailer has been negligent in not obtaining authorisation.

Problem with card receipts	Action
Errors in completing the card voucher **Non-processing** in error by the card issuer	Discrepancies which arise as a result of error can usually be dealt with quite quickly and efficiently by correspondence directly between the business and the card issuer.

Activity 8.4 — Level: Assessment

Reggie's Rubberwear is a retail shop which receives payment by cash, cheque and credit card. Each day's bankings are stored in a secure safe for banking on the following working day. Credit card vouchers are summarised daily on the bank's credit card summary.

The following summary relates to the week commencing Monday 27 November 20X7.

	Cash float at start of the day	*Cash/cheques for banking the day*	*Cash float at end of vouchers*	*Credit card sales vouchers*	*Credit card refund*
	£	£	£	£	£
Monday	24.16	684.08	37.05	104.28	-
Tuesday	37.05	504.27	12.60	202.96	-
Wednesday	12.60	691.41	19.40	124.17	37.26
Thursday	19.40	729.62	32.42	291.41	-
Friday	32.42	840.50	26.91	342.09	41.20

Tasks

(a) Prepare a schedule of each day's sales takings, showing cash/cheque sales and credit card sales separately for each day, and showing totals for the week.

(b) Three credit card sales vouchers and one credit card refund voucher were issued on Wednesday 29 November. Using the blank form below, complete for signature the retailer's banking summary for that day's credit card transactions.

HAVE YOU IMPRINTED THE SUMMARY WITH YOUR RETAILER'S CARD?

BANK Processing (White) copy of Summary with your Vouchers in correct order:
1. SUMMARY
2. SALES VOUCHERS
3. REFUND VOUCHERS
KEEP Retailer's copies (Blue & Yellow)
NO MORE THAN 200 Vouchers to each Summary
DO NOT USE Staples, Pins, Paper Clips

	ITEMS	AMOUNT	
SALES VOUCHERS (LISTED OVERLEAF)			
LESS REFUND VOUCHERS			
DATE	TOTAL £		

SUMMARY - RETAILER'S COPY

First Region Bank
FASTPASS

BANKING SUMMARY

RETAILER'S SIGNATURE

COMPLETE THIS SUMMARY FOR EVERY DEPOSIT OF SALES VOUCHERS AND ENTER THE TOTAL ON YOUR NORMAL CURRENT ACCOUNT PAYING-IN SLIP

(c) State what should be done with the banking summary you have prepared in (b).

Activity 8.5 — Level: Assessment

The following credit card receipts were processed on 22 May 20X7.

BPP PUBLISHING

Customer		*Amount*
		£
1		28.42
2		69.18
3		99.81
4		57.48
5	Refund	(21.14)
6		93.14
7		31.18
8		72.87
9	Refund	(34.69)
10		17.81

Task

Complete the credit card summary voucher and bank paying-in slip shown below.

HAVE YOU IMPRINTED THE SUMMARY WITH YOUR RETAILER'S CARD?

BANK Processing (White) copy of Summary with your Vouchers in correct order:
1. SUMMARY
2. SALES VOUCHERS
3. REFUND VOUCHERS

KEEP Retailer's copies (Blue & Yellow)
NO MORE THAN 200 Vouchers to each Summary
DO NOT USE Staples, Pins, Paper Clips

	ITEMS	AMOUNT	
SALES VOUCHERS (LISTED OVERLEAF)			
LESS REFUND VOUCHERS			
DATE	TOTAL		

SUMMARY - RETAILER'S COPY

Southern Bank FASTPASS

BANKING SUMMARY

RETAILER'S SIGNATURE

COMPLETE THIS SUMMARY FOR EVERY DEPOSIT OF SALES VOUCHERS AND ENTER THE TOTAL ON YOUR NORMAL CURRENT ACCOUNT PAYING-IN SLIP

DO NOT TICK OR MAKE ANY MARKS OUTSIDE THE LISTING AREA

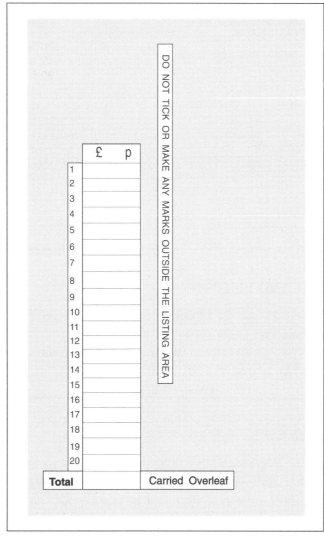

	£ p
1	
2	
3	
4	
5	
6	
7	
8	
9	
10	
11	
12	
13	
14	
15	
16	
17	
18	
19	
20	
Total	Carried Overleaf

Date ____________ Date ____________

A/c ____________

Cashier's stamp and initials   Cashier's stamp and initials

bank giro credit

Paid in by/Customer's Reference

8 | 83048231 | 92057419

Quality Bank

EALING BROADWAY BRANCH

A. B. BROWNE & CO   A/C no 30494713

Cash ____________

Cheques etc ____________

£

Fee

No of Cheques

Notes	£50	
	£20	
	£10	
	£5	
Coins	£1	
	50p	
	20p	
	Silver	
	Bronze	
	Cash £	
	Cheques	
	£	

Please do not write or mark below this line

101129   101129   20 27 48   30494713

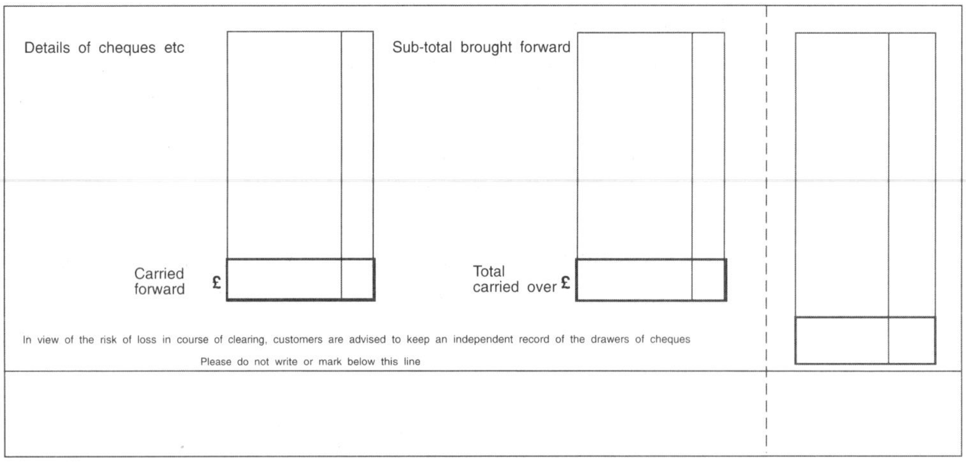
Details of cheques etc

Sub-total brought forward

Carried forward £

Total carried over £

In view of the risk of loss in course of clearing, customers are advised to keep an independent record of the drawers of cheques

Please do not write or mark below this line

6 BANKING AND EFTPOS

6.1 Where businesses use **EFTPOS** to process card receipts, there is no need to deposit the sale slips at the bank. The sales (and returns) are processed by the card issuers and credited **directly to the business bank account**, usually within two or three days. The narrative next to the bank account entry indicates the type of service (eg Switch, Visa and MasterCard).

'End of day' procedure

6.2 The retailer only knows what will be paid into his bank account if he has carried out the **'end of day' procedure**. This produces a **summary report of transactions** undertaken during the day. It should be carried out after closing time and can then be matched against amounts appearing on the bank statement.

6.3 The 'end of day' procedures will be something like the following (refer to the diagram of a terminal in Chapter 7).

SALE	REFUND

Step 1 Press the 'DEL' key. The display will change to:

REV	AUTH	TOTALS

Step 2 Press the 'F3' key. The display will change to:

X-TOT	REC	Z-TOT

Step 3 Press the 'F2' key. The display will change to:

WIPE SUP CARD

Step 4 Wipe the Supervisor Card through the terminal in the normal manner. The display will change to:

RECONCILE ALL?

Step 5 Press the 'F1' key to indicate that you wish to carry out an 'End of Day'/ Reconciliation with all the card companies. (Pressing the 'F3' key will cause the display to change showing each of the card companies in turn.) The terminal will display:

PLEASE WAIT

Followed by:

TEAR OFF	E

Step 6 Tear off the 'End of Day'/Reconciliation report and press the 'ENTER' key. Check the report to see that 'Session Totals Agreed' has been printed (which means that the card company's computer agrees with the number and value of transactions performed since the last 'End of Day' was completed).

The end of day report will appear in something like the following form.

A MERCHANT
HIGH STREET
ANYTOWN

RECONCILIATION

VISA	
M 1234567	
T06500015	R0023
VISA	
PREVIOUS	
0005	£0.89DR
0000	£0.00CR
TOTAL 0012-0018	
	£0.89
CURRENT	
0002	£50.50DR
0001	£25.25CR
TOTAL 0019-0023	
	£25.25
COMPLETED	
SESSION TOTALS AGREED	
DATE 06/07/X4	19:31

Step 7 It will then be necessary to match the summary to the credit entries in the company's bank statement when the relevant amounts are submitted by the card issuers. This might be quite straightforward where the figure in the bank statement is referenced, perhaps by date, but otherwise can prove quite difficult.

Retention of documents

6.4 In the event of queries regarding individual transaction or bank account credits, the retailer will need to produce relevant copies of the receipts. It is therefore essential that all copy receipts are kept in a safe place, preferably in date order, for a **minimum period of 6 months** and sometimes even longer.

6.5 It is usually most convenient to attach the day's sales and refund slips (with the copy of the customer's signature) to the **end of day reconciliation** and then to keep these in date order.

7 BANKING OTHER RECEIPTS

7.1 Some receipts, by their very nature, require no action on the part of the business to have them paid into its bank account; these include **direct debits, standing orders, BACS payments** and **telegraphic transfers**. Other receipts which must be paid into the business's bank account and which are relatively rare in a business account are banker's drafts and bank giro credits.

Banker's drafts

7.2 **Banker's drafts** are paid into the bank by the business in the same manner as cheques.

Bank giro credits

7.3 Bank giro credits can be paid into a bank account by the **customer of the business,** in which case the amounts will appear automatically on the business's bank statement.

Key learning points

- You should note the important theoretical and legal aspects of **banks, bankers and their relationship with their customers.**
  - How the clearing system works
  - Relationships between banker and customer
  - Rights and duties of banker and customer
- **Banking procedures** for various kinds of receipts should be fully understood and you should observe real transactions wherever possible.
- When **banking cash receipts**:
  - Cash must be properly counted and sorted
  - Notes and coins must be listed by denomination on the paying-in slip
- The details required on the paying-in slip when **cheques are banked** include:
  - Name of drawer (or endorser)
  - Amount of cheque
  - Total value of cheques banked
  - Number of cheques banked
- **Plastic card transactions** which are processed manually must be listed on a summary voucher for banking purposes. The processing copies are sent to the bank while the retailer retains two copies of each voucher (including the summary voucher).
- Credit, charge or debit card receipts via **EFTPOS** are credited directly to the retailer's bank account. He can agree the amounts received to the 'End of day' reconciliation produced by the terminal.

Quick quiz

1. What is 'clearing' in banking terms?
2. How long does a cheque take to clear?
3. What are the four types of relationship which may exist between a banker and customer?
4. What is a 'fiduciary relationship'?
5. How should coins be banked?
6. Which details from cheques should be included on the paying-in slip?
7. If you accept a stolen cheque in good faith, is it worth anything to you?
8. What happens if you accept a stolen credit card for an amount below your floor limit?

Answers to quick quiz

1. Clearing is the mechanism for obtaining payment for cheques.
2. Cheques take three working days to clear.
3. The relationships are: debtor/creditor; bailor/bailee; principal/agent; mortgagor/mortgagee.
4. A fiduciary relationship is one in which the superior party (the bank here) acts in good faith.
5. Coins should be banked in the plastic paying-in bags supplied by banks, with the correct number of coins as shown on the bag.
6. The drawer and the account should be noted on the paying-in slip.
7. No, you must pursue the person who forged the cheque to honour the debt.
8. If all security procedures have been followed, the issuer will usually honour the transaction.

9 Recording monies received

This chapter contains

1	Controls over recording receipts
2	The cash book
3	Cash registers
4	Cash received sheets (remittance lists)
5	Posting cash receipts to the general ledger

Learning objectives

On completion of this chapter you will have learned about:

- Relationship between accounting system and the ledger
- Organisational procedures for filing source documentation
- Types of business transactions and documents involved
- Types of discounts
- Operation of manual and computerised accounting systems
- Methods of handling and storing money, including the security aspects

Performance criteria

1.2.1	Receipts are checked against relevant supporting information
1.2.2	Receipts are entered in appropriate accounting records
1.2.4	Unusual features are identified and either resolved or referred to the appropriate person

Range statement

1.2.1	Receipts: cash; cheques; automated payments
1.2.2	Accounting records: cash book
1.2.3	Unusual features: wrongly completed cheques; out of date cheque, credit and debit cards; limits exceeded; disagreement with supporting documentation; under payments; over payments; cheques returned to sender

1 CONTROLS OVER RECORDING RECEIPTS

1.1 In practical terms, the first place that a receipt might be recorded is on a **cash register**, or on **cash received sheets** (see Section 4 in this chapter). For accounting purposes, however, the receipt is not recorded in the 'books' of the company until it has been entered in the **cash book**.

1.2 Recording receipts on cash received sheets or on cash registers is a method of **summarising cash transactions** which are then **recorded in summary form** in the cash book, which as we have seen is a **book of prime entry.**

1.3 The **controls** over recording receipts must be as good as controls over accepting and banking the money. If receipts are not recorded properly, how will we know whether we have received all the money that is due to us?

1.4 One of the main controls in this area is **segregation of duties**. As we saw in Chapter 7, this is where the **receiving and the recording functions are kept separate**. One person will receive, count and perhaps bank the money, while another person will record the money received. This is a way of avoiding theft, although collusion may occur between employees.

1.5 **Bank reconciliations** also help to control cash receipts. These are covered in Unit 3.

2 THE CASH BOOK

2.1 In its simplest form, a cash book consists of a single page divided into two halves by a vertical line. The left hand side of the page (the **debit** side) is used to record amounts of monies **received** by the business, while the right hand side (the **credit** side) is used to record **payments** of monies by the business. Periodically (often daily but perhaps only once a month) the entries in the book are totalled and the **balance of cash** available to the business is determined.

2.2 It is usual to maintain one main cash book to record the amounts received and paid through the **business bank account**. The 'cash' referred to in the title of the book will therefore consist normally of cheques, rather than notes and coins, depending on the nature of the business. But most businesses need a supply of notes and coins to pay for small everyday expenses such as postage, tea and coffee and so on. These amounts are usually recorded in a separate book of prime entry called a **petty cash book**. We will look at the petty cash book in Unit 2.

2.3 The simplified form of the cash book described above would very seldom be found in practice because it would not give enough detail about the nature of each receipt and payment. Most businesses instead use an **analysed cash book**. In this format each payment is recorded on the right hand side of the page not only in a single 'total' column, but also in one of a number of other columns with suitable headings such as 'Suppliers', 'Wages' and so on. Similarly, the left hand side of the page has columns in which cash receipts are analysed as 'Debtors', 'Cash sales' and so on.

2.4 An example of the receipts side of a cash book follows.

CASH BOOK

RECEIPTS

Date	*Narrative*	*Folio*	*Dis-count allowed*	*Total*	*Output VAT on cash sales*	*Receipts from debtors*	*Cash sales*	*Other*
20X7								
01-Sep	Balance b/d			900.00				
	(a) Cash sale			80.00	11.91		68.09	
	(b) Debtor pays: Hay	SL96	20.00	380.00		380.00		
	(c) Debtor pays: Been	SL632		720.00		720.00		
	(d) Debtor pays: Seed	SL501	40.00	960.00		960.00		
	(e) Cash sale			150.00	22.34		127.66	
	(f) Fixed asset sale			200.00				200.00
			60.00	2,490.00	34.25	2,060.00	195.75	200.00
			TD01	***CA01***	***VAT01***	***TD01***	***SA01***	***DIS01***
			CR	DR	CR	CR	CR	CR
			DA01					
			DR					

Discounts

2.5 The discount allowed column on the cash receipts page shows **how cash discounts are recorded.**

- Discounts allowed on sales are shown in a separate column which has nothing to do with the actual monies received; it is a **memorandum** column.
- The discount allowed column is required to show why the **full amount of a debt** has not been received from a customer.
- A list of the debts owed to the company will be recorded in the **sales ledger.** The individual discounts allowed will be posted to these individual's ledger accounts, thus clearing the **total** debt.
- A similar **summary** posting will be required to the total debtors account of the total cash received from debtors (£2,060) and the total discounts allowed (£60).

Bank statements

2.6 Every so often, a business will receive a **bank statement**. The bank statements should be used to check that the amount shown as a balance in the cash book reconciles with the amount on the bank statement, and that no cash has 'gone missing'.

Activity 9.1 — Level: Pre-assessment

Which of the following will *not* be entered in the cash book?

(a) Cheque received
(b) Payment to sales ledger customers
(c) Supplier's invoice
(d) Credit note
(e) Debit note
(f) Bank charges debited to the bank account
(g) Overdraft interest debited to the bank account
(h) Payment for a fixed asset purchased on credit
(i) Refund received from a supplier
(j) Depreciation

3 CASH REGISTERS

3.1 We have looked at how the cash book works, but the cash book itself is not always the first place that receipts are recorded. Sometimes it is more practicable to **record receipts somewhere else** and then **summarise them to record them in the cash book**. In this context we will look at:

- Cash registers
- Cash received sheets or remittance lists (see Section 4 of this chapter)

3.2 **Cash registers** in some form have been in use for a long time in retail shops. They used to be mechanically operated, but today most are computerised. The more sophisticated and larger stores will have cash registers which are all connected to a central computer; the cash registers will update the computer automatically as a sale takes place, and each cash register can be updated for price changes.

3.3 Cash registers can be very complicated but here we will look at an example of quite a simple **till**. It usually looks like a large typewriter with a drawer underneath it for the money. There is a **keyboard** and also a **till roll on a printer**. As we look at how the register operates we will look at its **built-in controls** which make modern tills accurate and secure. Not all registers will work in exactly the same way; this is only an example.

Keyboard

3.4 All cash registers will have a **keyboard** of this kind. The ringed letters correspond to the notes below.

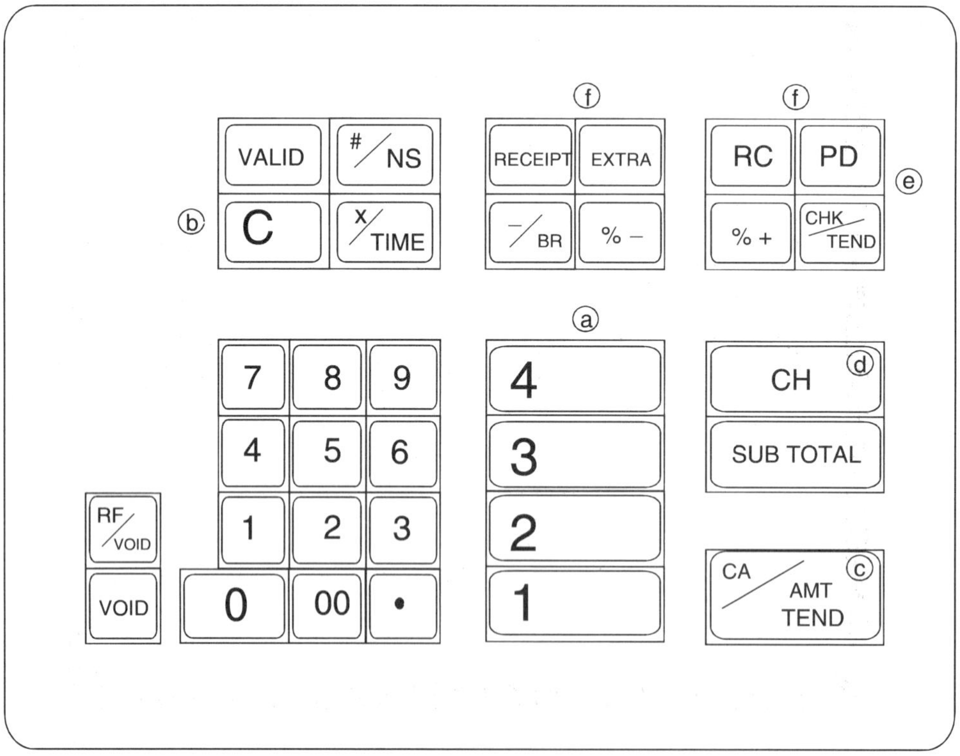

(a) These are **department number keys**, to help distinguish what kind of sale is being made (for example, in a newsagent they may be:

1 = Newspapers and magazines
2 = Confectionery and drinks

3 = Cigarettes
4 = Stationery)

(b) This is the **clear key** which clears a wrong entry.

(c) The **cash amount tendered key** allows the operator to key in how much cash is tendered so the register can work out how much change should be given.

(d) The **charge key** registers plastic card or sales.

(e) The **cheque tendered key** registers cheque sales.

(f) The **special function keys** include those which will:

- Add, subtract or multiply
- Deal with returned goods and refunds
- Deduct discounts
- Add premiums
- Issue a receipt
- Calculate value added tax (VAT)
- Perform foreign exchange calculations

Preset keys

3.5 Cash registers may also have **preset keys on a separate panel**.

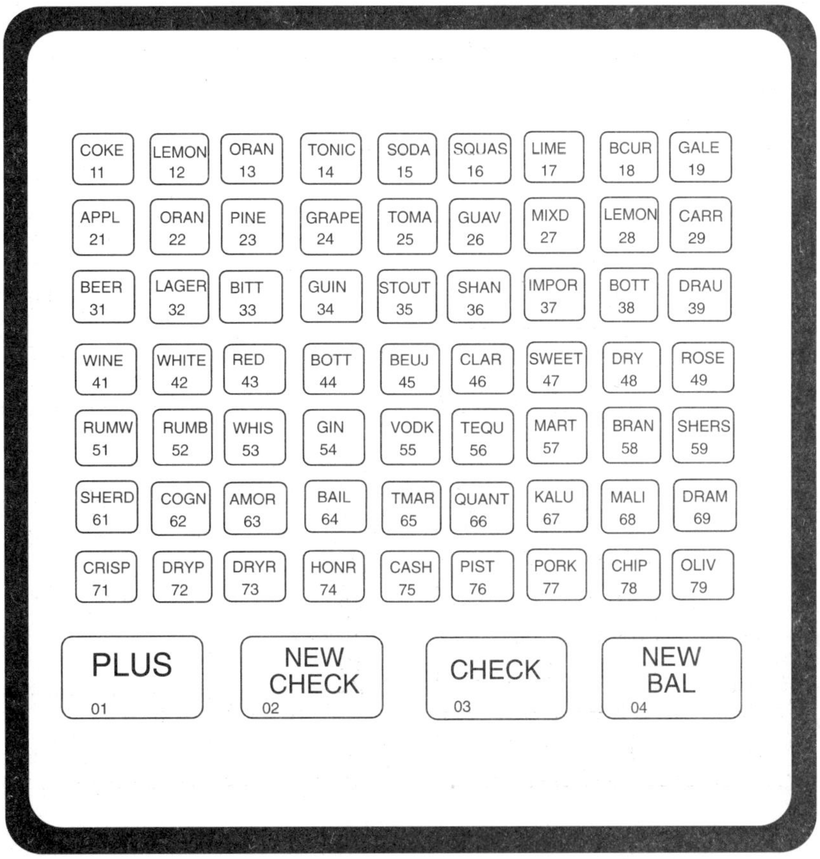

This is particularly useful in outlets where there is a limited range of set-priced items, for instance in a pub, which is where the example above comes from.

Mode access and switch keys

3.6 To operate the register it is necessary to have an **access key**. This is entered into the **mode switch** (which looks like a keyhole). The mode switch can be turned to a number of different positions or 'modes' but different access keys will restrict which modes are available to each access key holder. Access keys would include types similar to those listed here.

(a) **Operator key**. This only allows the standard operation of the register for sales.

(b) **Master key**. The mode switch can be turned to positions for processing refunds and reading sales records.

(c) **Owner key**. The mode switch can be turned to any position (explained below).

(d) Other keys are used elsewhere on the machine.

- **Clerk key** to identify who is using the machine
- **Printer key** to unlock the printer cover when replacing the paper roll
- **Cash drawer key** to open the cash drawer manually

3.7 The **mode switch** can be turned to the following settings.

(a) OFF. All keys are inserted and removed in the 'off' position.

(b) REG (Register). To process cancellations and registration errors.

(c) READ. For reading all sales records, including:

- Breakdowns of sales into cash, cheque and plastic card sales
- A specific department's sales data
- Periodic sales data

These records will be discussed below.

(d) Z (Reset). For reading all sales records *and* resetting the machine.

(e) PROGRAM. For programming all data such as the date, time, unit price and other standard information.

(f) RF (Refund). To process refund transactions by registering returned goods.

3.8 Access keys and the mode switch are good security features; they prevent unauthorised people from changing, say, the unit prices which are programmed into the register.

Tills and bar code readers

3.9 Many large retail organisations now use sophisticated **bar coding systems** in their stores.

- All stock items have a **bar code** attached as a tag, or on packaging.
- When the customer takes them to the till, the bar code is 'read' using a **hand-held scanner** which can recognise bar code patterns by the different reflection of light from the dark stripes and white spaces.
- The **stock code** given by the bar code is then used by the computer to pick up the relevant information from the central computer.

- A **display panel** on the till will display the information from the bar code, usually showing the type of item and the price.
- It may even ask the assistant to **check certain information.**

3.10 Even these tills will still have most of the **keys** shown in Paragraph 3.4 above, because of the need for occasional manual input, eg where a **bar code is missing** or unreadable or when a **price change has not been put into the computer**. This emphasises the point that the central computer, to which all the tills are connected, must be up to date so that, when the bar code is read, the till retrieves the correct information about that item of stock from the computer.

Cash register operations

3.11 We will look at the most straightforward operations which a modern cash register can perform.

Multiple item sale with change calculation

3.12 Suppose you wish to process the following sale (only one item is sold from each department).

Department	*1*	*2*	*3*	*4*
Unit price	£1.00	£2.00	£3.00	£4.00

The customer gives a £20 note to pay for the goods. The transaction would be entered as shown below. Note that the register will automatically insert the decimal point for pence; the operator in effect enters the number of pence in the price rather than pounds and pence.

	TILL ENTRIES	DISPLAY
100	1	1 1.00
200	2	2 2.00
300	3	3 3.00
400	4	4 4.00
	Sub total	10.00 TOTAL
2000	CA/AMT TEND	10.00 CHANGE

The cash register will print a receipt for the customer (and a record of the transaction on a second till roll which is kept in the printer).

***** ARNIE'S *****

VAT NO 423 4895 26

20 01 X3

1	.1,00	
2	.2,00	
3	.3,00	
4	.4,00	
	.10,00	ST
	.20,00	CA TD
	.10,00	CG

110000042

004 15:00

3.13 If the sale had been by cheque or credit card, then the keys used would have been similar except that, instead of the 'cash tendered' key being used, the 'cheque tendered' or 'charge card' keys would have been used.

3.14 Cash registers can also deal with sales where the customer tenders two, or even three, **different forms of payment** (cash and cheque, cash and credit card and so on).

3.15 We will not look at how all the other normal sales operations are entered, but remember that most cash registers can process quite complicated transactions.

Read and reset

3.16 The **'Read' function** is used to **confirm the sales data**. The read function can be used at any time of the day as the memory is not cleared after the read operation. Only the master and owner access keys can be used for this function. To activate the read function, the mode switch must be turned to 'X' and then the 'CA/Amt tendered' key pressed. A summary of sales data since the last reset will be produced.

3.17 The **'Reset' function** will perform the same function as 'read' but will clear the memory at the end of the print-out of sales data. Both the read and reset functions will be used to total the daily sales.

Recording cash received by the register

3.18 The total from the reset function will be used:

(a) To **check the amount of money** which is in the cash register at the end of the day against the summary; if there are any discrepancies, they can be investigated as we saw in Chapter 8.

(b) To **record receipts in the cash book**.

3.19 The entry in the cash book will be the total amount of cash received. This will be analysed into sales and VAT, so that it can be **posted to the general ledger** (see Section 5 of this chapter).

Security and controls

3.20 We have seen how accurate a cash register can be and how well it can **control receipts**; but the cash register will only act as an effective control if it is used properly.

(a) **Access keys** should be given to the appropriate members of staff and they should be kept in a safe and secure place. A spare set should be kept by the person in authority.

(b) Staff should be **trained in the use of the cash register** and their work should be observed for a period.

(c) The maximum possible amount of **preset information** should be programmed into the cash register. This saves cashier time and reduces the risk of fraud.

(d) **Periodic information** produced by the cash register such as average sales proceeds per customer, average sales value of the items sold and sales by clerk or operator should be analysed carefully by the manager or owner, with perhaps a brief weekly or monthly report being written. All variations should be investigated.

Activity 9.2 — Level: Assessment

The summary below analyses the number and value of sales made hourly on a particular day by a retail outlet called Spam at which you are employed. Such a summary is printed each day at the close of business. Spam opens daily at 9.00 am.

09:00 → 10:00	
14 NO	£77.41
10:00 → 11:00	
29 NO	£541.25
11:00 → 12:00	
35 NO	£1,096.99
12:00 → 13:00	
41 NO	£857.18
13:00 → 14:00	
24 NO	£1,148.58
14:00 → 15:00	
21 NO	£467.79
15:00 → 16:00	
33 NO	£405.26
16:00 → 17:00	
39 NO	£715.22

Tasks

The store manager wants certain information on the day's trading. Use the information from the summary to answer the following questions.

(a) What value of sales was made between 3.00pm and 5.00pm?

(b) In which two-hour period ('hour-to-hour') was there:

(i) The highest number of sales
(ii) The highest value of sales

(c) All sales were for cash except for £319.25 cheque and credit card sales. The cash float at the start of the day was £25.00. How much cash would you expect to find in the till at 5.00pm?

Activity 9.3 — Level: Assessment

During the day, different members of staff are on duty at the computerised till in Spam (see Activity 9.2). When a new member of staff takes over the till, the outgoing and incoming staff members are expected to count the contents of the till and put small change in bags for specified amounts provided by the bank. These bags are left in the till until the end of each day.

At 5.00pm when Ali Alaqat finished a two hour period on the till, it was found that the money in the till is £17.42 short. The amounts counted in the till at previous changes of duty during the day were as follows.

Time	*Outgoing till operator*	*Amount counted*
		£
11.00 am	John Walton	625.66
3.00 pm	Surinda Patel	4,196.20

Tasks

(a) State what the information given in Activities 9.2 and 9.3 tells us about the cash shortage and how it arose. Show any workings.

(b) Suggest what procedures could be adopted to make it possible for discrepancies in the amount of cash in the till to be discovered earlier and more easily than the procedure you have used in part (a).

4 CASH RECEIVED SHEETS (REMITTANCE LISTS)

4.1 Businesses which do not have a cash register still need to record money received from sales they have made. Very small shops or businesses will probably just write down on a piece of paper the money received as they sell something. (Note that 'cash' here means cash, cheques, cards or any other form of receipt.) This is a basic **cash received sheet.**

Apple Antiques

Sales Takings 22 July 20X1

	£
Two Victorian chairs: cheque	45.00
One Victorian table: cheque	155.00
Two Watercolours: cheque	100.00
Bookshelves: cash	40.00
One Edwardian chair: cheque	55.00
Pair Chinese vases: credit card	360.00
Two sidetables: credit card	180.00
Total for day	£935.00

4.2 Larger non-retail companies may have **pre-printed cash received sheets** or **remittance lists** on which they record receipts as they arrive through the post.

CASH RECEIVED SHEET 7141 (b)

DATE 10/4/X5

ARC BUILDING SUPPLIES LTD (a)

NAME		ACCOUNT	AMOUNT
P Jones and Son	1	00437	169.00
S Car & Co	2	01562	62.70
H M Customs & Excise	3	00002	55.00
Moblem Ltd	4	02137	3,233.99
Lobells plc	5	05148	244.91
Cannery Whiff	6	02420	9,553.72
Lymping Ltd	7	09370	62.20
Yorker plc	8	09682	322.41
Mowley Ltd	9	01433	43.30
Regalia plc	10	03997	978.50
Herod & Sons	11	05763	71.40
Forman & Co	12	07211	4,288.52
Thatchers	13	04520	610.00
Eggary & Co	14	08871	4,823.50
Redwood & Sons	15	08759	420.68
TOTAL		10000 (c)	24,939.83 (d)

(a) **Account number**. This is the ledger account number of the customer in the **sales ledger**. When the details from the cash received sheet are entered into the accounting system, this code number will tell the system (whether it is manual or computerised) which customer has paid off all or part of his debt. For non-sales ledger receipts, the code of the account in the general ledger is substituted. In this case 00002 is the code for Customs & Excise refunding VAT.

(b) **Cash received sheet number**. Preprinted cash received sheets may be sequentially numbered. This is a control which helps to make sure that all receipts have been recorded; a check can be carried out to make sure all cash received sheets are present.

(c) **Cash account number (10000)**. This is the ledger account number of the cash account in the general ledger.

(d) **Total receipts**. The money received is summarised here so only the totals need to be recorded in the cash book.

Activity 9.4 **Level: Assessment**

Glass 'I' Ltd manufactures glass and plastic containers of various colours which it sells to other companies in the food and drinks industry. All monies received are entered on cash received sheets which record details in separate columns, headed as follows.

(a) *Date*

(b) *Name*, showing the name of the firm or person from whom the money is received

(c) *Account number*, showing:

- For sales ledger receipts, the account number of the customer in the sales ledger, or
- For other receipts, the code for the ledger account to be credited

(d) *Amount*

In the week commencing 20 April 20X7, the post includes the items listed below. All cheques received were accompanied by a remittance advice.

20.4.X7 A cheque for £492.70 from Jill's Kitchen Co.
A cheque for £242.98 from G Edwards & Son.
A credit note for £124.40 from a supplier, Extrans Ltd.

21.4.X7 A cheque for £892.76 from Crystal Water Co.
A VAT repayment cheque of £487.50 from HM Customs & Excise.
A cheque for £500 from Green Gourmet Co, being part payment against invoice No 17201 which was for a total amount of £1,024.20.

22.4.X7 A cheque for £1,700.00 from BRM Motors in payment for a secondhand motor vehicle.
A cheque for £1,920.70 from Jennan Tonic Ltd.

23.4.X7 A cheque for £400 from Oliver's Organic Foods.
A debit note for £92.00 from Fender Foods plc.
A cheque for £3,208.00 from Parkers Preserves Ltd.

24.4.X7 A cheque for £4,920.75 from Pennine Springs Ltd
A statement of account from British Telecom plc, showing a balance of £382.44, to be paid by direct debit.

The following is a list of sales ledger account numbers.

	Account number		*Account number*
Crystal Water Co	C101	Jill's Kitchen Co	J211
Denny's Ltd	D024	Oliver's Organic Foods	O301
G Edwards & Son	E102	Parkers Preserves Ltd	P002
Fender Foods plc	F108	Pennine Springs Ltd	P004
Green Gourmet Co	G105	Spring Bottlers plc	S003
Jennan Tonic Ltd	J110	West, Key & Eiss	W402

The following list shows certain ledger account codes.

Cash	1000
Value added tax	1600
Motor vehicle disposals	1720
Telephones	1924

Tasks

(a) Draw up and total the cash received sheet for the week, using the blank sheet below.
(b) State how you would expect the cash receipts to be recorded in the cash book.

Cash received sheet			Number.......................
Date	Name	Account No.	Amount
			£
	Total	1000	

5 POSTING CASH RECEIPTS TO THE GENERAL LEDGER

ASSESSMENT ALERT

One of the key skills you must acquire for this Unit is the ability to post a summary of cash received in the accounts of the business. The Devolved Assessment will very likely require you to do this.

5.1 Back in Chapters 1 and 2 we saw that the aim of the accounting system was to document, record, summarise and present the financial transactions of a business. It is only when we **post the receipts side of the cash book to the cash (or bank) account in the general ledger that we can be said to have accounted for cash receipts.**

Book of prime entry	P O S T I N G	**Ledger account**
Cash book	→	Cash (or bank) account
Records cash receipts		*Summarises cash receipts*

5.2 Provided all the procedures have been followed correctly in preparing the cash book, posting it to the general ledger should be straightforward.

Step 1	**Add up** all the columns on the receipts side of the cash book.
Step 2	Check that the **totals of the analysis columns** (excluding the discount allowed memorandum column) add up to the total cash received column.
Step 3	**Identify general ledger accounts** which require posting by marking against cash book amount.
Step 4	Draw up a **posting summary** and post to the general ledger.

5.3 EXAMPLE: POSTING THE GENERAL LEDGER FROM THE CASH BOOK

Suppose we wished to post Robbie Jackson's cash received for 1 September 20X7 to his general ledger. The relevant general ledger accounts are as follows.

CASH ACCOUNT — CA01

		£		£
1 Sept	Balance b/d	900.00		

TOTAL DEBTORS — TD01

		£		£
1 Sept	Balance b/d	51,795.00		

SALES — SA01

		£		£
1 Sept			Balance b/d	200,403.00

VAT — VAT01

		£		£
1 Sept			Balance b/d	35,070.00

FIXED ASSET DISPOSAL — DIS01

		£		£

DISCOUNT ALLOWED — DA01

		£		£
1 Sept	Balance b/d	2,410.00		

5.4 SOLUTION

Step 1	The columns should be **added up** as follows (note that the 'total' columns total excludes the balance b/d - we do not want to double count).

ROBBIE JACKSON: CASH BOOK

RECEIPTS

Date	*Narrative*	*Folio*	*Discount allowed*	*Total*	*Output VAT on cash sales*	*Receipts from debtors*	*Cash sales*	*Other*
20X7								
01-Sep	Balance b/d			900.00				
	(a) Cash sale			80.00	11.91		68.09	
	(b) Debtor pays: Hay	SL96	20.00	380.00		380.00		
	(c) Debtor pays: Been	SL632		720.00		720.00		
	(d) Debtor pays: Seed	SL501	40.00	960.00		960.00		
	(e) Cash sale			150.00	22.34		127.66	
	(f) Fixed asset sale			200.00				200.00
			60.00	2,490.00	34.25	2,060.00	195.75	200.00
			TD01	***CA01***	***VAT01***	***TD01***	***SA01***	***DIS01***
			CR	DR	CR	CR	CR	CR
			DA01					
			DR					

Step 2 **Check the totals**

	£
Output VAT on cash sales	34.25
Receipts from debtors	2,060.00
Cash sales	195.75
Other receipts	200.00
Total cash received	2,490.00

Step 3 **Identify general ledger accounts.** We have marked the folio references for the general ledger accounts on the receipts page above.

TD01 ***Total debtors***

CA01 ***Cash account***

VAT01 ***VAT account***

SA01 ***Sales***

DIS01 ***Disposal of fixed assets***

DA01 ***Discounts allowed***

Step 4 Draw up the **posting summary** and post the general ledger.

			£	£
DEBIT	Cash account	CA01	2,490.00	
	Discounts allowed	DA01	60.00	
CREDIT	Total debtors	TD01		2,120.00
	VAT	VAT01		34.25
	Sales	SA01		195.75
	Disposal of fixed assets	DIS01		200.00

Being cash book receipts postings summary 1 September 20X7

Note that the credit to total debtors of £2,120 reflects £60 discounts allowed *plus* £2,060 received from them in cash.

CASH ACCOUNT — CA01

		£			£
1 Sept	Balance b/d	900.00			
1 Sept	Cash book	2,490.00			

TOTAL DEBTORS — TD01

		£			£
1 Sept	Balance b/d	51,795.00	1 Sept	Cash book	2,120.00

SALES — SA01

		£			£
1 Sept			Balance b/d		200,403.00
			1 Sept	Cash book	195.75

VAT — VAT01

		£			£
1 Sept			Balance b/d		35,070.00
			1 Sept	Cash book	34.25

FIXED ASSET DISPOSAL — DIS01

		£			£
			1 Sept	Cash book	200.00

DISCOUNT ALLOWED — DA01

		£			£
1 Sept	Balance b/d	2,410.00			
1 Sept	Cash book	60.00			

5.5 Remember that the general ledger *is* the double entry system and therefore all debits and credits on the posting summary must be equal: the **total cash received** represents the **debit** entry in the **cash account** (often called the **bank account**, or the **cash and bank account** in the general ledger).

- The **total of each analysis column** represents the credit entries in the general ledger accounts when cash has actually been received.
- The **discounts allowed** total is **debited to the discounts allowed expense account**, and **credited to the total debtors account**, where it reduces the total amount owed by debtors.

Activity 9.5 — Level: Assessment

Wagner Enterprises is a business selling marketing services to suppliers of opera companies. Most of its sales are to credit customers although there are a small number of cash sales. As at 15 February the receipts side of Wagner's cash book was as follows:

ARIA ENTERPRISES

RECEIPTS

Date	*Narrative*	*Folio*	*Discount allowed*	*Receipt total*	*VAT*	*Debtors*	*Cash sales*	*Other*
05-Feb	Carmen Carpets	SL0075	112.50	2,137.50		2,137.50		
08-Feb	Placido Players	SL0553		42.00	6.26		35.74	
11-Feb	Mehta Metronomes	SL0712		543.27		543.27		
14-Feb	Luciano Lighting	SL0009	19.00	361.00		361.00		
15-Feb	Tosca Tents	SL0473		4,000.00	595.74		3,404.26	
15-Feb	Magic Flute Instruments	SL0338	475.00	9,025.00		9,025.00		
	Bank interest			42.01				42.01
	Sale of delivery van			2,500.00				2,500.00

The business operates a memorandum sales ledger plus a sales ledger control account in the nominal ledger. Relevant nominal ledger codes and balances brought down are as follows:

Account	*Nominal code*	*Balance at 15/2*
		£
Cash	CAB 010	76,959 DR
VAT control account	VAT 094	10,500 CR
Sales ledger control account	SLC 040	152,744 DR
Sales discounts	DIS 340	7,050 DR
Sales	SAL 200	372,771 CR
Interest received	INT 270	0
Fixed asset disposal	FAD 028	0

Tasks

(a) Total the receipts side of the cash book and identify the postings to the nominal ledger.

(b) Prepare a posting summary. Open up the nominal ledger accounts and post the relevant amounts to them.

Tutorial note. Until now you have been used to seeing the term 'general ledger' and 'total debtors account' where 'nominal ledger' and 'sales ledger control account' are used above. In practice, and assessments, you will find that different terms are used in different contexts so you had better start getting used to it now!

Computerisation of receipts recording

5.6 It is quite rare to find a completely **computerised cash book in the books of prime entry**; companies with the most sophisticated general ledger computer systems will still often maintain a manual cash book. The 'bank account' in the ledger on the computer will reflect the same transactions as the manual cash book in the end. This may seem like a waste of time, but in fact it works quite well because some of the time the computer will update the manual cash book and some of the time it will happen the other way round.

5.7 What many businesses do have is a **computerised cash book** which *is* the **general ledger cash account**, so the recording of every cash transaction is effectively a posting to the general ledger cash account. This means that the company does not have to post totals from a book of prime entry, but has the disadvantage of making the general ledger huge in terms of the disk space it takes up.

5.8 For a computerised accounting system, when the cash book doubles as the cash account of the general ledger, we will look at two **different sources of receipts** and how they are recorded:

- Receipts from trade customers
- Miscellaneous receipts (sales of capital assets, refunds from suppliers and so on)

5.9 In a computerised accounting system, it is normal for receipts from trade debtors (who have balances owing on the sales ledger) to be **posted directly to the individual account on the computerised sales ledger**. At the end of the posting for a period (day or week, or even a month), the computer will produce a **posting summary**. An example is shown below.

SALES LEDGER POSTING SUMMARY 31 MARCH 20X4

	DR	£	CR	£
Sales	Total debtors	117.50	Sales	100.00
Output VAT			VAT	17.50
Cash received	Cash	90.00	Total debtors	90.00
		207.50		207.50

5.10 In some computer systems the sales ledger and general ledger are **interfaced** so they are connected and can update each other. If so, posting the sales ledger and the summary amounts can take place automatically. If the two systems are **not interfaced** then the posting will be input by the computer operator to the bank account in the general ledger.

5.11 The posting of the sales receipts to the sales ledger might be done from **cash received sheets** (remittance lists). A minimum amount of information would be posted.

Date	*Customer account number*	*Details*	*Reference number*	*Total amount* £
28.03.X4	37482	Receipt	469	349.57

The amount would be included in a total which would be posted to the bank account automatically.

5.12 It is not necessary to **summarise the receipts** before posting them to the sales ledger; each one could be entered individually. This method is often easier and saves time inputting into the computer. Sometimes a computer spreadsheet is used to provide a posting summary: when all the posted cash receipts are listed on it, it will automatically produce the posting entries.

5.13 **Miscellaneous receipts** will include sales of fixed assets, refunds from suppliers and perhaps VAT refunds from HM Customs & Excise. Such receipts do not normally appear in the sales ledger as it is unlikely that an invoice has been issued to tell the payer he owes money to the business. In this case the receipt can be recorded directly in a manual cash book and the cash book will be used to post such transactions to the cash account in the computer ledger. Alternatively, they can be journalled in.

Key learning points

- ***Controls* over the recording of cash receipts** include:
  - Segregation of duties
  - Bank reconciliations
- **Analysed cash books** show how much money has been received and paid, and what each amount was for, by placing it in the correct column. A cash book is a daybook or book of prime entry.
- **Cash registers** can be very useful in the control of cash receipts. They are accurate and they can be used to collect different kinds of sales information.
- **Cash received sheets**, or remittance lists are used to collect receipts ready for recording.
- **Computerised accounting systems** will often still have a manual cash book. The sales ledger will be used to update the cash book to reflect cash received.

Quick quiz

1. What is 'segregation of duties' when dealing with cash receipts?
2. The cash book reflects the movement of notes and coins through the business. True or false?
3. Why is a discount allowed column required in the cash book?
4. When bar codes are in use, why should a till have manual keys?
5. Is it easier for the operator if the computerised sales ledger and general ledger are interfaced?

Answers to quick quiz

1. The receiving and recording functions are kept separate to avoid theft.
2. False. The cash book records movements through the business bank account. Notes and coins are recorded in the petty cash book.
3. The discount allowed column shows why the full amount of a debt has not been received, for clearing the total amount in the sales ledger.
4. Manual keys are needed for items where barcodes are missing or a price change is required.
5. Yes, because both ledgers can be updated simultaneously for cash receipts from debtors.

10 Communications with debtors

This chapter contains

Learning objectives

On completion of this chapter you will have learned about:

- Send statements of account to debtors, where required
- Relevant understanding of the organisation's accounting systems and administrative systems and procedures
- House style for correspondence

Performance criteria

1.1.6 Statements of account are prepared and sent to debtors

1.1.7 Communications with customers regarding accounts are handled politely and effectively using the relevant source documents

1.2.4 Unusual features are identified and either resolved or referred to the appropriate person

Range statement

1.1.5 Communications: in response to queries; chasing payments

1.1.6 Source documents: aged debtors analysis

1.2.3 Unusual features: wrongly completed cheques; out of date cheques, credit and debit cards; limits exceeded; disagreement with supporting documentation; under payments; over payments; cheques returned to sender

1 THE STATEMENT OF ACCOUNT

1.1 The majority of credit transactions between businesses take place between parties which deal **regularly** with one another. Most businesses will have some customers to whom it sells regularly and some to whom it makes less frequent sales.

1.2 The number of customers which a business has will depend on the **nature of the business** as well as its **size**. Some businesses may have just one customer. Perhaps a defence contractor will sell only to the Ministry of Defence, or a motor component supplier might make all of its sales to a single large car manufacturer. We saw in Chapter 6 that this can mean that a business might not need a sales ledger as such at all.

1.3 The fact that a business usually sells on a regular basis to many of its customers means that there will probably be a steady flow of invoices to those customers. Some customers may be sent a handful of sales invoices each month; others may be sent rather more (again, depending on the nature of the business).

1.4 If a business expected its customers to pay **separately** for each individual sales invoice that it sent, the customer might have to prepare **several cheques** to send to the business each month. This would be wasteful in administrative time and resources. Instead, the seller will send out to the customer, in addition to separate invoices, a **statement of account.**

KEY TERM

A statement of account summarises the transactions undertaken over a given period and shows the total amount currently owed by the customer to the business. The customer will make periodic payments (say monthly), thereby reducing the balance on the account.

1.5 The statement of account is usually produced by a **computer**, though it may be **typed out by hand**. When talking about customers' statements of account, it is common to refer to them simply as 'statements'.

Frequency of the statement of account

1.6 Most organisations prepare customers' statements of account **monthly**. The statement issued at the end of the month will summarise all of the business which has taken place during that month.

What does the statement of account show?

1.7 The customer's statement of account will show the following.

Item(s)	Details
Amounts brought forward from previous statements which remain unpaid	This will be shown on the statement as the 'balance brought forward', or perhaps as the 'previous balance'. The total amount brought forward might be shown in a column headed 'balance'. Alternatively, the seller might actually list on the statement all the items from previous months remaining unpaid.
Invoices sent to the customer	These of course will increase the amount which the buyer owes to the seller, and will usually be shown in a column headed 'Debit'.
Credit notes issued to the buyer	These reduce the amount of the debt, and will be shown in a 'Credit' column on the statement.
Payments received from the customer	As we saw in Chapter 6, payments received from the customer are usually matched as far as possible against specific invoices, so that they and the payment 'disappear' from the statement in the following month. Unmatched cash would remain, however.
The total amount due at the end of the month	This will be shown at the foot of the statement.
Statement of terms	This will reiterate what is on the invoices, eg net 30 days, cash discount. Often a 'payment due' date is included.

Example of a statement of account

1.8 An example of a statement of account is set out below.

STATEMENT OF ACCOUNT

Pickett (Handling Equipment) Limited
Unit 7, Western Industrial Estate
Dunford DN2 7RJ

Tel: (01990) 72101 Fax: (01990) 72980 VAT Reg No 982 721 349

Accounts Department
Finstar Ltd
67 Laker Avenue
Dunford DN4 5PS

Date: 31 May 20X2

A/c No: F023

Date	Details	Debit £	p	Credit £	p	Balance £	p
30/4/X2	Balance brought forward from previous statement ①					492	22
3/5/X2	Invoice no. 34207 ②	129	40			621	62
4/5/X2	Invoice no. 34242 ②	22	72			644	34
5/5/X2	Payment received - thank you ④			412	17	232	17
17/5/X2	Invoice no. 34327 ②	394	95			627	12
18/5/X2	Credit note no. 00192 ③			64	40	562	72
21/5/X2	Invoice no. 34392 ②	392	78			955	50
28/5/X2	Credit note no. 00199 ③			107	64	847	86
	Amount now due				£	847	86

Terms: 30 days net, 1% discount for payment in 7 days. E & OE ⑤

Registered office: 4 Arkwright Road, London E16 4PQ Registered in England No 2182417

1.9 You can see from this statement that as at 31 May 20X2, according to the records of Pickett (Handling Equipment) Ltd, Finstar Ltd owes a total of £847.86 to Pickett.

1.10 Can you say how much of this is made up of invoices or credit notes from before May 20X2? The answer is not £492.22, as you will see that a payment by Finstar of £412.17 is shown on the statement with a date of receipt of 5 May 20X2. Almost certainly, this payment will relate to the items before May 20X2. Assuming that it does all relate to part of the balance brought forward on the May statement, you can see that £80.05 (£492.22 – £412.17) of the balance brought forward still remains unpaid.

Statements of account with remittance advice forms

1.11 A statement of account may be produced with a **remittance advice form** attached. The customer receiving the statement can tear off the remittance advice form and send it in with the payment to indicate to the supplier the invoices (less any credit notes) to which the payment relates. An example is set out below.

STATEMENT

Las Ninjos & Co
Belton Estate
Peterborough

TO:

ABC & Co
4 The Mews
Middlesborough

A/C REF: 12379
DATE: 0104X7
PAGE: 1

DATE	DETAILS		DEBIT	CREDIT
0202X7	Invoice	20381	96.27	
0502X7	Invoice	20414	113.44	
1102X7	Invoice	20522	84.95	
2102X7	C/note	C9410		22.00
0103X7	Cash received			272.66
1203X7	Invoice	20529	212.11	
1503X7	Invoice	20611	106.07	
2903X7	Invoice	22100	78.90	
3003X7	C/note	C9422		23.48

CURRENT	30 DAY	60 DAY	90 DAY	120+ DAY
373.60	0	0	0	0

AMOUNT DUE

£373.60

REMITTANCE ADVICE

Las Ninjos & Co
Belton Estate
Peterborough

FROM:

ABC & Co
4 The Mews
Middlesborough

A/C REF: 12379
DATE: 0104X7
PAGE: 1

DATE	DETAILS		DEBIT	CREDIT
0202X7	Invoice	20381	96.27	
0502X7	Invoice	20414	113.44	
1102X7	Invoice	20522	84.95	
2102X7	C/note	C9410		22.00
0103X7	Cash received			272.66
1203X7	Invoice	20529	212.11	
1503X7	Invoice	20611	106.07	
2903X7	Invoice	22100	78.90	
3003X7	C/note	C9422		23.48

OUR TERMS 30 DAYS. YOUR PROMPT SETTLEMENT WOULD BE APPRECIATED. THANK YOU.

AMOUNT DUE

£373.60

1.12 If the amount being paid is not the full amount due per the statement, then the customer might indicate on the remittance advice form which he sends to the supplier why there is a difference, as shown on the following page.

REMITTANCE ADVICE

Las Ninjos & Co
Belton Estate
Peterborough

FROM: ABC & Co
4 The Mews
Middlesborough

A/C REF: 12379
DATE: 0104X7
PAGE: 1

DATE	DETAILS		DEBIT	CREDIT
0202X7	Invoice	20381	96.27	
0502X7	Invoice	20414	113.44	
1102X7	Invoice	20522	84.95	
2102X7	C/note	C9410		22.00
0103X7	Cash received			272.66
1203X7	Invoice	20529	212.11 ✓	
1503X7	Invoice	20611	106.07 ✓	
2903X7	Invoice	22100*	78.90	
3003X7	C/note	C9422		23.48 ✓

* Credit due - ref. our letter 31/3/X7

OUR TERMS 30 DAYS. YOUR PROMPT SETTLEMENT WOULD BE APPRECIATED. THANK YOU.

AMOUNT DUE

£294.70 ~~£373.60~~

1.13 Often debtors will not make use of a remittance advice sent to them, but will instead send an internally-generated remittance advice which indicates how the payment is made up.

Activity 10.1 — Level: Assessment

You work for Muzak Ltd in the sales ledger department. A new assistant, Boris Thug, has recently been taken on to help you. He is keen, but as he is so inexperienced you have made it a policy to review his work.

You were ill for a couple of days, at the time you normally send out reminder letters to late paying debtors. To help you out, Boris has drafted some for you.

One such letter refers to a customer, J L Baudrillard plc, who has *two* accounts with you. On your sales ledger, these appear as:

- J L Baudrillard plc Head Office (A/c no BA01)
- J L Baudrillard plc Robotics (A/c No BB01)

J L Baudrillard plc is an old and valued customer, and has done increasing amounts of business with Muzak Ltd over the years. J L Baudrillard plc has recently appointed a new finance director, Mr Martin Jacques.

Muzak Ltd's sales ledger is computerised.

Tasks

(a) Review Boris's letter to J L Baudrillard plc in the light of:

  (i) The most recent statement on *each* J L Baudrillard plc account

  (ii) Your own Screen Enquiry of the Customer Reference file

  (iii) The notes Boris himself made on September 7 regarding the balances on the J L Baudrillard plc accounts at that date

  (iv) Your own common sense

  And note down *anything* and *everything* in Boris's draft which you regard as incorrect or inappropriate. Boris regards his letter as ready for posting.

(b) State any matters which have been raised about your accounts with J L Baudrillard plc and what action you would take as a consequence.

Boris's draft letter to J L Baudrillard plc

Finance Director

Baudrilard
Charles House
Postmodern Industrial Estate
Frontage, Wilts

14/9/X7

Dear Mr Baudrilard

We've got problems with your account which you will see from the statement I sent you two weeks ago. Your always going overdrawn and this month you don't seem to have paid us. Please do something about it, or I might have to call in a soliciter or debt collector.

I remain, sir, your obedient servant,

Boris Thug, Assistant

Boris's screen enquiry 7/9/X7

Boris has also noted down the following details from an enquiry he made of the system on 7 September 20X7.

SALES LEDGER BALANCE ENQUIRY NOTE

	Amount outstanding £
BA01 Baudrillard PLC Head Office	35,752.62
BB01 Baudrillard PLC Robotics	25,978.41

DATE 7/9/X7

Statements of account

MUZAK LTD

99 Bleak Street, London N3
Phone: 0151 234 5678 Fax: 0151 234 5679
VAT reg: 231 1423

STATEMENT OF ACCOUNT

J L BAUDRILLARD PLC ROBOTICS
SIMULACRA HOUSE,
CYBERNETIC STREET,
STEPFORD,
LINCS

Account BB01

Date 31/8/X7

Date	Item	£ p	£ p	£ p
1/8/X7	BALANCE FROM STATEMENT 31/7/X7			25,011.92
3/8/X7	CREDIT NOTE 975		7,121.07	17,890.85
4/8/X7	CREDIT NOTE 977		985.72	16,905.13
10/8/X7	PAYMENT RECEIVED - THANK YOU		7,429.49	9,475.64
25/8/X7	INVOICE 9491	11,071.32		20,546.96
31/8/X7	BALANCE			20,546.96

Reg office: 99 Bleak Street, London N3 Reg no: 231 1423

MUZAK LTD

99 Bleak Street, London N3
Phone: 0151 234 5678 Fax: 0151 234 5679
VAT reg: 231 1423

STATEMENT OF ACCOUNT

J L BAUDRILLARD PLC HEAD OFFICE
CHARLES HOUSE
POSTMODERN INDUSTRIAL ESTATE
FRONTAGE
WILTS

Account BA01

Date 31/8/X7

Date	Item	£ p	£ p	£ p
1/8/X7	BALANCE FROM STATEMENT 31/7/X7			25,553.01
4/8/X7	INVOICE 0483	7,121.07		32,674.08
9/8/X7	INVOICE 3448	985.72		33,659.80
14/8/X7	PAYMENT RECEIVED - THANK YOU		17,639.56	16,020.24
25/8/X7	INVOICE 9372	8,131.41		24,151.65
31/8/X7	BALANCE			24,151.65

Reg office: 99 Bleak Street, London N3 Reg no: 231 1423

Details from screen enquiry 14/9/X7

Customer: J L Baudrillard plc Robotics BB01
Simulacra House
Cybernetic St
Stepford
Lincs

Phone 01941 821010

Fax 01941 821013

Credit Limit £20,000 Last reviewed 1/1/20X2

Customer:	J L Baudrillard plc Head Office Charles House Postmodern Industrial Estate Frontage Wilts	BA01
Phone	01711 468246	
Fax	01711 468247	
Credit Limit £50,000		Last reviewed 1/1/20X6

SALES LEDGER RUN 31/8/X7

CUSTOMER: J L BAUDRILLARD PLC ROBOTICS DIVISION — ACCOUNT NO: BB01

ADDRESS: SIMULACRA HOUSE, CYBERNETIC STREET, STEPFORD, LINCS

PHONE: 01473 979149

Date	Trans ref	DR £ p	CR £ p	Balance £ p
30/6/X7				19,215.68
9/7/X7	Invoice 3448	985.72		20,201.40
10/7/X7	Invoice 3492	7,429.49		27,630.89
15/7/X7	Cash book 15/7		9,740.04	17,890.85
31/7/X7	Invoice 0483	7,121.07		25,011.92
3/8/X7	Credit note 975		7,121.07	17,890.85
4/8/X7	Credit note 977		985.72	16,905.13
10/8/X7	Cash book 10/8		7,429.49	9,475.64
25/8/X7	Invoice 9491	11,071.32		20,546.96
		26,607.60	25,276.32	

SALES LEDGER RUN				31/8/X7
CUSTOMER:	J L BAUDRILLARD PLC HEAD OFFICE		ACCOUNT NO:	
ADDRESS:	CHARLES HOUSE, POSTMODERN INDUSTRIAL ESTATE, FRONTAGE, WILTS		BA01	
PHONE:	01711 468246			
Date	Trans ref	DR £ p	CR £ p	Balance £ p
30/6/X7				15,504.66
8/7/X7	Invoice 0107	8,312.50		23,817.16
14/7/X7	Cash book 17/4		19,372.50	4,444.66
21/7/X7	Invoice 0252	17,639.56		22,084.22
28/7/X7	Invoice 0371	3,468.79		25,553.01
4/8/X7	Invoice 0483	7,121.07		32,674.08
9/8/X7	Invoice 3448	985.72		33,659.80
14/8/X7	Cash book 14/8		17,639.56	16,020.24
25/8/X7	Invoice 9372	8,131.41		24,151.65
		45,659.05	37,012.06	

2 DEALING WITH DEBTORS' QUERIES

2.1 Sending out statements of account is a **regular routine**. Other aspects of communications with debtors arise on a less regular basis, depending upon whatever discrepancies, unusual features or queries occur. Such communications may involve **telephone calls** as well as **written forms of communication**.

2.2 EXAMPLE: BUSINESS LETTER

An example of a business letter involving a debtor is set out below. Britton Trading Co plc has received a complaint from one of the firm's regular customers, UK Freight plc. UK Freight have informed the company that they have received a statement indicating that payment of their account is overdue and that settlement must be made immediately. The amount stated to be outstanding is £2,340.20. UK Freight plc says that a cheque for this amount was paid on 23 August 20X3 but no acknowledgement of receipt was received.

Investigations have revealed that an incorrect ledger entry was made on 26 August 20X3. Payment of £2,340.20 was actually credited to the account of UK Carriage plc. August was a month in which there were staff changes in the office.

2.3 SOLUTION

BRITTON TRADING CO PLC
WOLVERHAMPTON
WEST MIDLANDS

UK Freight plc
Tingeley Street
MANCHESTER
M12 4RS

22 September 20X3

Ref: YN/87/33

Dear Sirs

PAYMENT OF ACCOUNT: £2,340.20 [1]

I was sorry to learn of your complaint regarding a statement received from us indicating that payment of your account is overdue[2].

Having investigated the matter[3], I may confirm that we did receive a cheque for £2,340.20[4] from you on the 23 August. I regret that this payment was incorrectly credited as a result of unforeseen pressures on our accounting procedures at that time[5]. I am pleased to report that the error has been rectified: your account is fully paid up and I have taken steps to ensure that its creditworthiness is not impaired by this incident[6].

Please accept my sincere apologies for the concern caused to you[7]. We do not anticipate any recurrence of our temporary problem, but if I can be of any further assistance please do not hesitate to contact me directly[8].

Yours faithfully

R Coe

R Coe
Senior Accounts Clerk
Extension 3320

2.4 Note the following features in the above letter, which should be borne in mind whenever a business letter is sent.

Letter feature	**Comments**
[1] Letter title	Always be as clear as possible about the matter covered in the letter - a brief letter title is ideal.
[2] Tone	This letter is polite and appropriately apologetic, without being grovelling, defensive or impertinent.
[3] Action taken	Always state what action has been taken when investigating a customer complaint.
[4] Amounts and dates	Stating the exact amounts and the dates of disputed transactions is vital for the customer to understand what you are saying.

Letter feature	Comments
5 Cause of error	It is not strictly necessary to give an explanation for why something went wrong (in theory, the customer is simply concerned that it has been corrected) but it lets the customers see that you have control of the overall situation, even if mistakes are made occasionally.
6 Future action	Consider what effect an error might have on a customer in the future, and reassure them.
7 Apologise	It is polite and reassuring to the customer for you to apologise for the mistake, and to reassure them.
8 Further contact	Reassure the customer that any further queries on the matter will be readily dealt with; make sure your name, and preferably your extension number, are clear on the letter.

2.5 EXAMPLE: SHORT INFORMAL REPORT

The complaint from UK Freight plc has been received by Mr Case who asks for a **short informal report** on the matter.

REPORT ON CUSTOMER COMPLAINT: UK Freight plc payment of £2,340.20

TO:	Mr Case	Ref: IRC/85/20
FROM:	R Coe	Date: 21 September

1 *Background*

I have investigated the situation with regard to this complaint. I have consulted all ledger entries relevant to this account, and to accounts of similar names, at the time of the claimed payment. The last week in August was a time of extraordinary staff turnover and therefore unusual stress in the office.

2 *Findings*

A cheque for £2,340.20 was indeed received from UK Freight plc on 23 August as claimed. On 26 August this amount was credited in error to the account of UK Carriage plc. and an acknowledgement of receipt issued to them. The incorrect entry may have been made by temporary staff.

3 *Action taken*

I have corrected the ledger entries for UK Freight plc and UK Carriage plc, and ensured that the creditworthiness of the former account is not affected. I have written a letter of apology and explanation to UK Freight plc (copy attached), and I have issued a warning to the accounts clerks about the ease with which such an error can be made. I have also explained the erroneous receipt to UK Carriage plc and apologised for the mistake.

R Coe, Senior Accounts Clerk

2.6 Members of the sales ledger department of a business may well be in **fairly regular contact** with the purchase ledger department of the business to whom they sell their goods and services. It is of course the buyer's purchase ledger department (or 'bought ledger' department) which will be responsible for processing the seller's invoices and which will receive and take action on the seller's statements of account. There will be various queries which may need to be sorted out between the two departments of the different businesses.

2.7 Much of this contact will probably be by telephone, perhaps with **later confirmation in writing**. **Fax machines** are particularly useful where the information needed to settle a query, such as a copy of an invoice, cannot easily be read out over the telephone. Major matters, and matters where some formal documentation is necessary, will probably need to be dealt with by **letter**.

2.8 Whether a query is received by telephone or in writing, it should be dealt with **promptly** and **courteously**. This is really a matter of good business sense and will help to ensure that good relations are maintained with customers of the business.

Examples of debtors' queries

2.9 In the following paragraphs, we look at a number of different enquiries which a sales ledger department might have to deal with and at what response might be appropriate. In each of these examples, the situations described are set in the **sales ledger department of Pickett (Handling Equipment) Ltd** and involve other departments of that company, as appropriate. Highlight for yourself what you consider to be the key areas of each situation, and check that they are included in the solution.

Situation 1: opening a customer account

2.10 The Buying Manager of Cash Factories plc has held meetings with Pickett's Sales Manager Paul Morley on a number of occasions with a view to becoming a regular customer of Pickett. The first firm orders have already been placed, and the Sales Manager has asked for a **credit account to be set up for this new customer**.

You obtain a credit reference agency report on Cash Factories plc which indicates that the company is financially sound and recommends a credit limit of up to £100,000. Paul Morley considers that the maximum balance of the new account is unlikely to exceed £20,000 at any one time and requests that the credit limit for Cash Factories plc be set at £50,000. The Financial Director authorises this proposed limit.

Draft a letter dated 2 June 20X2 to R Staite, the Buying Manager of Cash Factories plc, at 630 Atlantic Avenue, Dunford DN9 9TB, confirming the opening of the new account and the credit limit allocated, and the standard credit terms (30 days net, a discount of 1% for payment within 7 days, statements of account issued monthly).

Pickett (Handling Equipment) Limited
Unit 7, Western Industrial Estate
Dunford DN2 7RJ

Tel: (01990) 72101 Fax: (01990) 72980 VAT Reg No 982 721 349

R Staite Esq
Buying Manager
Cash Factories plc
630 Atlantic Avenue
Dunford DN9 9TB

2 June 20X2

Dear Mr Staite

Following your recent meetings with our Sales Manager Paul Morley, I write to confirm that a sales account has been opened for your company.

The reference number for the account is CO24 and the credit limit applying to the account is initially £50,000.

Our terms are 30 days net, and a discount of 1% is given for payment within 7 days. Statements of account are issued monthly.

Yours sincerely

N Norman

N Norman
Financial Controller

Situation 2: prospective customer with financial difficulties

2.11 On 7 June 20X2, Tryiton Ltd submitted a purchase order for goods to be supplied on credit to the value of £2,400 approximately. Tryiton Ltd does not currently have a sales ledger account with Pickett and is unable to provide any references. A report obtained from a credit reference agency suggests that Tryiton Ltd may be in financial difficulties and declines to recommend any credit limit.

Draft a letter to Tryiton Ltd, of 124 Luton Avenue, Dunford DN10 6RB, explaining that credit cannot be extended.

> **Pickett (Handling Equipment) Limited**
> **Unit 7, Western Industrial Estate**
> **Dunford DN27 7RJ**
>
> Tel: (01990) 72101 Fax: (01990) 72980 VAT Reg No 982 721 349
>
> Tryiton Limited
> 124 Luton Avenue
> Dunford DN10 6RB
>
> 7 June 20X2
>
> Dear Sirs
>
> Thank you for your purchase order No P9093.
>
> I regret that we are unable to extend credit to your company, although we would be able to supply the goods you require if you make payment in advance. Should you wish to trade with us on this basis, please contact our Sales Manager, Paul Morley.
>
> We look forward to hearing from you.
>
> Yours faithfully
>
> *N Norman*
>
> N Norman
> Financial Controller

Situation 3: payment not received

2.12 An Accounts Assistant at Finstar Ltd telephones on 1 June 20X2, thanking you for the Statement of Account for May 20X2 (see Paragraph 1.8). The Assistant says that the statement is incorrect, as it does not show the payment of £117.77 made on 28 May 20X2 which she says cleared invoices 34207, 34242, credit note 00192 and all amounts relating to periods earlier than May 20X2.

Write down what you would say in responding on the telephone to this call. Include in your response an indication of whether you accept the caller's claim about the make-up of the payment made.

- The reason why the payment made on 28 May is not shown in our statement dated 31 May, is probably that the payment was **in the post** or **waiting to be processed** by our sales ledger department at the time the statement was prepared.
- Assuming that the payment is received, it will be reflected in the next statement of account issued at the end of June.
- A payment of £117.77 does not completely clear the items which you specify.

		£
Invoice	34207	129.40
	34242	22.72
Credit note	00192	(64.40)
Balance brought forward		492.22
Payment received		(412.17)
		167.77
Payment sent		117.77
Amount remaining unpaid		50.00

Requests for credit notes

2.13 Many communications with debtors will involve **requests by customers for credit notes against goods or services already invoiced.**

(a) If goods have been damaged in transit

(b) Or the amount delivered is less than the amount invoiced.

The buyer will need to inform the seller and to request that a credit note be issued.

2.14 Until a credit note is issued against an invoice, the statement of account will simply show the full amount invoiced. **Many businesses will therefore wait until any credit notes claimed are issued before paying a specific invoice.** This will encourage the seller to issue credit notes quickly to minimise any delay in payment being received.

Activity 10.2 Level: Assessment

You work for Tune Ltd. The company sells a variety of products, including Divas (two models - the *Callas* and the *Sutherland*) and Super Conductors. Divas are made to order, and it takes about four weeks to produce them. One of your customers is Beethoven plc. Beethoven plc's purchase ledger clerk, Herbert V Karajan, has rung you with a query regarding an invoice.

He is questioning invoice number 4321. He says he only received one Diva, not the two as he was billed on that invoice. Karajan also says that he's owed a 10% trade discount.

You dig out file copies of invoice 4321 and the corresponding delivery note.

Task

Address the following questions.

(a) What would you do to find out more about Karajan's claim? What has gone wrong?

(b) How would you deal with Karajan's query for rectification? What documentation is involved? Draft a written reply to him covering the discrepancy and the discount.

INVOICE

TUNE LTD
Discord Street, Crochety, Sussex

Date/tax point: 1/7/X7
Invoice no: 4321

Please quote number 379

Beethoven plc
Symphony Promenade
Quavertree, Essex

	List price per unit £ p	Trade discount	Invoice £ p	VAT 17½% £ p	Total £ p
1 super conductor	705.99		705.99	123.55	829.54
2 'Callas' divas	211.88		423.76	74.16	497.92
Total			1,129.75	197.71	1,327.46

Comments

Delivery note ref 4321

Reg office: Discord Street, Crochety, Sussex Reg no: 451 059
VAT reg no: 678 9012

4321

DELIVERY NOTE

TUNE LTD

Date/tax point: 1/7/X7

Beethoven plc
Symphony Promenade
Quavertree, Essex

Qty	Item	Order	Signature (checked and accepted)
1	super conductor	897	H V Karajan for Beethoven plc
2	'Callas' divas	897	H V Karajan for Beethoven plc
			1 diva returned because not a Callas diva, but a Sutherland diva

Date delivered Driver

Reg office: Discord Street, Crochety, Sussex Reg no: 451 059
VAT reg no: 678 9012

Yellow copy to customer | Pink copy to the warehouse | Blue copy to accounts

3 DEMANDS FOR PAYMENT

3.1 Not all customers pay on or before the due date for payment!

- The mildest form of letter to a customer to point out that their account is overdue may be called a '**request for payment**', and is likely to be sent out at a specific period after the failure to pay a debt.
- As a debt becomes longer overdue, **more strongly worded reminders** and demands may be called for in an attempt to secure payment.

A credit sale is a legally binding contract, and accordingly the creditor can sue the debtor for payment if payment is not made under the terms of the contract.

3.2 For simple reminders or further demands for payment, it may be simplest for a business to use **standard letters**. Some computerised accounting packages are able to print off standard letters for sending out to customers whose debts are overdue and these will be sent at certain specified times after invoicing, for example when the debt has been overdue 2 weeks, 1 month, 5 weeks and so on. Personal contact with the customer concerned may be important in eliciting the most favourable response.

3.3 While standardised letter formats have the advantage of costing little in staff time to send out, the lack of the '**personal touch**' may unfortunately result in customers simply ignoring them. For '**key account**' **customers** (discussed a little later in this chapter), or for customers whose debt is long overdue, a more personal approach may be necessary.

3.4 An individually written debt collection letter will have the following features.

1	**Statement of amount due** and other relevant details (account no, date). Reference to previous reminders sent, if accounts long overdue.	A collection letter is brief and business-like, so state the purpose and relevant details immediately.
2	(a) Reminder of **terms agreed for payment**. (b) Other relevant information: where/ how to pay, discounts for quick payment etc	Other information will depend on whether this is a first, second or final request. Be helpful but firm.
3	**Request for payment**, action to be taken if payment not forthcoming.	Your tone should be firm but not aggressive. Even final warnings can be made courteously.

3.5 Standard forms of collection letter used by a business might look similar to those below.

Letter 1

> Dear Customer
>
> I write to inform you that the balance on your account of £xxx.xx has not been settled for over 30 days. As a result of this, I have to inform you that we cannot offer a discount on this occasion.
>
> I look forward to receiving payment and hope you will take advantage of our cash discount arrangements in the future.
>
> Yours faithfully

Letter 2

> Dear Customer
>
> It has come to our attention that settlement of your account now exceeds 60 days but still it has not been paid. I take this opportunity to remind that we now require a payment of £xxxx.xx in settlement of your account.
>
> If you have any queries regarding this account, then please contact us as soon as possible to resolve any possible problems.
>
> I must inform you that if payment is not forthcoming, then we will find it necessary to take action on this matter.
>
> Yours faithfully

4 CREDIT CONTROL

KEY TERM

Credit control is the task of ensuring that payments are received from debtors on a timely basis and that late payers are followed up promptly.

4.1 Larger businesses will have special **credit control departments**, whose work is often very important in maintaining the cash flow of the business.

4.2 Customers can gain some **cash flow advantage** from paying as late as they can. Human nature being what it is, some customers will seek to exploit this advantage, however unfair this may seem. In many businesses, some customers become known as habitually **late payers** and these customers are likely to occupy much of the time of the credit control department.

4.3 As in the case of other communications with debtors, the **telephone** and the **letter** will both be important methods of communication to the credit controller. A good credit controller will be persistent as well as persuasive. The new credit controller will soon learn that one often cannot take 'the cheque's in the post' for an answer!

Objectives of credit control

4.4 Credit control may be described as the **management of debtors**. The objectives of debtor management can be summarised as being:

(a) To ensure that all sales are paid for, within the agreed period of credit, without alienating customers.

(b) To administer and collect debts with minimum cost.

Setting out customer terms

4.5 In communicating with debtors, it is important that **credit terms are stated clearly**, as well as the conditions in which any cash discounts are available. Credit terms and cash discount terms should be set out in documentation for customers to see:

(a) When the customer **order is acknowledged**
(b) When the customer is **invoiced**
(c) When the customer is sent a **statement of account**

4.6 Abbreviated phrases such as '2% 14 days' are less clear and therefore more open to misinterpretation than the words '2% cash discount may be deducted if payment is received within 14 days of the invoice date'.

4.7 Once established, a policy of credit terms and cash discounts will need to be **enforced properly**. Enforcement of a cash discount policy becomes difficult if customers adopt a practice of taking the discount whether or not they pay on time. If widely accepted, this practice makes the cash discount 'policy' rather pointless.

Credit rating and credit limits

4.8 A business which simply supplies goods on credit to any customer in any quantity without applying any **credit limit** is exposing itself to considerable risk because some customers may not pay in the end. However, it is important to balance that risk against the need to allow **sufficient credit to allow the business to prosper**. An accountant who is extremely cautious and sets very low customer credit limits may avoid any bad debts, but if as a result the business has made much lower sales than it should have been able to, then the accountant's policy may be damaging to the business.

4.9 It is good practice for a business to set credit limits for all customer accounts. Credit limits will be based on the business's assessment of the customer's ability to pay. How can this be assessed?

- For major customers, a business will obtain copies of the **annual accounts**.
- Many businesses also make use of the services of one of the **credit rating agencies** (for example Dunn & Bradstreet).
- Obtain **trade and bankers' references**. A new customer may be asked to provide the names of referees. As with all references, it will be necessary to 'read between the lines' of the information supplied. A bank will be particularly sensitive about the risk that they could be seen to be defaming a customer, and so it will word a reference on a doubtful customer with the greatest of care. Like all references, references on customers are often more significant for what they do *not* say than for what they do say!
- **Credit managers** get together on a regular basis to **exchange information** on **customer credit risks**. This can be very useful, as it may be credit managers who are first alerted to financial problems which a company may be having. Such information often takes rather more time to reach the files of credit rating agencies.
- In some cases, particularly when the customer is a small limited company, the business may require **personal guarantees** from the company's directors.

Activity 10.3 **Level: Assessment**

Stravinsky Products Ltd, a company with whom you, as sales ledger clerk for Tune Ltd, have had no prior business relationship, writes to you. It wishes to set up an account. Stravinsky is promising a lot of business, and wants a large credit limit to match.

Tasks

(a) Set out what information about the prospective customer you need to open the account. What further measures would you undertake to ensure that the credit limit asked for is appropriate?

(b) Explain what you would do to set up the account.

'Key account' customers

4.10 In a typical business, 20% of the customers account for 80% of the sales of the business, and therefore for 80% of the customer debts. In many businesses, such customers will receive special treatment in the sales effort, and it is appropriate that **in managing the debts of these 'key account' customers, special treatment is given.**

4.11 It will be important for managers to establish a **good working relationship** with whoever makes the **payment decisions** in the customer organisation. For large debts, it may be a good idea to telephone well before the due date so that any problems may be resolved and a promise of payment may be obtained. The credit manager will then ring back on the due date if the payment is not received thus confronting the customer with the fact that the promise has been broken.

Putting an account on stop

4.12 Specific time periods should be set for issuing **letters of demand**, such as those set out earlier in this chapter. When payment becomes very long overdue, a time will be reached at which **deliveries to the non-paying customer should be stopped**.

4.13 In stopping deliveries, as well as in other respects of credit control, it is important for the **credit control department to liaise with the sales management team.** 'Insensitive' credit control procedures could damage relations with customers.

Solicitor's letter

4.14 There will be some point at which a business will seek **outside help** to collect an overdue debt. As with stopping deliveries, it is likely that plenty of warning will have already been given to the customer that this next step is about to be taken.

4.15 The best known form of outside help is probably **legal help from a solicitor**. However, other organisations whose assistance may be enlisted include **trade organisations** in certain industries, and **debt collection agencies**.

4.16 **Bringing in outside help costs money** of course, and the work of collecting overdue debts involves staff time which also has a cost even though this cost may not be so visible as the fees of outside agencies, which may exceed the value of the debt itself.

Key learning points

- A **statement of account** is sent periodically (usually monthly) to the credit customers of a business. It summarises the business which has taken place in the month with that customer and shows the total amount due from the customer.
- **Dealing with queries** from customers **involves the use of different communication media**, including written communication, telephone and fax.
- While the communication medium used should be appropriate to the task involved, whatever medium is used the **response to customers' queries** should always be **prompt** and should always be **courteous**.
- The **credit control function** in an organisation has the task of ensuring that all sales are paid for within the agreed credit period while maintaining customer relations. The **credit controller** is charged with the task of administering and collecting debts with minimum costs being incurred in doing so. Major debtors may receive particularly careful treatment as '**key account**' **customers**.
- **Credit limits** are set for customers on the basis of an assessment by the business of the customer's ability to pay. To make this assessment, the business may refer to the customer's annual accounts, to credit rating agencies, or to other sources of information from their own business or the industry.
- If **debts become long overdue**, eventually the **legal process** or other **outside agencies** may need to be brought in. If a **customer goes into liquidation**, the **business is unlikely to recover more than a small proportion of its debt.**

Quick quiz

1. What is the purpose of a statement of account?
2. What is a remittance advice for?
3. If the supplier makes a mistake, why might he give the customer an explanation as to why things went wrong?
4. When would you use a fax for communicating with debtors?
5. A credit sale is a legally binding contract. True or false?
6. What is credit control?
7. When would you put an account "on stop"?

Answers to quick quiz

1. It summarises the transactions entered into by a customer over a given period and shows the amount currently due.
2. A customer returns a remittance advice with his payment to indicate the invoices (less credit notes) to which the payment relates.
3. It shows that the supplier is in control and knows about his own system. This will be reassuring to the customer.
4. When the information being communicated is too complicated to be given over the telephone. For more formal purposes, a letter would be more appropriate.
5. True.
6. Credit control is the task of ensuring that payments are received from debtors on a timely basis.
7. If payments are long overdue. Senior authority is required.

Part D

Basic law

11 Business law

This chapter contains

Learning objectives

On completion of this chapter you will have learned about:

- Basic law relating to contract law, sale of goods act and document retention policies

1 INTRODUCTION: CONTRACT LAW

ASSESSMENT ALERT

Contract law is not likely to come up in an assessment. It is more likely that you will need to show an understanding of business law within your portfolio.

1.1 Business organisations can be involved in many different types of activity. However, all organisations do business by entering into **transactions** with individuals and with other organisations.

- Transactions for the buying and selling of materials and goods
- For the provision of services
- For securing labour
- For receiving and offering payment for any or all of the above

Contract law

1.2 These transactions are conducted by **agreement** between the parties involved. Business life is full of such agreements. A standard framework is required to control the terms and fulfilment of business agreements, so that people do not:

- Promise one thing and deliver another
- 'Take the money and run'
- Take the goods and run *without* paying!

This is where the **law of contract** comes in.

KEY TERM

Contract law comprises the rules in statutes and case law governing the ways in which people contract with each other. It is *civil* law.

1.3 **Contract law** is the main area of the law relevant to this Unit. Much law is detailed and complex. You might think (quite rightly) that it is best left to lawyers. However, the law forms a general and important background to all business activity, and you need to have some grasp of:

- What particular laws are trying to achieve
- Broadly how the laws work.

Criminal and civil law

1.4 The English legal system distinguishes between two branches of the law.

(a) **Criminal law** deals with conduct which is **prohibited by law**.

- The **State** (the police and Crown Prosecution Service) is usually the **prosecution** in a criminal case, because it is the community that suffers as a result of a law being broken: murder, theft or drink-driving, say.
- The criminal is the **accused.**
- The **burden of proof** lies with the state, which must prove the accused guilty '**beyond reasonable doubt**' in order to gain a conviction.

- Penalties or **punishments** for crimes include fines and imprisonment.

(b) **Civil law** exists to **regulate disputes over the rights and obligations of persons dealing with each other**.

- The State is not involved.
- The matter lies between the **parties concerned**.
- The person bringing the complaint is the **plaintiff**; the other party is the **defendant.**
- The case can be proved on the '**balance of probability**': the plaintiff bears the **burden of proof** and must demonstrate that it is more likely than not that what he says is true.
- The action is pursued to reach a **settlement** (not a punishment), perhaps in the form of compensation, or damages.

	Criminal law	Civil law
Parties to a case	State - prosecution	Individual - plaintiff
	Individual - accused	Individual - defendant
Burden of proof	With prosecution, beyond reasonable doubt	With plaintiff, on the balance of probability
Objective	Punishment	Settlement
Examples	Murder, fraud, drink-driving	Contract, divorce

1.5 EXAMPLE: CIVIL AND CRIMINAL WRONGS

A business person is on his way to visit a client after spending an afternoon in the pub. He crashes his car and injures a pedestrian. What type of legal proceedings might ensue?

(a) The police will initiate a **prosecution** for the offence of drunken driving. This would be a **criminal action**.

(b) The pedestrian might wish to sue the business person for compensation for pain and suffering resulting from the wrong. This is a **civil action**.

1.6 The main area of civil law relevant to this Unit is **contract law**. There are special provisions for the **sale of goods** which we will discuss later, but there are also important general principles defining **what makes a valid contract**, and when such a contract can be regarded as fulfilled or 'discharged'.

2 FORMATION OF A CONTRACT

KEY TERM

A **contract** is an agreement which legally binds the parties to it.

2.1 What kinds of contract have you entered into, as an individual? If you have bought a property, you will have signed a **contract of purchase** and 'exchanged' it with the vendor. You may have a signed **contract of employment**, setting out your hours of work, your holiday entitlement and the required period of notice.

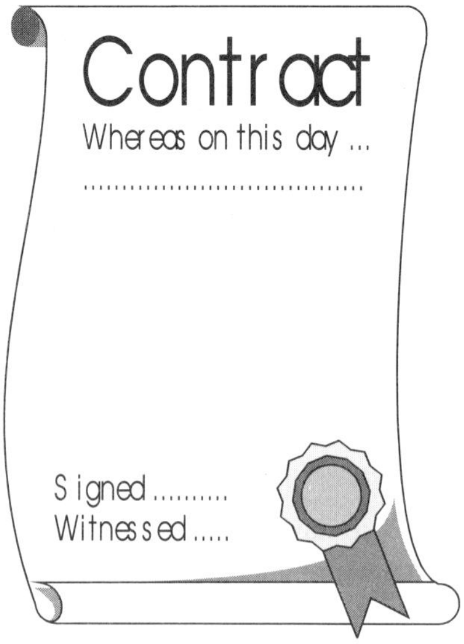

2.2 EXAMPLE: A SIMPLE CONTRACT

What happens if you buy some paperclips for your employer? You and the retailer do not draw up and sign a written contract. However, if you have paid money, you have a reasonable expectation that you will get your paperclips. If you have the paperclips, the retailer has a reasonable expectation that you will pay for them. There is a mutual agreement here: one party 'agrees' to sell, and the other to buy, the goods concerned. **This is a contract**.

2.3 It is important to note that a contract does **not** have to be in **writing**, and may not be clear-cut, explicit or specific. So **what makes a contract?**

- There must be an **intention to create legal relations**. (Both parties intend and understand the same outcome from the relationship and agreement between them.)
- There must be **offer and acceptance**.
- The obligations assumed by one party must be supported by **consideration** given by the other.

We will look at each of these elements in turn.

Intention to create legal relations

2.4 Both parties must intend and understand the agreement between them to be **legally binding**. In the majority of contracts this is not explicitly stated, so the courts apply two presumptions.

- **Social, domestic and family arrangements** are *not* usually intended to be binding.
- **Commercial agreements** are usually intended by the parties to be legally binding.

Sometimes, a commercial agreement may be worded to show that legal relations are *not* intended. In such cases, because of the presumption above, the burden of proof is on the party seeking to escape liability to show that there was no intention to enter into legal relations.

2.5 EXAMPLE: LEGAL RELATIONS

A company, negotiating over the terms for making an employee redundant, gave him the choice either of withdrawing his total contributions from their contributory pension fund or of receiving a paid-up pension. It was agreed that if he chose the first option, the company would make an *ex gratia* payment to him. He chose the first option; his contributions were refunded but the *ex gratia* payment was not made. He sued for **breach of contract**. The defendant (the company) argued that the use of the phrase *ex gratia* showed no intention to create legal relations. The court decided that this was a commercial arrangement, and the company was not able to rebut the presumption of legal relations: it had to make the payment.

Activity 11.1 **Level: Pre-assessment**

Commercial agreements are usually intended by the parties to be legally binding. True or false?

Offer and acceptance

2.6 A binding contract is formed by an initial agreement (or offer and acceptance of terms). This means that new terms cannot be introduced afterwards unless both parties agree.

The offer

KEY TERM

An **offer** made in the proper sense (with the intention that it shall become binding when accepted) forms a binding contract when accepted. The person making the offer is the offeror. The person to whom it is made is the offeree.

2.7 Case law shows that an offer must be distinguished from:

- An invitation to make an offer (an invitation to 'treat' or negotiate)
- The mere supply of information
- An advertisement

2.8 Here are some illustrations of **what does *not* constitute an offer.**

(a) **Invitation to make an offer**. A supermarket selling food is not legally making an 'offer' to you. Instead it is inviting **you** to make an 'offer' to buy the goods. (In the old days, you would bargain, so putting goods on sale is an invitation to negotiate – rather like buying a house.)

(b) **Supply of information**. For example you may receive details of goods through the post. The seller may decide not to sell you the goods: the supply of information in a catalogue, say, is not an 'offer' strictly speaking.

(c) **Advertisement**. An advertisement of goods for sale is an attempt to induce people to offer to buy the goods and is therefore classified as an invitation to make an offer.

2.9 EXAMPLE: OFFER AND ACCEPTANCE

Can you identify the offer and the acceptance in the following typical business transaction?

(a) Grant publishes an advertisement showing range of goods and prices of each item.
(b) Hurley telephones Grant in response to the advertisement.
(c) Grant sends a complete price list or quotation to Hurley.
(d) Hurley sends a completed purchase order to Selkirk.
(e) Grant supplies the goods to Hurley.
(f) Grant invoices Hurley.
(g) Hurley pays for the goods.

2.10 SOLUTION

Grant's initial **advertisement** is not an offer. Neither is his sending of a price list, since this can be described as a **supply of information**. Hurley's **purchase order** constitutes an offer. Grant's **supply of the goods** constitutes **acceptance**.

Consider what would happen if either the advertisement or the supply of information *did* constitute an offer: by sending a purchase order, Hurley would have accepted the offer and created a binding contract. However, a supplier of goods usually obtains credit references in respect of new customers. It will also wish to check the status of the account of an existing customer before despatching goods, as the customer may have exceeded its credit limit or may have failed to pay off the due balance on its account. The supplier would be unfairly penalised if it had to satisfy every purchase order it received at risk of breach of contract! This is not the commercial position which the law seeks to achieve.

The acceptance

KEY TERM

Acceptance of an offer forms a contract, provided:

- It is in response to an offer
- There is some act on the part of an offeree to signal acceptance
- It is unqualified (not a counter-offer)
- It is communicated to the offeror
- It is not subject to contract

2.11 Acceptance of an offer may be by express words. It may also be **implied** from the conduct or actions of the accepting party. There must be **some act on the part of the offeree** to indicate his acceptance. Passive inaction is not acceptance.

2.12 Acceptance must be **unqualified agreement** to the terms of the offer. Acceptance which introduces any new terms is defined at law as a **counter-offer.** This is treated as a rejection of the original offer. (If a counter-offer is made, the original offeror may accept it, but if he does not, his original offer is no longer available for acceptance.)

2.13 There are laws about the sending of **unsolicited** (un-asked-for) goods; the recipient is not bound to accept such goods.

2.14 Acceptance must be **communicated to the offeror**, and is not effective unless this has been done.

- Where acceptance by means of a letter, sent through the post, is reasonably expected by both parties, the acceptance is effective as soon as the letter (correctly addressed and stamped) is put in the post - even if it is then delayed or lost in the post. This is called the **postal rule**.
- If an offer is made over the telephone, the offeree must ensure that his acceptance is understood. If interference on the line prevents the offeror from hearing the reply, no contract is formed.
- The offeror may **call for acceptance by specified means**, but unless he states very precisely that this is the only means that will suffice, acceptance by other suitable means would constitute a valid acceptance.

2.15 Acceptance **subject to contract** is neither acceptance, rejection nor a request for information. It means that the offeree is agreeable to the terms of the offer but that the parties should negotiate a formal (usually written) contract on the basis of the offer. Neither party is bound until the formal contract is signed.

KEY TERM

The **postal rule** states that, where both parties expect that the post may be used, the acceptance is complete and effective as soon as a letter (if it is correctly addressed and stamped and actually put in the post) is posted.

Termination of offer

2.16 An offer might be terminated by:

- **Rejection**, either outright or by the making of a counter-offer
- **Expiring after a specified time** set in the offer
- **Expiring after a reasonable time** if there is no express time limit set. What is reasonable depends on the circumstances of the case, on what is usual and to be expected.
- The offeror **revoking (withdrawing) the offer at any time before acceptance and actually communicating revocation to the offeree**, unless he has bound himself under a separate contract (or option agreement) to keep the offer open for the whole of a specified time.

  The offer may be revoked by an **express statement**, or by some **action** by the offeror indicating that he no longer regards the offer as in force. (*Note:* there is no postal rule here). The **communication of the revocation takes effect only when it is received**.

Activity 11.2 — Level: Assessment

As accountants assistant, it is your responsibility to dispose of any motor vehicles which are surplus to the company's requirements. You place an advertisement in the local paper asking a price of £4,000 for a car. Jenson telephones you saying he will buy the car for £3,000. You say that you would accept £3,500 and he tells you he will need to think about it but would like to have a test drive at the weekend. Then you receive a call from Eddie and agree to sell him the car for £3,300. When Jenson rings back to arrange the test drive he is furious to hear that the car has been sold and threatens you with an action for breach of contract.

(a) Was there at any point a valid contract between Jenson and you? Yes/No
(b) Explain briefly the reason for your answer.

Activity 11.3 — Level: Assessment

You advertise a consignment of goods for sale at the standard price of £600 per batch. Ajax telephones you and you offer to sell him the goods at £550 per batch. He says he will pay £480 but you refuse to reduce your price. The following day you receive an order by post from Ajax for five batches at £550 each.

(a) Has a valid contract been formed? Yes/No
(b) Explain briefly the reason for your answer.

Activity 11.4 — Level: Assessment

You are assistant to the chief accountant at Bold & Co. Vim, the site administration manager, rings you to say that he has received a telex directory with a note which says that unless it is returned within fourteen days it will be assumed that the recipient has bought it for £49.95.

(a) Does a valid contract exist? Yes/No
(b) Explain briefly the reason for your answer.

Consideration

2.17 The third essential element for a binding contract is **consideration**. In distinguishing the characteristics of a contract, the law looks for an **element of bargain**. To be binding or contractual, a promise cannot be 'free': something must be given in exchange.

Someone telephones you and tells you that, as a special promotion, he will clean your car free of charge on the following day. If he then fails to turn up, you cannot sue him for breach of contract. There is **no contract**. You have not provided any consideration.

There is one exception to this rule. A promise for free is binding if it is made by **deed**. An example is an annual payment to a charity, made by **deed of covenant**.

KEY TERM

Consideration is what the promisee (the person who seeks to enforce the promise) must give in exchange for the promisor's promise to him. Consideration may consist of an act or another promise to do something in return.

Activity 11.5 — Level: Assessment

Harry of Super Sounds Ltd has recently sent out a quotation to Sally at The Music Store offering to sell her 20 CD players for £85 each plus VAT. In reply she sends him a fax saying that The Music Store would like to accept the offer provided that the units can be delivered by Saturday.

(a) At this stage, does a valid contract exist between the two companies? Yes/No

(b) Briefly explain the reason for your answer.

Activity 11.6 — Level: Assessment

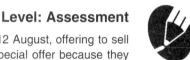

Super Sounds Ltd has placed a display advertisement in a hi-fi magazine for a new line of car CD players. The price stated in the magazine is £29.99 for each CD player, but an error has been made by the printer and the price should have been £129.99. Harry of Super Sounds Ltd receives a phone call from Billy who wants to place an order for 30 CD players. Chris tells him of the mistake but Billy insists that the company must honour its offer and supply them at £29.99 each.

(a) Does Super Sounds Ltd have to supply the CD players at £29.99 each? Yes/No

(b) Explain briefly the reason for your answer

Activity 11.7 — Level: Assessment

Suzy of Security Ltd telephones Jeanne of Home Designs Ltd on 12 August, offering to sell her 30 burglar alarm systems which are being disposed of as a special offer because they are surplus stock. Jeanne, on being told that the offer is open for ten days, expresses interest and so Suzy faxes full details, including price and contract terms, on 13 August. On 14 August Jeanne faxes back saying she is 'definitely interested' and will reply by post within a week. She posts an acceptance of the offer on 16 August and Suzy receives this on 19 August. The alarm systems are despatched on 21 August, invoiced on 23 August and delivered on 24 August. Home Designs Ltd pays by credit transfer on 2 September.

(a) On what date was a contract for the sale of the burglar alarm systems formed between Security Ltd and Home Designs Ltd?

(b) Briefly explain the reason for your answer.

Activity 11.8 — Level: Assessment

Security Ltd receives an enquiry from Great Fires Ltd to purchase 230 smoke alarms. A quotation is sent out offering to supply these for £2.20 each. Two days later, Suzy of Security Ltd realises that a mistake has been made and that the quoted price should have been £3.20 each. She writes to Great Fires Ltd telling them of the mistake and saying that the smoke alarms cannot be supplied as per the quotation. The following day, Julius telephones from Great Fires Ltd, thanks her for her letter and tells her that he wants to accept the offer contained in the original quotation. He insists that Security Ltd must honour the contractual price of £2.20.

(a) Does a valid contract exist between Security Ltd and Great Fires Ltd? Yes/No

(b) Explain briefly the reason for your answer.

Activity 11.9 — Level: Assessment

Wang sees an advertisement placed by his local electrical retailer in his local paper for a multimedia PC for £1,025 including VAT. He immediately rushes along to the shop to buy one. One of the store assistants tells him that they are out of stock but that they can supply one at the advertised price on the next day: Henry agrees and signs an order form.

(a) Does a valid contract exist between Henry and the retailer? Yes/No

(b) Explain briefly the reason for your answer.

3 CONTRACTS FOR THE SALE OF GOODS

3.1 An important area of contract law is the law concerning the **sale of goods**. The main statute on this is the Sale of Goods Act 1979, the terms of which have been extended to cover contracts where the **supply of services** is the major part of the contract; for example, contracts of repair, where the supply of goods may be incidental to the provision of a service.

KEY TERM

A **contract for the sale of goods** is defined in the Act as 'a contract by which the seller transfers, or agrees to transfer, the property in goods to a buyer for a money consideration, called the price'. This includes immediate sales and agreements by which the seller is to transfer ownership at a future date. Note that it covers *sellers* and *buyers* - a retailer cannot avoid the provisions of the 1979 Act by claiming that any breaches of its terms are the fault of the maker of the goods or other person who supplied the retailer.

3.2 There must be a **money consideration**, or **price**. A situation in which goods are exchanged for other goods does not give rise to a 'sale of goods'. Provided that *some* money changes hands - as with a trade-in arrangement for a car - there is a contract for the sale of goods.

3.3 Imagine that you are about to enter into a contract for the purchase of some goods. What might you be concerned about?

- If you wanted the goods for a particular occasion or **date**, you would want to be sure they would be available to you by then.
- You would be interested to know whether the goods are stolen, ie whether the seller has a **right to sell the goods**.
- If you had been sent a **description or sample** of the goods, you would expect the goods to be the same type and quality as the description or sample.
- You would want the goods to be of **reasonable quality** and **suitable for their purpose**.

3.4 The Sale of Goods Act covers these matters and a number of other important issues. Its provisions are regarded as **implied terms** of most contracts for the sale of goods: they apply, whether stated or not, and under the Unfair Contract Terms Act 1977 **cannot be excluded from any contract involving a consumer**. They can only be excluded from non-consumer contracts to the extent that it is reasonable to do so.

3.5 We will look at some of the key statutory rules that apply, as implied terms, to all contracts for the sale of goods.

ASSESSMENT ALERT

The provisions of the Sale of Goods Act are a potential source of questions in the Devolved Assessment. Make sure you understand the basic principles discussed in this section.

Implied terms

3.6 A sale of goods is subject to the following provisions of the Sale of Goods Act.

- The effect of delay in performance (s 10)
- Title, or the seller's right to sell the goods (s 12)
- Description of the goods (s 13)
- Quality of the goods (s 14(2))
- Fitness of the goods for the purpose for which they are supplied (s 14(3))
- Sale by sample (s 15)

Time of performance

3.7 If goods arrive too late, they may be useless. The terms of the contract will determine whether a particular timescale is a condition of performance: if it is, a breach of such terms entitles the injured party to treat the contract as discharged. In commercial contracts for the supply of goods for business or industrial use, it will be assumed that **time is of the essence**, even where there is no express term to that effect.

Seller's title

3.8 You cannot sell something that is not yours to sell. It is an implied condition that the seller has a **right to sell the goods**, or will have, at the time when ownership of the goods is to be transferred. If the seller delivers goods to the buyer without having the right to sell, the buyer does not obtain the ownership of the goods which is the essential basis of the contract. If the buyer subsequently has to give up the goods to the real owner, he may recover the entire price from the seller.

3.9 EXAMPLE: SELLER'S TITLE

R bought a car from D which D had unknowingly bought from a thief. When this was discovered, the car was returned to the true owner, and R sued D for the return of the full purchase price (as damages). The court decided that, although R had used the car for several months, he had not had ownership of it, which is what he had paid for. D therefore had to repay the full amount.

Goods to correspond with contract description

3.10 If you have agreed to buy goods that have been described to you, you expect the goods to correspond to the description. (Similarly, if a seller has agreed to supply goods on the basis of your description of your requirements, you expect the goods to correspond to your description.) This is implied, under the Act, in any contract for sale of goods 'by description'. The description may be of ingredients, components, age, date of shipment, packing, quantity etc.

3.11 EXAMPLE: SALE BY DESCRIPTION

A seller advertised a second-hand reaping machine, describing it as new the previous year. The buyer bought it without seeing it. When it arrived he found that it was much more than a year old and rejected it. The seller sued for the price but it was held that this was a sale by description, the goods had not corresponded to the description, and the buyer was therefore entitled to reject the goods.

3.12 The provisions of the Trade Descriptions Act 1968 may also be relevant if the seller uses a **false description**: this is a *criminal* offence.

Satisfactory quality

3.13 All goods supplied under a contract for the sale of goods **in the course of a business** must be of '**satisfactory quality**': that is, they should meet the standard that a reasonable person would regard as satisfactory, taking account of any description of the goods, the price and other relevant circumstances. The condition of satisfactory quality was introduced by the **Sale and Supply of Goods Act 1994**. Under the 1979 Sale of Goods Act, there was a corresponding condition of 'merchantable quality'. Its replacement by the term 'satisfactory' was designed to extend the law to cover more minor (though genuine) defects which cause consumer dissatisfaction.

3.14 Some of the attributes to be taken into account in deciding whether or not goods are of satisfactory quality are as follows.

(a) **Fitness for all the purposes for which goods of the kind in question are commonly supplied.** A hot water bottle that deteriorated when filled with hot water, for example, would not be of satisfactory quality. This is a clear-cut example, because the goods are only used for *one* purpose - and failed in that.

Where goods are multi-purpose, they must be suitable for *all* purposes for which people usually buy them, and for which they could reasonable be expected to be used. A bucket, for example, would be needed to hold a variety of substances, and be handled in a variety of ways, without leakage, damage, immediate deterioration and so on.

(b) **Appearance and finish**. Previous to 1994 goods with superficial damage, but which operated properly in the main, could be of merchantable quality: satisfactory quality includes freedom from dents, marks, scratches and so on - unless they have clearly been allowed for in the description and price of the goods.

(c) **Freedom from minor defects**.

(d) **Safety**.

(e) **Durability**. Under the old law, it was generally accepted that goods had to be of merchantable quality only at the time of sale, but they now have to remain of satisfactory quality for a period which could be expected by a reasonable person.

Activity 11.10 **Level: Assessment**

Peter buys an electronic keyboard from his local catalogue store. He pays £199 for it. He returns to the store the next day complaining that, although the main keys work, none of the pre-set rhythm buttons seem to function. He demands an immediate refund. The sales assistant refuses to given him a refund or take back the goods, and instead gives him a card with the name and address of the manufacturer, suggesting that Peter contacts them to obtain a refund or a replacement.

(a) Was the sales assistant legally justified in refusing to give a refund? Yes/No

(b) Give briefly a reason for your answer.

Fitness of goods for a disclosed purpose

3.15 If you tell a seller (explicitly or by implication) that you intend to use goods for a particular purpose, whether or not it is the 'usual' purpose of such goods (as in paragraph 3.14(a) above), you expect the goods supplied to be reasonably fit for that purpose. This is an implied term, under the Act, unless it can be shown that:

(a) The buyer did not rely
(b) It was unreasonable for him to rely

On the skill or judgement of the seller in stating whether or not the goods were fit for the buyer's disclosed purpose. (In other words, the seller may not have known whether the goods were suitable for a purpose which was not familiar to him and the buyer may have been in a better position to tell.)

Like 'satisfactory quality', this condition only applies to goods sold **in the course of a business**.

Sale by sample

3.16 If you have agreed to buy goods on the basis of inspecting a sample of the goods, you have the implied right to expect that:

(a) The bulk of the delivery will be of the **same quality** as the sample

(b) You will have a reasonable opportunity to **compare** the bulk of the delivery with the sample

(c) The bulk of the goods contain no defects (rendering their quality unsatisfactory) which would not be noticeable from reasonable **inspection** of the sample.

3.17 EXAMPLE: SALE BY SAMPLE

A child buys a catapult. Because of its faulty construction, it breaks, causing him to lose an eye. He successfully sues the shopkeeper, under the Act, for failure to supply goods which are of satisfactory quality and fit for the purpose for which they were supplied. The shopkeeper had bought the catapults by relying on a sample, which he had tested by pulling on the elastic. He sues the wholesaler for breach of the implied terms related to sale by sample under the Act. The court would find that the shopkeeper made a reasonable examination, which did not reveal the defect: the wholesaler would be liable to the shopkeeper.

Passing of property and risk

3.18 Sections 10-15 of the Act, described above, deal with the goods themselves. Another important issue in any transaction for the sale of goods is determining **the point at which property (ownership) passes** from one person to another.

This is important because the **risk (and cost) of accidental damage or loss is, as a general rule, borne by the owner of goods**.

> **KEY TERMS**
>
> - **Specific goods** are goods which have been identified and agreed upon at the time that the contract of sale is made: for example, 'this Ford Mondeo, registration number N123 AAT'.
> - **Unascertained goods** are goods which are not specified, for example, 'a red Citroen Xantia', 'six reels of newsprint' or '2 tonnes of winter barley'. When such goods are positively identified, they become **ascertained goods.**

3.19 The key rules (set out in ss 16-18 of the Act) are as follows.

(a) **Property (or ownership) cannot pass from one party to another in relation to goods which are unascertained** and not yet specifically identified as the goods to be sold under the contract (s 16).

(b) The property in specific or ascertained goods is **transferred to the buyer at the time when the parties *intend* it to be transferred**. Their intention may be deduced from the terms of the contract, the conduct of the parties and the circumstances of the case (s 17).

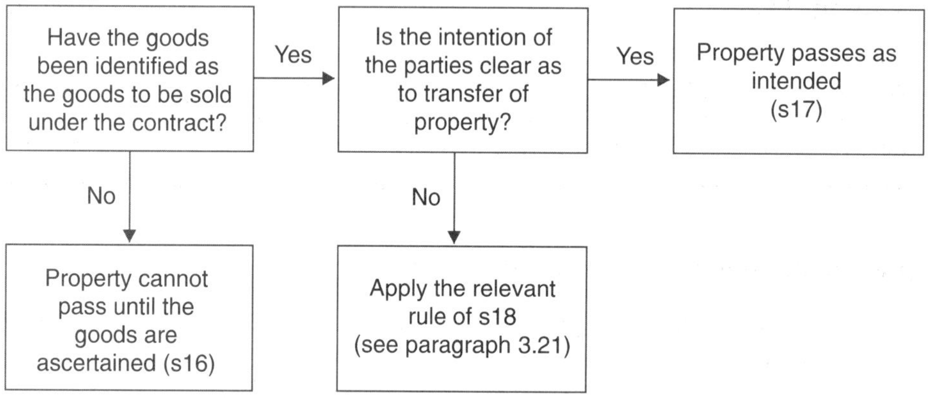

3.20 Note that **property** is not the same as **possession**. Despite the old adage 'possession is nine-tenths of the law', property (ownership) passes when the parties *intend* it to pass - not necessarily when possession of the goods change hands.

(a) A buyer may gain ownership of goods (property), while the seller retains possession of them: prior to delivery, for example.

(b) A buyer may gain possession of goods (by delivery), while the seller retains property in them: for example, under a contract stating that the seller retains title/ownership until the buyer has settled all debts due to him. (Terms like these are designed to protect the seller in case the buyer goes bankrupt and is unable to pay in full: the seller will still have the goods, provided he can regain possession of them of course.)

Such clauses are known as **retention of title** or **Romalpa** clauses (after an important 1976 case in this area). You may well find similar terms printed on the back of invoices which you process in your everyday work.

3.21 If the intention of the parties is not clear as to the transfer of property, **the rules of section 18 are applied to ascertain the point of transfer**. As brief examples of the detailed provisions:

(a) **Rule 2** states that where there is a contract for the sale of specific goods, and the seller has to do something to the goods in order to get them into a **deliverable state**, the property does not pass until that thing is done *and* the buyer has notice that it has been done. (Imagine that your company has entered into a contract for the purchase of a new machine, to which certain safety hoods and noise-reduction baffles are to be fitted prior to delivery. Before the suppliers can do this work, the machine is destroyed by a fire at their warehouse; they still demand payment from you, since you had effectively purchased the machine. Relying on rule 2, you could claim that the goods had not reached a deliverable state, and that property had therefore not yet passed.)

(b) **Rule 3** states that where there is a contract for the sale of specific goods in a deliverable state *and* the seller is bound to **weigh, measure or test them to fix the price**, property passes when he has done so and the buyer has notice of it. (The rule does not apply when it is the *buyer* who must take this action.)

Activity 11.11 **Level: Assessment**

Your company has entered into a contract for the purchase of some envelopes. Under the contract the envelopes are to be stamped with the company logo by the supplier. Before the supplier can do this work, the envelopes are damaged in a flood at the supplier's warehouse; he brings an action for the price against you. What is your legal position?

Acceptance and rejection of goods or services

3.22 The third important area in sale of goods contracts is **acceptance and rejection**. Once you have 'accepted' goods, it is (in general) too late to claim a breach of contract if you find that the seller has breached an implied condition (such as satisfactory quality). A buyer is deemed to have accepted goods if :

- He informs the seller that he accepts them
- He acts in a way that is inconsistent with the seller's continuing ownership, for example by re-selling the goods to a third party
- After the lapse of a reasonable time, the buyer retains the goods without informing the seller that he has rejected them

3.23 Obviously, you want to discover any defects or breaches of conditions **before** you do or say anything that implies acceptance (like signing for a delivery)! Under the Act, the **buyer must be given a reasonable opportunity to examine the goods on delivery**, before accepting them.

3.24 EXAMPLE: ACCEPTANCE OF GOODS

A company buys goods from a manufacturer and resells them to a customer, with delivery direct from manufacturer to customer. The customer complains that the goods are defective. In these circumstances, the company would be permitted to reject the goods - despite the resale - because it had not been given the opportunity, as buyer, to inspect them.

Remedies for non-payment

3.25 If a buyer wrongfully neglects, or refuses, to pay for goods, the seller may pursue one of a number of remedies, depending on the circumstances. Remedies fall into two categories:

(a) **Remedies against the buyer**. The seller has a right to sue the buyer for the **price** of the goods. (This is the '**action for the price**' described earlier.) This can be pursued if property in the goods has passed to the buyer. (If it has not, the appropriate remedy is an action in **damages**.);

(b) **Remedies 'against the goods'**, or 'real remedies'.

- (i) **Lien** is the right to retain physical possession of the goods. The seller may refuse to hand the goods over to the buyer until the buyer pays for them.
- (ii) **Stoppage in transit** is the right to recover the goods from an independent carrier to whom they have been entrusted, and to hold them until the buyer pays for them.
- (iii) **Right of resale** is the right, under certain circumstances (for example, where the goods are perishable), to sell the goods to a third party.

Activity 11.12 **Level: Assessment**

A customer fails to pay for goods which he ordered from you and which you have supplied. What remedy for breach of contract are you most likely to pursue?

---

4 RETAINING FILES

Preparing documents for filing

4.1 When documents containing information have been received, acknowledged, acted upon or have otherwise fulfilled their immediate purpose, they are ready to be added to the storage system.

4.2 The following procedures might be followed when adding new information to the organisation's storage system.

(a) The document containing the information is **indicated as being ready for filing** - perhaps initialled by the recipient or supervisor. This is a signal to the filing clerk that it is OK to go ahead and file it.

(b) **Paper clips and binders are removed** leaving flat sheets for filing, and punched holes appropriate to the storage method are created so that documents can be inserted.

(c) Documents are placed at **random in a filing tray**, or kept in rough order in a **concertina file**.

(d) If the document is an internally generated one it may have a **file reference** on it already (this will often be what the numbers and letters following 'Our reference ....' mean at the head of letters your receive). If not, a **reference number** will have to be determined.

(e) The **reference number**, or **name** or **subject** of the file into which the document is to be inserted should be shown on the document.

(f) Batches of documents can then be **sorted** (by each name, subject and so on) and put into the appropriate filing sequence (chronological, numerical or whatever).

(g) Documents are **inserted in the appropriate place** in appropriate files. This process should be carried out daily at a set time, to avoid pile-ups and disorganisation.

Opening a new file

4.3 If there is no file existing for a document a **new file** will be opened. This will involve the following.

(a) In a centralised filing system, a **request** and **authorisation** for a new file to be opened. This is to check for duplication or misnaming of files.

(b) **Appropriate housing** for the document - a **folder** or **binder**, noting size, colour and so on as necessary. An extra pocket may have to be inserted in sequence for suspended files.

(c) **Identification**. This will mean writing the number or name on files or suspension pockets or on a suitable tag or label. Colour coding may also be used.

(d) **Adding** the new file name/number to the index, file list, and cross-referencing system.

4.4 The procedure will be much the same as when a file cannot hold any more documents, and a **continuation file** is needed. Simply mark the cover of the original file 'Volume 1' and add the range of dates its subject matter covers. Then open a new file marked 'Volume 2'.

Activity 11.13 — Level: Pre-assessment

What matters should you take account of when you are considering opening a new file for some documents in your possession?

Activity 11.14 — Level: Assessment

The following is an extract from your organisation's permanent file on customer number 476/23/3.

Company:	Folworth Ltd
Address:	47 Bracewell Gardens London EC2
Directors:	Robin Folworth Margaret Foster Laurence Oldfield
Purchasing manager:	John Thornhill

You have just had a letter from this company which is shown on the next page.

Your task is to update the permanent file as necessary.

FOLWORTH (Business Services) Ltd

Crichton Buildings
97 Lower Larkin Street London EC4A 8QT

GETTING THINGS DONE

D. Ashford
Sales Department
Bosley Products Ltd
Ducannon House
4-6 West Brook Road
LONDON W12 7LY

8 August 20X6

Dear Mr Ashford

Account No. 476/23/3

I should be grateful for a reply to my letter of 30 July regarding the above account.

Yours sincerely

D Simmonds

D. Simmonds
Purchasing Manager

Folworth (Business Services) Ltd, Registered Office:
Crichton Buildings, 97 Lower Larkin Street, London, EC4A 8QT

Registered in England, number 9987654

Directors:
R. Folworth, BA ACA; J. Crichton; M. Foster; L. Oldfield MA; T. Scott; J. Thornhill BSc

---

Retaining information

4.5 When information contained within files is no longer needed on a daily basis, it is not automatically thrown away (as you may be forgiven for thinking). It is generally dealt with in one of the following ways.

(a) **Microfilmed or microfiched** for long-term storage.

(b) Retained in its original form and stored elsewhere (this is generally known as **archiving**) for a certain period of time.

(c) **Securely destroyed**.

4.6 Imagine how distressed you would be if you needed to refer to a legal document that had been filed some years ago, and you found out that it had been thrown away by a filing clerk during the latest office spring-clean! (Alternatively, imagine trying to find an urgently needed current file, with *all* the paperwork of the organisation's history still in the active filing system!)

4.7 In order to streamline the system, information which is no longer current, but which may need to be referred to at some point in the future, should be given a revised **status**: no longer active, but semi-active; no longer semi-active, but non-active - in which case, a prime candidate for the **archive**!

KEY TERM

A **retention policy** is the amounts of time decided on for the holding of various types of information.

4.8 **Retention periods** vary. Documents concerned with the legal establishment of the organisation will have to be kept permanently, as will the annual accounts. Simple legal contracts will have to be kept for six years, and more important sealed ones for twelve. Other documents may be kept at the organisation's discretion but the principle overall is: if you think you might need it, for as long as you might need it - keep it!

Some recommended retention periods you might find interesting include the following.

Document	**Years**
Agreements	12
Balance sheets	30
Bank statements	6
Cheque counterfoils	1
Correspondence files	6
Credit notes	6
Customs and Excise VAT records	6
Delivery notes	1
Directors' reports	30
Expense claims	1
Insurance claims forms	6
Leases, expired	12
Licences for patents	30
Medical certificates	1
Patents, expired	12
Paying-in books	1
Powers of attorney	30
Prospectuses	30
Purchase orders	6
Quotations, out	6
Royalty ledgers	30
Sales invoices	6
Share applications	12
Specifications, product	6
Tax records	6

4.9 Try to find out what your organisation's policy is for the retention of documentation.

Archiving information

4.10 Even non-active files may need to be kept so that information can be retrieved from them when required. In most organisations, office space is scarce, and filing space is limited. Information that needs to be retained is therefore often stored away in boxes in storage spaces such as storehouses, spare cupboards and inaccessible places. Such storage of files is known as **archiving.**

Activity 11.15 — Level: Assessment

Dribble Ltd, a very small company, file their correspondence as follows.

(a) All incoming mail is placed on a 'current' file initially. It is usually actioned within a week after which the correspondence is filed permanently.

(b) Business customers each have their own separate correspondence file.

(c) Correspondence with domestic customers is placed on a single file; only one file has been needed per year since the business started in 1944.

(d) Letters relevant to the latest year's accounts are filed in a file entitled 'Auditors'.

(e) There is also an extremely thick file entitled 'Miscellaneous 1959 -'.

This is the theory, and Derek Dribble, who founded the business, was an enthusiastic filer. His son, Dominic, however, sees himself as a dynamic entrepreneur and cannot be bothered with it. The current file has not been reviewed for several years and presently includes the following documents.

1 Letter from Miskimin Ltd dated 9.9.04 returning goods.

2 Undated letter from Jacksnares School concerning jumble sale.

3 Letter from London Borough of Greenwich dated 31.12.05 concerning Business Rates.

4 Letter dated 21.7.98 from Dribble Ltd to Mr T N Clipper requesting payment in advance. This has 'Pending - 28.7.98' written across it in red ink.

5 Letter dated 4.3.06 from A J Butterworth Esq requesting '2 × green spats (pair), 1 × red spats (pair)'.

6 Letter from Landlord notifying rent increase as from 1.9.02

7 Letter dated 26.5.96 from Hardman and Free Shoes Ltd ordering '20 pairs spats'.

8 Memo to 'all staff including secretaries' concerning the staff Christmas lunch. This is dated 3.12.03.

9 Letter from Jacksnares School dated 7.5.06 thanking Dribble Ltd for their 'generous donation but unfortunately returning goods unsold'.

10 Letter from Dudley Theatre Company dated 14.4.06 ordering '7 pairs of spats in white'.

11 Letter dated 14.2.06 from Major John Cummings asking for a brochure.

12 Letter dated 14.3.06 from Major John Cummings ordering '1 pair in a conservative colour'.

13 Letter from Miskimin Ltd dated 24.8.04 ordering '2 dozen pairs in white'.

14 Letter from Mr Howard P Wisebacker dated 17.2.00 congratulating Dribble Ltd on 'keeping up a fine old tradition'.

15 Letter dated 17.11.05 from Period Costumiers Ltd ordering '50 pairs, 10 in each colour'.

16 Letter from London Borough of Greenwich notifying dates of refuse collection as from 3.12.05.

17 Letter from Period Costumiers Ltd dated 12.1.06 ordering '50 pairs, 10 in each colour'.

18 Letter dated 15.3.06 from Mrs A J Butterworth returning goods.

19 Letter regarding insurance claim dated 19.4.99.

20 Memo to 'all staff' about summer outing in July 2006.

Task

It is November 2006. Which of these documents would you remove from the current file and where would you place them?

Do you have any suggestions for improving the system?

Deleting or destroying information

4.11 Once information becomes **out-of-date,** it may be **deleted or destroyed**. Be aware that screwing up a piece of paper and throwing it in the bin is not destroying it. Even if information (particularly financial information) is out-of-date it may still be damaging if it falls into the wrong hands. Waste paper bins are the first place that the wrong eyes will look!

Many organisations have **shredding devices** for such documents, or a system of disposal which involves **special confidential waste bags**. Find out what your organisation's system is and be sure to use it.

Key learning points

- The English legal system recognises a distinction between **criminal law** and **civil law**, each of which has different objectives.
- A **contract** is an agreement which legally binds the parties to it. The essential elements of a contract are that there is an **intention to create legal relations** and that it is an agreement made by **offer and acceptance** in which the obligations assumed by each party are supported by **consideration**.
- The most important single topic in the law of **contracts for the sale of goods** is the protection given to a buyer of goods by the conditions implied by ss 12-15 of the Sale of Goods Act 1979. These are designed to ensure that a buyer can obtain goods which are of **satisfactory quality** and **in accordance with his requirements**. The second key area is the question of **when property passes** and so of who bears the loss if goods are damaged or destroyed while the transaction is in progress.
- There is in practice an overlap between the basic law of contract and the law relating to sale of goods. This is to be expected, as the sale of goods is really a particular, and common, kind of contract. **Basic contract law** is therefore of as much importance as statutory rules in any sale of goods.
- **Adding new information** to an information storage system involves the following.
  - Indicating that the information is ready for filing
  - Removing any paperclips or binders
  - Placing information in a filing tray or concertina file
  - Allocating a reference number if there is not already a file reference
  - Sorting batches of documents containing information
  - Inserting the documents into the appropriate place in appropriate files

- Information is usually **destroyed** by using shredding devices or by placing in confidential wastebags.
- In general, when information is no longer needed on a daily basis, it is retained in its original form and stored elsewhere; this is known as **archiving**.
- A **retention policy** is the amount of time decided on by an organisation for the holding of various types of information.
- Material containing information **must be kept in good condition** and stored in an appropriate location.

Quick quiz

1. What are the three essential elements which make a contract?
2. When is an offer taken to have been accepted in such a way as to create a binding contract?
3. List the aspects of goods subject to implied conditions, under sections 10-15 of the Sale of Goods Act.
4. What are the criteria for defining goods as being of 'satisfactory quality' under the Sale and Supply of Goods Act 1994?
5. Under section 17 of the Sale of Goods Act, when is property in ascertained goods transferred to the buyer?
6. What remedies (a) against the buyer and (b) against the goods does a seller have when the buyer refuses to pay for the goods?
7. How is information that is no longer needed on a regular basis dealt with?

Answers to quick quiz

1. In order to create a contract:

   (a) There must be an intention to create legal relations

   (b) There must be offer and acceptance

   (c) The obligations assumed by one party must be supported by consideration given in exchange by the other.

2. An offer is taken to have been accepted when there is some expression or act on the part of the offeree, indicating unqualified agreement to the terms of the offer, which is communicated to the offeror by any suitable means. (Under the postal rule, acceptance dates from the time of posting of an acceptance by means of a correctly stamped and addressed letter, where this is recognised by both parties as a reasonable means of reply.)

3. A sale of goods may be subject to conditions with regard to:

   (a) The time of (or effect of delay in) performance
   (b) Title, or the seller's right to sell the goods
   (c) Description of the goods
   (d) Satisfactory quality of the goods
   (e) Fitness of the goods for a particular (disclosed) purpose
   (f) Sale by sample

4. Goods of 'satisfactory quality' must be:

   (a) Fit for all purposes for which they are commonly supplied
   (b) Adequate in appearance and finish
   (c) Free of minor defects
   (d) Safe
   (e) Durable

   With reasonable regard to description, price and other relevant circumstances.

5 Property in ascertained (identified) goods is transferred at the time when the parties intend (as deduced from the terms of the contract) that it be transferred.

6 Remedies against the buyer: action for the price, action in damages. Remedies against the goods: lien, stoppage in transit, right of resale.

7
- Microfilmed or microfiched
- Archived
- Destroyed

Answers to Activities

Answers to Chapter 1 activities

Answer 1.1

An **enterprise** is the most general term, referring to just about any organisation in which people join together to achieve a common end. In the context of accounting it can refer to a multinational conglomerate, a small club, a local authority and so on.

A **business** is also a general term, but it does not extend as widely as the term 'enterprise': for example, it would not include a charity or a local authority. But any organisation existing to trade and make a profit could be called a business.

A **company** is an enterprise constituted in a particular legal form, usually involving limited liability for its members. Companies need not be businesses; for example, many charities are constituted as companies.

A **firm** is a much vaguer term. It is sometimes used loosely in the sense of a business or a company. Some writers, more usefully, try to restrict its meaning to that of an unincorporated business (ie a business not constituted as a company, for example a partnership).

Answer 1.2

The missing words are:

separate; owners; all; company; owners; limited.

Answer 1.3

Transaction	*Assets*	=	*Capital*	+	*Liabilities*
(a)			Increase		Decrease
(b)	Decrease				Decrease
(c)			Decrease		Increase
(d)	Decrease		Decrease		
(e)	Increase		Increase		
(f)	Increase				Increase

Answer 1.4

We have assets of £2,500 (cash), balanced by liabilities of £2,500 (the amounts owed by the business to Liza and Phil).

- The £1,750 owed to Liza clearly falls into the special category of liability labelled **capital**, because it is a sum owed to the proprietor of the business.
- To classify the £750 owed to Phil, we would need to know more about the **terms of his agreement** with Liza.
- If they have effectively gone into **partnership**, sharing the risks and rewards of the business, then Phil is a proprietor too and the £750 is 'capital' in the sense that Liza's £1,750 is.
- If Phil has no share in the profits of the business, and can expect only a repayment of his 'loan' plus some interest, the amount of £750 should be classified under **liabilities**.

Answer 1.5

(a) Assets (cash) increase by £5,000; liabilities (amount owed to the bank) increase by £5,000

(b) Assets (cash) decrease by £800; assets (stock) increase by £800

(c) Assets (cash) decrease by £50; capital decreases by £50 (the proprietor has taken £50 drawings for her personal use; in effect, the business has repaid her part of the amount it owed)

(d) Assets (cash) increase by £440; assets (stock) decrease by £300; capital (the profit earned for the proprietor) increases by £140.

(e) Assets (cash) decrease by £5,270; liabilities (the bank loan) decrease by £5,000; capital decreases by £270 (the proprietor has made a 'loss' of £270 on the transaction).

Answers to Chapter 2 activities

Answer 2.1

(a) A **steel manufacturer** would have a high proportion of its asset values locked up in fixed assets (factory premises, heavy machinery). It might also hold large stocks of raw materials and finished goods, and the value of debtors might be significant too.

(b) A **bank's** main asset is its debtors, namely the people to whom it lends money by way of loan or overdraft. Curiously enough, cash holdings may be much smaller than debtor balances, because banks aim to *use* cash (ie lend it or invest it) rather than merely sitting on it. In the case of a bank with a large number of branches, land and buildings will also be a significant item, but still not as great as debtors.

Answer 2.2

Asset	**Business**	**Current or fixed**
Van	Delivery firm	Fixed
Machine	Manufacturer	Fixed
Car	Car trader	Current

Answer 2.3

(a) Fixed asset
(b) Current asset
(c) Current liability
(d) Current asset
(e) Fixed asset
(f) Current liability

Note that the same type of item can be categorised differently according to how it is used and the business which owns it.

Answer 2.4

Assets	=	*Capital*	+	*Liabilities*
£(85,500 + 15,800)	=	£94,700	+	£6,600
£101,300	=	£101,300		

Answer 2.5

You may have said three of the following.

- Salaries of managers and office staff
- Rent and rates of offices
- Insurance
- Telephone and postage
- Printing and stationery
- Heating and lighting of offices
- Advertising

Answer 2.6

If you succeeded in filling in all the figures then well done! If you struggled, work through this answer *very* carefully to see where you went wrong.

Step 1 *Cash*

	£
Borrowed from bank 1 June 20X7	2,000
(a) Interest charges (3 × £25)	(75)
(b) Van hire	(1,000)
Van running expenses (3 × £300)	(900)
(c) Part-time helper (3 × £100)	(300)
(e) Cash sales	8,900
Credit sales (all paid)	1,100
(f) Purchase of ice cream (6,200 – 700)	(5,500)
(g) Telephone and postage	(150)
(h) Drawings (3 × £300)	(900)
Balance in hand at 31 August 20X7	3,175

Step 2 *Accounting equation at 1 June 20X7*

Assets	£	=	*Capital*	£	+	*Liabilities*	£
Cash	2,000			0		Bank loan	2,000

Accounting equation at 31 August 20X7

Assets	£	*Capital*	£	*Liabilities*	£
Cash	3,175	Profit	1,375	Bank loan	2,000
		Drawings	(900)	Melted Ltd	700
	3,175		475		2,700

Step 3 *Business equation (to check retained profit figure)*

P = I + D – C

P = £475* + £900 – £0

= £1,375

* Increase in net assets = Net assets at 31 August less net assets at 1 June £(3,175 – 2,700) – £(2,000 – 2,000)

= £475

Step 4 MR WHIPPY
BALANCE SHEET AS AT 31 AUGUST 20X7

	£	£
Current assets		
Cash	3,175	
Current liabilities		
Bank loan	2,000	
Trade creditors	700	
	2,700	
Net assets		475
Capital		
Proprietor's opening capital		0
Net profit for period		1,375
Drawings		(900)
		475

Answer 2.7

The missing words are: used; purchased; current; fixed; one.

Answer 2.8

(a) Capital expenditure

(b) The legal fees associated with the purchase of a property may be added to the purchase price and classified as capital expenditure

(c) Capital expenditure (enhancing an existing fixed asset)

(d) Revenue expenditure

(e) Capital income (net of the costs of sale)

(f) Revenue income

(g) Capital expenditure

(h) If customs duties are borne by the purchaser of the fixed asset, they may be added to the cost of the machinery and classified as capital expenditure

(i) Similarly, if carriage costs are paid for by the purchaser of the fixed asset, they may be included in the cost of the fixed asset and classified as capital expenditure

(j) Installation costs of a fixed asset are also added to the fixed asset's cost and classified as capital expenditure

(k) Revenue expenditure

Answers to Chapter 3 activities

Answer 3.1

(a) In a cash transaction you pay cash for the goods at the time they are supplied. In a credit transaction you do not pay until some time after the goods have been supplied.

(b) (i) It is usual for shops to provide a **till receipt**, although the customer does not always take it or retain it. This is the only piece of business documentation that would need to change hands.

(ii) This is a **much more complicated** transaction, and is likely to involve the following documents.

(1) A letter of enquiry
(2) A quotation
(3) An order
(4) An order acknowledgement
(5) A delivery note
(6) An invoice

The quotation or the order acknowledgement might include details of the supplier's terms and conditions of business. If any part of the work is unsatisfactory, or if the firm overcharges, a credit note may also be issued.

Answer 3.2

(a) The copies of the sales order set may be distributed as follows.

(i) The top copy might be sent to the **customer** to confirm the order.

(ii) A copy must be passed from the sales department to the **warehouse** or production department so that delivery can be arranged.

(iii) Another copy might be kept in the **sales department** to help deal with customer queries.

(iv) Another copy would be passed to **accounts** as a means of requesting accounts to 'raise' (ie produce) an invoice.

(v) One copy can be used as a **delivery note** and another as an **advice note**. The delivery note might be returned to accounts to be matched with the invoice to ensure that the invoice is not sent out until the goods have been delivered.

(vi) A copy might be kept in the warehouse for the **warehouse records**, in case of a query.

(b) The parts of a purchase order set might be used as follows.

(i) The top copy is sent to the **supplier**, possibly to confirm a telephone order.

(ii) A copy is kept by the **department placing the order** for reference and possibly to be compared with the supplier's delivery note. (Alternatively, a copy may go to the warehouse for checking against the delivery note.)

(iii) Another copy may be given to the **accounts department** to be matched with the supplier's invoice when it comes in.

Answer 3.3

This is a significant digit code. The digits are part of the description of the item being coded. '1' in 100000 clearly represents fixed assets, the '2' in 100200 represents plant and machinery etc.

Answer 3.4

The main advantage of computerised accounting systems is that a large amount of data can be processed very quickly. A further advantage is that computerised systems are more accurate than manual systems.

Ivan's comment that 'you never know what is going on in that funny box' might be better expressed as 'lack of audit trail'. If a mistake occurs somewhere in the system it is not always possible to identify where and how it happened.

Answer 3.5

	£
List price	22,000
Less 10% trade discount	2,200
	19,800
Less 2½% cash discount £19,800 × 2½%	495
	19,305

(a) If Quickpay pays after 20 days it will receive only the trade discount. The business will therefore pay £19,800.

(b) If payment is made within 20 days, the business will be able to take advantage of the cash discount and pay only £19,305.

Note. The cash discount is calculated as a percentage of the list price **net of trade discount**.

Answer 3.6

(a) VAT for product A = 17.5/117.5 × £705.60 = £105.08936 = £105.08. (So net price was £705.60 – £105.08 = £600.52)

(b) VAT for product B = 0.175 × £480.95 = £84.16625 = £84.16 (So gross price was £480.95 + £84.16 = £565.11)

Answer 3.7

The VAT is calculated as if **all discounts** are taken, so the VAT is the same for both (a) and (b), ie 17½% × £19,305 = £3,378.37.

Answers to Chapter 4 activities

Answer 4.1

	Rate of discount	*Goods total*	*Discount*	*Net total*
	%	£	£	£
1	15	94.92	14.24	80.68
2	25	125.20	31.30	93.90
3	10	242.10	24.21	217.89
4	20	572.63	114.53	458.10
5	10	421.74	42.17	379.57
6	0	62.00	-	62.00
7	10	160.60	16.06	144.54
8	20	34.17	6.83	27.34
9	20	721.47	144.29	577.18
10	0	84.89	-	84.89
		2,519.72	393.63	2,126.09

Note. The totals have been calculated in order to carry out the check:

£2,519.72 – £393.63 = £2,126.09

Answer 4.2

(a) (1)

WORKBASE OFFICE SUPPLIES LTD

63 Conduit Street
Liverpool L1 6NN

Telephone: 0151-432 2222
Fax: 0151-432 2210

VAT Reg No. 924 4614 29

Invoice No. 7010

Order No. 3017

Account No. F003

Date/Tax point 30 April 20X7

Fawsley's & Co Ltd
74 Green bank Road
Blackley
Liverpool L6 4NP

Product code	*Description*	*Quantity*	*Unit price* £	p	*Total amount* £	p
A87724	Tara 6-tray file trolley (300 size)	1	65	00	65	00
A87725	Tara 12-tray file trolley	1	94	00	94	00
A87821	Tara Tower 300 filing tray	18	4	92	88	56
F10577	Ambience 9-drawer card filing cabinet	1	484	50	484	50
F58110	Ambico 6-shelf unit	2	126	00	252	00
			Goods total		984	06
			Less 10% discount		98	41
Comments			NET TOTAL		885	65
			VAT @ 17 ½%		154	98
			GRAND TOTAL		1,040	63

Registered Office: 63 Conduit Street, Liverpool L1 6NN   Registered No: 822 4742

(2)

WORKBASE OFFICE SUPPLIES LTD

63 Conduit Street
Liverpool L1 6NN

Telephone: 0151-432 2222
Fax: 0151-432 2210

VAT Reg No. 924 4614 29

Invoice No. 7011

Order No. Letter 14/4/97

Account No. K010

Date/Tax point 30 April 20X7

Keats & Joyce
24 Fore Street
Bourneley
L24 6PN

Product code	*Description*	*Quantity*	*Unit price* £	p	*Total amount* £	p
A22410	420 Heavy duty perforator	3	23	45	70	35
A22500	120 Min-punch	10	1	64	16	40
G14392	Fine point Hi-lite Jumbo markers (black)	12		94	11	28
G14003	Office Star pencils 'B' Packs of 12	2	2	58	5	16
G14000	Office Star pencils 'HB' Packs of 12	3	2	58	7	74
			Goods total		110	93
			Less 15% discount		16	64
Comments			NET TOTAL		94	29
			VAT @ 17 ½%		16	50
			GRAND TOTAL		110	79

Registered Office: 63 Conduit Street, Liverpool L1 6NN Registered No: 822 4742

(3)

WORKBASE OFFICE SUPPLIES LTD

63 Conduit Street
Liverpool L1 6NN

Telephone: 0151-432 2222
Fax: 0151-432 2210

VAT Reg No. 924 4614 29

Invoice No. 7012

Order No. Telephone

Account No. R001

Date/Tax point 30 April 20X7

Rabbit Fast Food Franchises Ltd
62 Hellon Avenue
Bourneley
L24 6BS

Product code	*Description*	*Quantity*	*Unit price* £ p	*Total amount* £ p
F71620	Chequers 474E Typist's chair (Colour: Fern)	2	136 00	272 00
F71630	Chequers 474E Typist's chair (Colour: Charcoal)	1	136 00	136 00
			Goods total	408 00
			Less 25% discount	102 00
Comments			NET TOTAL	306 00
			VAT @ 17 ½%	53 55
			GRAND TOTAL	359 55

Registered Office: 63 Conduit Street, Liverpool L1 6NN   Registered No: 822 4742

(b) (i) Fawsley's invoice is over £800 before VAT and so would be referred to the sales manager for authorisation.

(ii) To see which despatches would be delayed, we need to carry out a simple calculation.

Customer	*Fawsley*	*Keats and Joyce*	*Rabbit*
Credit limit	£2,000	£1,000	£500
	£	£	£
Currently owed	500.00	900.00	-
Invoice	1,040.63	110.79	359.55
Total	1,540.63	1,010.79	359.55

Goods ordered by Keats and Joyce would not be despatched until they had reduced their outstanding debt.

Answer 4.3

(a)
(i) The customer account number should read W011.

(ii) The correct product code for the Chequers 474E Typist's chair in Charcoal is F71630. (Alternatively, the invoice might be for an oatmeal chair.)

(iii) The total amount for two Exeter 420L Executive chairs should be £592.

(iv) The goods total has been added incorrectly.

(v) The discount allowed should be 10%.

The correct calculation is summarised below.

	£
2 × F74700 @ £296.00 each	592.00
1 × F71610 @ £136.00 each	136.00
Goods total	728.00
Less 10% discount	72.80
Net total	655.20
VAT at 17½%	114.66
Grand total	769.86

(b)
(i) The invoice is not numbered.

(ii) The price of item F55650 is incorrectly stated as £85.15. The price should be £104.25, as stated in the company's price list.

(iii) The discount of 10% which all customers receive for orders over £100 has not been given.

(iv) The total amount for product A22588 has been incorrectly calculated.

(v) VAT has been subtracted from the net total instead of being added to it.

The correct calculation is summarised below.

	£
1 × F55650 @ £104.25	104.25
1 × F10430 @ £186.20	186.20
5 × A22588 @ £20.47	102.35
Goods total	392.80
Less 10% discount	39.28
Net total	353.52
VAT at 17½%	61.86
Grand total	415.38

Answer 4.4

(a)

WORKBASE OFFICE SUPPLIES LTD

63 Conduit Street
Liverpool L1 6NN

Telephone: 0151-432 2222
Fax: 0151-432 2210

VAT Reg No. 924 4614 29

Credit Note No. C422

Account No. R001

Date/Tax point 9 May 20X7

Rabbit Fast Food Franchises Ltd
62 Hellon Avenue
Bourneley
L24 6BS

Product code	*Description*	*Quantity*	*Unit price* £ p	*Total amount* £ p
F71620	Chequers 474E Typist's chair (Colour: Fern)	1	136 00	136 00
			Goods total	136 00
			Less 25% discount	34 00
Reasons for credit:			NET TOTAL	102 00
Faulty goods returned (Inv No. 7012)			VAT @ 17 ½%	17 85
			TOTAL CREDIT	119 85

Registered Office: 63 Conduit Street, Liverpool L1 6NN   Registered No: 822 4742

(b) A credit note should be issued for the items incorrectly delivered, and the correct items re-invoiced. This process will generate a delivery note for the re-delivery. The credit note will appear as below.

WORKBASE OFFICE SUPPLIES LTD

63 Conduit Street
Liverpool L1 6NN

Telephone: 0151-432 2222
Fax: 0151-432 2210

VAT Reg No. 924 4614 29

Credit Note No. C423

Account No. L004

Date/Tax point 9 May 20X7

For the attention of Mrs French
Lexicon Translators
67 Back Lane
Mountford L22 7FE

Product code	*Description*	*Quantity*	*Unit price* £	p	*Total amount* £	p
A89811	Priory System 3 triple tier tray sets (Colour: Grey)	8	14	27	114	16
			Goods total		114	16
			Less 10% discount		11	42
Reasons for credit:			NET TOTAL		102	74
Incorrect items delivered (Inv No. 7038)			VAT @ 17 ½%		17	97
			TOTAL CREDIT		120	71

Registered Office: 63 Conduit Street, Liverpool L1 6NN   Registered No: 822 4742

Answers to Chapter 5 activities

Answer 5.2

DINERS' SUPPLIES LIMITED		No: 121	
Journal Entry			
Date 18 March 20X7			
Prepared by A Technician			
Authorised by			
Account	Code	DR £ p	CR £ p
Debtors' ledger control account	0210	733-38	
Sales C	2010		146-82
Sales G	2020		310-34
Sales E	2030		119-97
Sales X	2040		47-01
VAT control account	4000		109-24
Totals		733-38	733-38

Note. Answer 5.1 is on page 310.

Answer 5.1

DINERS' SUPPLIES - SALES DAY BOOK

Date	Invoice No.	Customer No.	Total	C	G	E	X	VAT
17/3/X7	I2060	K02	141-00	58-00	62-00			21-00
17/3/X7	I2061	B09	151-62		55-32	62-09	11-63	22-58
17/3/X7	I2062	Cancelled						
17/3/X7	I2063	P11	104-11		34-47	26-31	27-82	15-51
18/3/X7	I2064	A01	141-00		120-00			21-00
18/3/X7	I2065	N04	59-07	50-27				8-80
18/3/X7	I2066	D06	45-98			31-57	7-56	6-85
18/3/X7	I2067	M09	90-60	38-55	38-55			13-50
	TOTAL		733-38	146-82	310-34	119-97	47-01	109-24

Answer 5.3

DINERS' SUPPLIES LIMITED		No: 132	
Journal Entry			
Date 24 March 20X7			
Prepared by A Technician			
Authorised by			
Account	Code	DR £ p	CR £ p
Debtors' ledger control account	0210		231-60
Sales returns C	2310	38-55	
Sales returns G	2320	158-55	
VAT control account	4000	34-50	
Totals		231-60	231-60

Answer 5.4

(a) (i) £12,572.50 is owed by Diners' Supplies Ltd to HM Customs & Excise.

(ii) The credit balance on the VAT control account represents a *liability* for Diners' Supplies Ltd.

(b)

Account	*Credit or debit balance?*	*Answer*
Sales	CREDIT	Revenue
Sales returns	DEBIT	Expense
Debtors' ledger control account	DEBIT	Asset
Discounts allowed	DEBIT	Expense
Cash	CREDIT	Liability

Answers to Chapter 6 activities

Answer 6.1

A sales ledger record could look like this.

Customer:	Joe Bloggs	Account No: 00001
Address:	Bloke Estate	
	Geezertown	Credit limit: £???
	Chapshire CH1 ONO	
Telephone:	XXX XXXX	Payment terms: 1.5% 30 days

Date	*Item*	*Debits*	*Credits*	*Balance*
		£	£	£

Answer 6.2

Tutorial note. If you could not begin to answer this question, you have not really got the point of the chapter! There is no point learning the mechanics of a process unless you know what it is *for*.

The situation describes one of the basic reasons for setting up a sales ledger system.

Your answer should have mentioned that you would keep a set of inter-related record books, rather than just the nominal ledger. The key record books which you would require are as follows.

(a) The *nominal ledger* (as at present), where the double entry of a transaction is recorded. However, instead of posting individual amounts due from debtors on each invoice to a single account in this ledger, you should consider setting up a separate sales ledger to record the detail and simply post a monthly total to the sales ledger control account in the nominal ledger.

(b) The *sales ledger*, which is a memorandum ledger divided into individual customer accounts. This will enable you to keep track of your dealings with each customer. You might also have suggested the use of a sales day book.

(c) A *sales day book* is used as the book of prime entry for recording the details of sales invoices raised by the company. (A book of prime entry is a book where entries are made straight from source documents, rather than posted from other records. The purpose of the whole process described here is largely to prevent the use of the nominal ledger as a book of prime entry.)

A thorough answer to this activity might have identified *how* and *when* postings are made to each of the above books.

(a) As soon as invoices are raised (daily/weekly), details are posted to the sales day book.

(b) From the sales day book, the total of each invoice is posted to the relevant customer's account in the sales ledger.

(c) When cash is received in settlement of debts, it is recorded as cash received in the cash book (a book of prime entry) and posted to the credit of individual accounts in the sales ledger. The sales ledger will show the balance outstanding from each customer, together with a transaction history, which may be useful.

(d) At the end of each accounting period, the nominal ledger can be updated. This will involve the following procedures.

    (i) A debit to the sales ledger control account from the gross sales total in the SDB.

(ii) A credit to the VAT control account (or output VAT account) from the VAT total in the SDB.

(iii) A credit to the sales (revenue) account from the net sales total in the SDB.

(iv) A debit to the cash account from the cash received total in the cash book.

(v) A credit to the sales ledger control account from the cash received total in the cash book.

(e) Finally, to ensure that you have not missed anything, you must check that:

(i) The closing balance in the cash book agrees with the cash account balance in the nominal ledger.

(ii) The total of the individual account balances in the sales ledger agrees with the sales ledger control account balance in the nominal ledger.

Answer 6.3

(a)

CUSTOMER NAME: Arturo Aski

ACCOUNT 001

ADDRESS: 94 Old Comedy Street, Vaudeville, 1BR, W. Meds

CREDIT LIMIT: £2,200

Date	Description	Transaction Ref	DR £	DR p	CR £	CR p	Balance £	Balance p
Brought forward 1/1/X7							2,050	37
1/1/X7	Inv	100	85	00			2,135	37
1/1/X7	Inv	102	16	99			2,152	36
1/1/X7	Inv	106	76	34			2,228	70

CUSTOMER NAME: Maye West

ACCOUNT 030

ADDRESS: 1 Vamping Parade, Holywood, Beds, HW1

CREDIT LIMIT: £1,000

Date	Description	Transaction Ref	DR £	DR p	CR £	CR p	Balance £	Balance p
Brought forward 1/1/X7							69	33
1/1/X7	Inv	101	98	15			167	48

CUSTOMER NAME: Naguib Mahfouz

ACCOUNT 075

ADDRESS: 10 Palace Walk, London NE9

CREDIT LIMIT: £1,500

Date	Description	Transaction Ref	DR £	DR p	CR £	CR p	Balance £	Balance p
Brought forward 1/1/X7								
1/1/X7	Inv	104	123	10			123	10

CUSTOMER NAME: Josef Sveik

ACCOUNT 099

ADDRESS: 99 Balkan Row, Aldershot

CREDIT LIMIT: £700

Date	Description	Transaction Ref	DR £	DR p	CR £	CR p	Balance £	Balance p
Brought forward 1/1/X7							353	71
1/1/X7	Inv	105	35	72			389	43
1/1/X7	Cred	C44			353	71	35	72

CUSTOMER NAME: Grace Chang	ACCOUNT 132
ADDRESS: Red Dragon Street, Cardiff, CA4	
CREDIT LIMIT: £1,200	

Date	Description	Transaction Ref	DR		CR		Balance	
			£	p	£	p	£	p
Brought forward 1/1/X7							1,175	80
1/1/X7	Inv	103	20	21			1,196	01

(b) *Double entry*

The sales ledger (ie the list of credit-related transactions analysed by customer) is a memorandum account.

So, the *double entry* from the sales day book and sales returns day book is as follows.

			£	£
(i)	DEBIT	Sales ledger control account	455.51	
	CREDIT	Sales		387.67
		VAT control account		67.84
			455.51	455.51
(ii)	DEBIT	Sales returns	301.03	
		VAT control account	52.68	
	CREDIT	Sales ledger control account		353.71
			353.71	353.71

(c) *Additional items*

(i) Did you check the sales return to the original invoice?

(ii) More importantly, did you notice that Arturo Aski (customer 001) has now exceeded his credit limit? How can this have slipped through the net?

(1) The customer may have told the person who took the order that a cheque was 'in the post'.

(2) The invoice might have been given the incorrect account code.

(3) The person receiving the order might not have checked the customer's credit status.

(4) The credit limit may have been raised, but you have not yet been told about it.

In any case, the matter should be referred to your boss for checking.

(iii) Grace Chang has an outstanding balance of £1,196.01. When she next makes an order, the account must be checked to see that she has reduced the balance outstanding, as it is near her credit limit. In any case, you may wish to monitor the account to ensure that she is not having cashflow problems (and therefore represents a risk to you). If her business is expanding and she is settling debts promptly (which you will be able to ascertain by looking at the ledger history), it may be appropriate to review her credit limit.

Answer 6.4

(a)

CUSTOMER: RANJIT SINGH ACCOUNT 1124
ADDRESS: 19 AMBER ROAD, ST MARY CRAY

Date	*Transaction reference*	*Debit* £ p	*Credit* £ p	*Balance* £ p
Brought forward				NIL
1/1/X7	236	405.33		405.33
2/2/X7	315	660.72		1,066.05
3/2/X7	317	13.90		1,079.95
5/2/X7	320	17.15		1,097.10
15/2/X7	Cash 004		1,066.05	31.05
21/2/X7	379	872.93		903.98
25/3/X7	Cash 006		500.00	403.98
31/3/X7	443	213.50		617.48
15/4/X7	Cash 007		500.00	117.48
1/5/X7	502	624.30		741.78
15/5/X7	Cash 031		500.00	241.78
	514	494.65		736.43
19/5/X7	521	923.91		1,660.34
20/5/X7	Cash 038		500.00	1,160.34
22/5/X7	538	110.00		1,270.34
20/6/X7	Cash 039		500.00	770.34
22/6/X7	Cash 042		923.91	(153.57)
1/7/X7	618	312.17		158.60
2/7/X7	619	560.73		719.33
8/7/X7	CRN 32		110.00	609.33
		5,209.29	4,599.96	609.33

(b) From the sales ledger which you have reconstructed, it seems that Ranjit Singh owes you £609.33. How is this made up?

	£
Invoices raised	5,209.29
Specific payments	(1,989.96)
Payments on account	(2,500.00)
Credit note	(110.00)
Balance	609.33

Working back from the most recent items on the account:

(i) Credit note number 32 for £110.00 can be matched against an invoice
(ii) Cash receipt ref 042 for £923.91 can be matched against an invoice
(iii) Invoice 619 for £560.73 is not settled
(iv) Invoice 618 for £312.17 is only part settled.

This may look odd - invoice 618 being part settled when the only subsequent credit on the account (the credit note) relates to a different item - but it arises because the cash receipts on 20 June and 22 June led to the account being overpaid, ie it was in *credit.* This means that the excess credit was allocated against the next available debit, invoice 618.

You might have reached the same position by tracking *forward* through the account, eliminating 'matched' items and working through the payments on account, as follows.

Payments on account amounted to £2,500. This is deemed to cover the invoices as follows.

		£
Invoice	317	13.90
	320	17.15
	379	872.93
	443	213.50
	502	624.30
	514	494.65
	618 - part (ie balance)	263.57
		2,500.00

The balance remaining is:

618 - unpaid part	48.60
619	560.73
	609.33

(*Note*. Invoice 618 is £312.17, being £263.57 paid and £48.60 unpaid.)

Answers to Chapter 7 activities

Answer 7.1

Customer	*Amount of sale*	*Amount tendered*	*Change due (a)*	*Notes/coin in change (b)*
	£	£	£	
1	7.42	10.00	2.58	£2 coin, 50p coin, 5p coin, 2p coin and 1p coin
2	29.21	30.00	0.79	50p piece, 20p piece, 5p piece and two 2p pieces
3	7.98	10.00	2.02	£2 coin and 2p coin
4	44.44	45.00	0.56	50p coin, 5p coin and 1p coin
5	39.25	40.00	0.75	50p coin, 20p coin and 5p coin
6	57.20	57.20	-	-
7	9.46	10.46	1.00	£1 coin
8	10.17	10.50	0.33	20p coin, 10p coin, 2p coin and 1p coin
9	59.62	60.12	0.50	50p coin
10	12.93	20.00	7.07	£5 note, £2 coin, 5p coin and 2p coin
Totals	277.68	293.28	15.60	

The calculations may be checked as follows: £293.28 – £277.68 = £15.60.

Answer 7.2

	£
Cash float at start of the day	36.40
Sales in the day	277.68
Cash held at the end of the day	314.08

Answer 7.3

(a) The date on the cheque is incorrect. However, the cheque cannot be accepted even if the date is corrected because the sort code on the cheque does not agree with the sort code on the cheque card. Barry should ask whether the customer presented a card relating to another account in error.

(b) The date on the cheque is again incorrect. Perhaps Barry has been telling customers the incorrect date! It will be necessary for the customer to sign or initial a change in the date.

The amount in words and the amount in figures do not agree. Again, the customer must initial or sign any change.

The cheque guarantee card expired at the end of July 20X7. The customer needs to use his new replacement card, or some other method of payment entirely.

(c) The year has been omitted from the date. Barry should ask the customer to complete this. The cheque guarantee card details show that the card is not yet valid. This is probably because the customer has only recently been sent the card. Barry should ask the customer whether he has a card covering the period up to August 20X7.

Answer 7.4

(a) 'You can pay by quarterly **direct debit**. You need to complete a direct debit mandate form which authorises us to debit amounts from your bank account. We will send you a bill in the usual way each quarter, and the amount due will be debited from your account 14 days after the date of the bill, so you'll know how much is to be debited well in advance. If an error is made, either the bank or ourselves must put it right.'

(b) 'Normally, any balance due to us when the sale is completed will be paid by **banker's draft** or by **BACS**. A banker's draft or BACS is considered to be as good as cash, and of course cash would be acceptable but it is unusual and not so convenient to pay such a large amount in cash.'

Tutorial note. A builder may accept a cheque for a *deposit* put down on a house, but is very unlikely to accept a cheque when the sale is 'completed', as that is when he must hand over the keys and there is a risk that the cheque could be dishonoured.

(c) 'We do not advise you to send cash through the post, as we cannot accept responsibility if it is lost. We suggest that you pay by **postal order**, obtained from your post office. The post office will charge a fee for this service.'

(d) 'In order to pay by a cheque supported by a **banker's card**, it is necessary for the person whose signature appears on the card to sign and date the cheque in the presence of the payee - in other words, in our store. This rule is a standard rule of all of the banks. Please therefore ask your friend to call in to make the payment herself, unless you wish to pay by some other means, such as cash.'

Answers to Chapter 8 activities

Answer 8.1

The cheque from your son is an instruction from the drawer (your son) to his bank to pay to you the sum stated on the cheque. When you pay it in at the branch here, we as the 'collecting' bank need to claim payment of the amount from your son's bank (the 'paying' bank). To deal with the large number of cheques going through the banking system each day, this is done by means of a centralised 'clearing' process. All of the cheques must be sorted, and when your son's bank receives and 'honours' the cheque they will debit the amount to his account and credit us. Only then will we know that the money represents 'cleared funds', and the clearing process usually takes about three working days. This is no reflection on your son's creditworthiness, it is simply a process which all cheques must go through.

Writing 'not negotiable' across the cheque is a way of 'crossing' the cheque. The words mean that if the cheque is stolen, the thief (or anybody he passes the cheque to) cannot become the true owner. Since your son's cheque is made out to you, this presents no problem. If someone had tried to pay the cheque into an account in another person's name, the cashier would need to make some enquiries before accepting it.

Answer 8.2

Date 10 June 20X7
A/c Easter & Co
Cashier's stamp and initials

Cash 2,292.13
Cheques etc 2,902.83
£ 5,194.96

Date 10 June 20X7
Cashier's stamp and initials

Fee
No of Cheques 8

bank giro credit
Paid in by/Customer's Reference

8 | 72-27-28 | 45046221

First Region Bank
BARRINGTON BRANCH

EASTER & CO
A/C no 16966117

Notes £50	100	00
£20	100	00
£10	970	00
£5	210	00
Coins £1	804	00
50p	40	00
20p	24	00
Silver	34	85
Bronze	9	28
Cash £	2,292	13
Cheques	2,902	83
£	5,194	96

Please do not write or mark below this line

101129 C101129C 72D2728A 16966117

Details of cheques etc	£	p
B Wyman	940	00
Pacific Ltd	1,721	50
S McManus	94	26
A Singh	19	29
P L Ferguson	57	37
Dex Ltd	42	91
M Green	12	50
Carried forward £	2,887	83

Sub-total brought forward	2,887	83
Postal order	15	00
Total carried over £	2,902	83

B Wyman	940	00
Pacific Ltd	1,721	50
S McManus	94	26
A Singh	19	29
P L Ferguson	57	37
Dex Ltd	42	91
M Green	12	50
S R Sykes (Postal order)	15	00
	2,902	83

In view of the risk of loss in course of clearing, customers are advised to keep an independent record of the drawers of cheques

Please do not write or mark below this line

Answer 8.3

(a) The words on each of the cheques have been written by the bank in order to indicate why the cheques have not been 'paid'. The fact that the cheques cannot be paid means that the bank will have debited the amounts of the returned cheques from the firm's bank account in order to cancel the part of the credit entry which was made in respect of these cheques when they were paid in. Action should be taken as follows.

First cheque. These words mean simply that the cheque has not been signed by the drawer (our customer). We should return the cheque to our customer asking him either to sign it or to issue a new cheque.

Second cheque. In this case, the cheque has been paid in to the bank before its due date: before the date written on the cheque. Since this cheque has been given a date after the date at which it was received by the firm, it is called a 'post dated' cheque.

Unless we want to ask the customer to send us a fresh cheque with an earlier date on it, we will have to wait until the due date of the cheque and try to pay it in again then.

Third cheque. The bank has presented this cheque to the paying bank (the drawer's bank) but that bank has declined to honour it. Most businesses will have had at some time customers who have run into financial difficulties, and this may have happened here.

It may be necessary to make further enquiries if we do not already have knowledge of the customer's difficulties. If we are not able to secure payment from the customer, we may have to instruct our solicitor to help us to recover the debt.

(b) MEMORANDUM

To: A Smith
General Manager
7 May 20X7

From: A Technician

Subject: *Cheques returned unpaid by the bank*

You asked about the returned cheques shown on the bank statement dated 2 May 20X7 and the bank charges relating to them.

Two of the three cheques should clearly not have been paid in to the bank. One of these had no drawer's signature and another was a post-dated cheque.

Recommendation

A checklist should be prepared for use by the staff member preparing cheques for banking. A brief check list will be more easily used and memorised than a lengthy list. The checklist should cover the following points as a minimum.

(i) Is the cheque 'in date'?
(ii) Is payee name/endorsement in order?
(iii) Do words and figures agree?
(iv) Is it signed?

The third cheque was returned with the words 'refer to drawer', possibly indicating that the customer is in financial difficulties. The possibility that from time to time difficulties in recovering some debts will involve some cheques being returned unpaid is something which a business may just have to accept. A business may avoid some of these problems by being careful to whom it sells on credit. However, problems may still arise where customers who were thought to be creditworthy unexpectedly ran into financial difficulties later on.

Recommendation

The sales ledger department (the credit controller) should be informed of all cheques returned as 'refer to drawer'. If such items are occurring frequently it may be time to review the credit policy of the business.

Answer 8.4

(a)

Week beginning 27.11.X7	*Cash/cheques takings* £		*Credit card takings* £		*Total takings* £
Monday	696.97	(684.08 + 37.05 – 24.16)	104.28		801.25
Tuesday	479.82	(504.27 + 12.60 – 37.05)	202.96		682.78
Wednesday	698.21	(691.41 + 19.40 – 12.60)	86.91	(124.17 – 37.26)	785.12
Thursday	742.64	(729.62 + 32.42 – 19.40)	291.41		1,034.05
Friday	834.99	(840.50 + 26.91 – 32.42)	300.89	(342.09 – 41.20)	1,135.88
	3,452.63		986.45		4,439.08

(b)

HAVE YOU IMPRINTED THE SUMMARY
WITH YOUR RETAILER'S CARD?

BANK Processing (White) copy of Summary with your Vouchers in correct order:
1. SUMMARY
2. SALES VOUCHERS
3. REFUND VOUCHERS
KEEP Retailer's copies (Blue & Yellow)
NO MORE THAN 200 Vouchers to each Summary
DO NOT USE Staples, Pins, Paper Clips

	ITEMS	AMOUNT	
SALES VOUCHERS (LISTED OVERLEAF)	3	124	17
LESS REFUND VOUCHERS	1	37	36
DATE 22.11.X7	TOTAL £	86	91

SUMMARY - RETAILER'S COPY

First Region Bank
FASTPASS

BANKING
SUMMARY

RETAILER'S SIGNATURE

COMPLETE THIS SUMMARY FOR EVERY DEPOSIT OF SALES VOUCHERS AND ENTER THE TOTAL ON YOUR NORMAL CURRENT ACCOUNT PAYING-IN SLIP

(c) As stated on the banking summary form, a summary should be completed for every deposit of sales vouchers and the total should be entered on the usual current account paying-in slip. The summary will be handed over at the bank with the credit card vouchers and the rest of the day's takings.

Answer 8.5

DO NOT TICK OR MAKE ANY MARKS OUTSIDE THE LISTING AREA

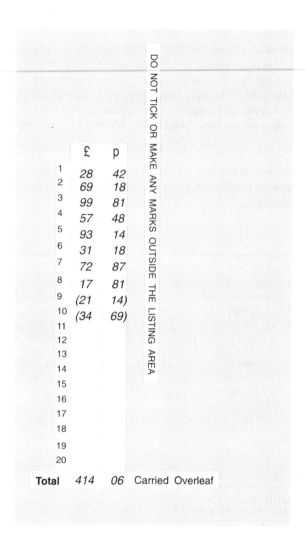

	£	p
1	*28*	*42*
2	*69*	*18*
3	*99*	*81*
4	*57*	*48*
5	*93*	*14*
6	*31*	*18*
7	*72*	*87*
8	*17*	*81*
9	*(21*	*14)*
10	*(34*	*69)*
11		
12		
13		
14		
15		
16		
17		
18		
19		
20		
Total	*414*	*06* Carried Overleaf

HAVE YOU IMPRINTED THE SUMMARY WITH YOUR RETAILER'S CARD?

BANK Processing (White) copy of Summary with your Vouchers in correct order:
1. SUMMARY
2. SALES VOUCHERS
3. REFUND VOUCHERS

KEEP Retailer's copies (Blue & Yellow)
NO MORE THAN 200 Vouchers to each Summary
DO NOT USE Staples, Pins, Paper Clips

	ITEMS	AMOUNT	
SALES VOUCHERS (LISTED OVERLEAF)	*8*	*469*	*89*
LESS REFUND VOUCHERS	*2*	*(55*	*83)*
DATE *22.5.X7*	TOTAL £	*414 :*	*06*

SUMMARY - RETAILER'S COPY

Southern Bank FASTPASS **BANKING SUMMARY**

RETAILER'S SIGNATURE

COMPLETE THIS SUMMARY FOR EVERY DEPOSIT OF SALES VOUCHERS AND ENTER THE TOTAL ON YOUR NORMAL CURRENT ACCOUNT PAYING-IN SLIP

Date 22/5/X7	Date 22/5/X7	**bank giro credit**
A/c 30494713	Cashier's stamp and initials	Paid in by/Customer's Reference

	£	p
Notes £50		
£20		
£10		
£5		
Coins £1		
50p		
20p		
Silver		
Bronze		
Cash £		
Cheques	414	06
£	414	06

6 | 83048231 | 92057419

Quality Bank
EALING BROADWAY BRANCH

Fee

No of Cheques: 1

A B BROWNE & CO — A/C no 30494713

Please do not write or mark below this line

	£	p
Notes £50		
£20		
£10		
£5		
Coins £1		
50p		
20p		
Silver		
Bronze		
Cash £		
Cheques	414	06
£	414	06

101129 ⑈101129⑈ 20⑉2748⑆ 47318221⑈

Details of cheques, etc.		
Carried Forward £		

Sub-total brought forward		
Fastpass	*414*	*06*
Total Carried over £	*414*	*06*

In view of the risk of loss in course of clearing, customers are advised to keep an independent record of the drawers of cheques

Please do not write or mark below this line

Fastpass	
414	*06*
414	*06*

BPP PUBLISHING

Answers to Chapter 9 activities

Answer 9.1

Tutorial note. The cash book records money received and money paid. If something does not involve money coming into or going out of the business, it will not result in an entry in the cash book.

The following will *not* be entered in the cash book.

(c) Supplier's invoice
(d) Credit note
(e) Debit note
(j) Depreciation

A cheque received (a) and a payment to sales ledger customers (b) comprise a receipt and a payment respectively. But receiving a supplier's invoice (c) is not a receipt or payment of money: the invoice establishes a debt, which might not be paid until some time later. Similarly, issuing (d) a credit note or (e) a debit note does not involve money changing hands. Bank charges (f) and overdraft interest (g) are both paid (by the business, to the bank) when debited to the bank account, and these need to be recorded in the cash book. A fixed asset purchased on credit will have been invoiced previously; the payment for it (h) must be recorded in the cash book. A refund from a supplier (i) would be included as it is a monetary item (ie it is *not* a credit note). Depreciation of fixed assets (j) may be necessary, but the accounting entries for it do not involve money changing hands.

Answer 9.2

(a) £405.26 + £715.22 = £1,120.48.

(b) (i) 11.00am to 1.00pm (see working)
(ii) 12.00 noon to 2.00pm (see working)

Working

Two hour period	*Number of sales*	*Value of sales*
		£
9.00 - 11.00	43	618.66
10.00 - 12.00	64	1,638.24
11.00 - 1.00	76 Highest (i)	1,954.17
12.00 - 2.00	65	2,005.76 Highest (ii)
1.00 - 3.00	45	1,616.37
2.00 - 4.00	54	873.05
3.00 - 5.00	72	1,120.48

(c) Total sales can be calculated from two-hour periods as in the working for (b).

Period	*Value of sales*
	£
9.00 - 11.00	618.66
11.00 - 1.00	1,954.17
1.00 - 3.00	1,616.37
3.00 - 5.00	1,120.48
Total sales	5,309.68
Add float	25.00
Less credit card and cheque sales	(319.25)
Total in till	5,015.43

Answer 9.3

(a) Assuming that the times at which the members of staff concerned took over the till are precisely as stated compared with the times on the till's own clock, we can calculate the amounts expected to be counted in the till at each change of duty.

	Expccted		*Actual*	*Difference*
	£		£	£
11.00 am	643.66	(£618.66 + £25.00)	625.66	– 18.00
3.00 pm	4,214.20	(£618.66 + £1,954.17 + £1,616.37 + £25.00)	4,196.20	– 18.00

At both 11.00am and 3.00pm the cash counted is £18.00 short. It would appear that a shortage of £18.00 occurred while John Walton was operating the till and that an excess of 58p occurred between 3.00pm and 5.00pm while Ali Alaqat was on duty. This has led to a net shortage of £17.42 at the close of business.

(b) On each change of staff duty, a report could be obtained from the cash register giving a subtotal of sales for the day up to that time. This total could be added to the amount of the float at the start of the day to give a figure for the amount expected in the till at that time. Preferably, the subtotal should be obtained after the till operators have written down their own count. Otherwise the till operators may be tempted not to bother to carry out their own count.

Answer 9.4

(a)

Cash received sheet *Number.......................*

Date	*Name*	*Account No.*	*Amount*
			£
20.4.X7	Jill's Kitchen Co	J211	492.70
20.4.X7	G Edwards & Son	E102	242.98
21.4.X7	Crystal Water Co	C101	892.76
21.4.X7	H M Customs & Excise	1600	487.50
21.4.X7	Green Gourmet Co	G105	500.00
22.4.X7	BRM Motors	1720	1,700.00
22.4.X7	Jennan Tonic Ltd	J110	1,920.70
23.4.X7	Oliver's Organic Foods	0301	400.00
23.4.X7	Parkers Preserves Ltd	P002	3,208.00
24.4.X7	Pennine Springs Ltd	P004	4,920.75
	Total	1000	14,765.39

(b) The cash receipts will be recorded on the debit side of the cash book, probably on a single line showing the cash received sheet number.

Answer 9.5

(a)

WAGNER ENTERPRISES

RECEIPTS

Date	Narrative	Folio	Discount allowed	Receipt total	VAT	Debtors	Cash sales	Other
05-Feb	Carmen Carpets	SL0075	112.50	2,137.50		2,137.50		
08-Feb	Placido Players	SL0553		42.00	6.26		35.74	
11-Feb	Mehta Metronomes	SL0712		543.27		543.27		
14-Feb	Luciano Lighting	SL0009	19.00	361.00		361.00		
15-Feb	Tosca Tents	SL0473		4,000.00	595.74		3,404.26	
15-Feb	Magic Flute Instruments	SL0338	475.00	9,025.00		9,025.00		
	Bank interest	**INT270 CR**		42.01				42.01
	Sale of delivery van	**FAD028 CR**		2,500.00				2,500.00
			606.50	18,650.78	602.00	12,066.77	3,440.00	2,542.01
			DIS340 DR SLC040 CR	**CAB010 DR**	**VAT094 CR**	**SLC040 CR**	**SAL200 CR**	

(b)

WAGNER ENTERPRISES

CASH BOOK RECEIPTS POSTING SUMMARY 15 FEBRUARY

Narrative	Nominal ledger account	DR	CR
		£	£
Cash and bank	**CAB010**	18,650.78	
Sales discounts allowed	**DIS340**	606.50	
VAT control	**VAT094**		602.00
Sales ledger control	**SLC040**		12,066.77
	SLC040		606.50
Sales	**SAL200**		3,440.00
Interest received	**INT270**		42.01
Fixed asset disposal	**FAD028**		2,500.00
		19,257.28	19,257.28

CASH — CAB 010

		£		£
15 Feb	Bal b/d	76,959 00		
	Cash book	18,650.78		

VAT CONTROL ACCOUNT — VAT 094

	£			£
		15 Feb	Bal b/d	10,500.00
			Cash book	602.00

SALES LEDGER CONTROL ACCOUNT SLC 040

		£			£
15 Feb	bal b/d	152,744.00	15 Feb	Cash book	12,066.77
				Cash book	606.50

SALES DISCOUNTS DIS 340

		£			£
15 Feb	Bal b/d	7,050.00			
	Cash book	606.50			

SALES SAL 200

		£			£
			15 Feb	Bal b/d	372,771
				Cash book	3,440

INTEREST RECEIVED INT 270

		£			£
			15 Feb	Cash book	42.01

FIXED ASSET DISPOSALS FAD 028

		£			£
			15 Feb	Cash book	2,500

Answers to Chapter 10 activities

Answer 10.1

(1) Finance Director
Baudrilard
Charles House
Postmodern Industrial Estate
Frontage, Wilts

(1) (2)

14/9/X7

Dear Mr *Baudrilard*

(3) (4) (5)

We've got problems with your *account* which you will see from the *statement* I sent you *two* weeks ago. *Your* always going *overdrawn* and this month you don't *seem* to have paid us.

(9) (6) (7) (8)

Please do *something about* it, or I might have to call in a *soliciter* or debt collector.

(14) (10) (11) (12) (13)

I remain, sir, your obedient servant,

(15)

Boris Thug, Assistant

(a) 1 (i) Wrong spelling; should be Baudrillard.
(ii) Boris should have used the proper name of the company, J L Baudrillard plc.

2 The Finance Director, to whom Boris is writing, is called Martin Jacques. (Should the letter go to the Finance Director?)

3 Who? Boris hasn't used headed notepaper, nor given any address, so the relevant personnel at J L Baudrillard plc are likely to be mystified.

4 Which account? Both of them? One of them? Boris has not clearly explained what he is referring to.

5 Again, there are two accounts and so two statements would have been sent.

6 Better: (i) To give the precise date you sent them
(ii) To give the statement date, ie 31 August 20X7

7 You are.

8 You are not J L Baudrillard plc's banker. Baudrillard has exceeded his credit limit, but an overdraft is when you owe a bank money on your current account.

9 Statement is dated 31 August. The letter is dated 14 September. Boris's last enquiry was 7 September. The statement reveals that Baudrillard usually pays on the 10th or 11th of each month. Boris should have waited and checked to see if there were any receipts.

10 Like what? Why not just say 'clear the outstanding debt'?

11 Boris would not be doing that sort of thing, as he is far too junior.

12 Threatening solicitors or debt collectors is completely inappropriate at this stage. This is a first reminder.

13 Solicitor.

14 'I remain ... servant' is absurdly pompous in this context. (Boris has obviously been reading the letters page of one of the newspapers.)

15 The letter is unsigned. This is extremely discourteous.

In short, the letter cannot be sent in its current form.

- It fails to identify the sender.
- It does not precisely describe the problem.
- It is not properly addressed.
- It is far too aggressive.
- There are basic errors in spelling and grammar.

(b) While Boris Thug's approach to debtor relations is brutal and potentially disastrous, there are a number of valid questions raised by the situation, and the following actions are appropriate.

(i) Check to see if Baudrillard and/or Baudrillard Robotics have paid in the time which has elapsed since September 7.

(ii) Check that the invoices received since the last statement and the invoices on the statement have been posted to the correct account (ie Baudrillard plc Head Office or Baudrillard plc Robotics).

(iii) Examine the credit limits offered to Baudrillard, on both accounts.

(1) The 'A' account has never breached the credit limit. The credit limit was reviewed last year.

(2) The Robotics Division's credit limit has not been reviewed for nearly eight years.

(iv) If Baudrillard Robotics is continually breaching its credit limits, the issue is important enough to bring up with Martin Jacques.

(1) It may be that a new arrangement with the company should be negotiated, covering both Head Office and Robotics division.

(2) Alternatively, perhaps a simple solution is that the Robotics Division's credit limit should be raised to reflect the increase.

The matter certainly merits discussion.

(v) If it is simply the case that Baudrillard Robotics holds on to its money for as long as possible, then offering a settlement discount or charging interest on overdue balances might encourage more prompt payment.

Answer 10.2

(a) The goods were mispacked. Beethoven plc has been billed for two Callas Divas when only one was received.

(i) Check the sales order, and confirmation to see that two Callas Divas were in fact ordered, rather than one Sutherland and one Callas.

(ii) Check the sales returns day book to see that one Sutherland Diva was returned.

(iii) Check that you do in fact offer a 10% trade discount to Beethoven plc.

(b) There are a number of ways you could deal with it. The simplest is probably to do the following.

(i) Issue a credit note for £1,327.46 to cancel, in its entirety, invoice 4321.

(ii) Issue a new invoice for the Superconductor and the one Callas Diva already received by Beethoven plc, taking the discount into account. This amounts to (£705.99 + £211.88) – 10% = £826.08, + VAT = £970.64.

(iii) Issue an invoice for the other Callas Diva when it is delivered.

TUNE LTD
Discord Street, Crochety, Sussex

Beethovern plc
Symphony Promenade
Quavertree, Essex

Date ....
Our Ref ....
Your Ref ....

Attn: H V Karajan

Dear Mr Karajan,

Re: Invoice 4321

Further to our conversation today, I write to inform you that:

(a) you will be issued a credit note for the entire amount of Invoice 4321 (£1,327.46);

(b) you will also be sent an invoice for the Superconductor and the Callas Diva you have already received;

(c) the second Callas Diva is in the course of construction, and will be sent to you when it is completed. You will be billed separately.

As you are entitled to the 10% trade discount, the invoiced amounts will reflect this fact.

Please accept my apologies for any inconvenience caused.

Yours sincerely

A Clerk

A Clerk

Answer 10.3

(a) Basic information needed is as follows.

- Customer name, in full
- Business address and telephone number
- Delivery address, if different from the business address
- Address of registered office
- VAT registration number, for checking purposes
- The name of a person you can deal with
- A reference number

In order to offer credit, you would need to know whether the company is able to use it responsibly. If a substantial amount of credit is requested you might need to know more about the customer's business, such as its profitability and trading history, as these will affect the assessment of how risky it is to give substantial credit. You can also make an assessment of what proportion of their purchases will come from you. If the planned percentage is high, you should consider the company as high risk.

You might insist that Stravinsky trades on a 'cash only' basis for a short period. You can also ask for references, either through the company, who should be asked to nominate other suppliers who you can contact, or from the company's bank or through the trade generally. (Care should be exercised: it has been known from habitual late-payers who withhold payment of bills as long as possible to select two suppliers for regular prompt payment and then to quote these two whenever they are asked for references!)

(b) Setting up an account involves:

(i) Assigning a code number to the account
(ii) Writing to the customer detailing the terms on which you operate
(iii) Setting up the requisite ledger accounts in the accounting system
(iv) Notifying subordinates of the new account
(v) Assigning credit limits and payment terms
(vi) Obtaining all the information in (a) above

Finally, make sure that you have followed your own organisation's procedure for obtaining authorisation to open the account.

The account should be monitored closely for the first, say, six months, to ensure that credit terms are adhered to and Stravinsky pays regularly.

Answers to Chapter 11 activities

Answer 11.1

True

Answer 11.2

(a) No

(b) Your advertisement is not an offer, but an 'invitation to make an offer'. It invites other parties to make an offer to purchase.

Jenson makes an offer to purchase the car for £3,000 which you reject, by making a 'counter-offer' to sell the vehicle to him for £3,500. He can accept or reject your counter-offer. He rejects it. At this point there is no contract between you and Jenson.

You then reach agreement with Eddie to sell the car to him; at this point a contract comes into force between you and Eddie. Jenson cannot therefore successfully sue you for breach of contract as there is no contract between you and him at any point.

Answer 11.3

(a) No

(b) Your newspaper advertisement is not an offer for sale but an invitation to make an offer. You make an offer when you offer to sell the goods to Ajax for £550. In offering £480, he makes a counter-offer. This has the effect of terminating your offer. An acceptance of an offer must be unqualified acceptance of all the terms of the offer. Therefore when the telephone call ends there is no contract and no open offer. Thus Ajax's subsequent order is an offer to purchase which you are free to accept or reject. You are not bound to sell him the goods at £550 per batch.

Answer 11.4

(a) No

(b) For an agreement to be valid there must be offer and acceptance. Each must be communicated to the other party. There must be some action on the part of the 'offeree' (the person to whom the offer is made) to indicate acceptance. The offeror cannot impose acceptance merely because the offeree does not reject the goods.

Goods sent to a person who did not request them are not 'accepted' merely because he does not return them to the sender. Silence cannot constitute acceptance. (The Unsolicited Goods and Services Act 1971 also addresses this area of the law.)

Answer 11.5

(a) No

(b) Acceptance of an offer must be unqualified acceptance. Sally has stipulated that the CD players must be delivered by Saturday and, because she is introducing a new term into the contract, her purported acceptance is not valid.

Answer 11.6

(a) No

(b) The advertisement in the magazine is an invitation to make an offer. It is not an offer which is capable of being accepted. When Billy rings up to order 30 units, he is making an offer to purchase the goods. Super Sounds Ltd does not have to accept that offer.

Answer 11.7

(a) 16 August

(b) Where it is within the contemplation of the parties that acceptance might be made by using the post, the acceptance is complete and effective as soon as a letter of acceptance is posted. This means that the contract is also complete at that time. This is referred to as the postal rule.

Answer 11.8

(a) No

(b) The offer to supply burglar alarms at £2.20 each has been withdrawn (revoked) before acceptance and that revocation was actually received by Great Fires. Once an offer is revoked, it is no longer open for acceptance.

Answer 11.9

(a) Yes

(b) Although the advertisement is an invitation to make an offer, there is an agreement between Wang and the retailer, consisting of offer and acceptance. (It could be said that the store assistant's offer to supply the PC by the next day is a legal offer accepted by Wang when he completes the order form, but it is more likely that Wang's completion of the order form is an offer which is legally accepted when the store accept the order form for fulfilment of the order.)

Answer 11.10

(a) No

(b) Contracts of sale are between the buyer and the seller, not between the buyer and the manufacturer.

Answer 11.11

S 18 rule 1 states that if the contract is unconditional and the goods are specific or identified, property passes when the contract is made. If this applies, it does not matter that the seller has not yet delivered the goods or that the buyer has not yet paid for them.

Rule 2 states that where there is a contract for the sale of specific goods and the seller is bound to do something to the goods for the purpose of putting them into a deliverable state, the property does not pass until the thing is done and the buyer has notice that it has been done.

In this case, rule 2 applies and so property in the goods (ownership) has not passed. Risk of ownership has therefore not passed either, and the action will fail.

Answer 11.12

An action for the price.

Answer 11.13

A good deal of thought needs to go into the opening of new files.

(a) Is there already a file for this purpose?

(b) What other files are related to this purpose? In other words, what cross-referencing needs to be done?

(c) Are the documents to be filed of an unusual size or material, requiring special storage facilities?

(d) Are the documents confidential?

(e) Will the documents be needed by you frequently, so that a personal or departmental file would be more appropriate than a central one?

(f) What title should be given to the file to make it clear to all potential users what it contains?

(g) How should documents be arranged within the file?

You may have thought of other points in addition to the above. Point (a) is the most important.

Answer 11.14

The updated file should show the following information.

Company:	Folworth (Business Services) Ltd
Address:	Crichton Buildings 97 Lower Larkin Street London EC4A 8QT
Directors:	Robin Folworth BA ACA J..................... Crichton Margaret Foster Laurence Oldfield MA T........................ Scott John Thornhill BSc
Purchasing manager:	D Simmonds

Note that space has been left to fill in the new directors' first names.

Answer 11.15

Business customers' files	*Domestic customers' files*	*Auditors' file*	*Miscellaneous file*
13, 1	5, 18	3	2, 9
7	11, 12		14
10			
15, 17			

(a) Given its date, document 3 is likely to be relevant to the current year, 2006.

(b) Document 4 may as well be thrown away.

(c) Document 6 should be placed on the auditors' file for 2002.

(d) Documents 8 and 20 can be thrown away, or kept with personnel records, perhaps in a file for 'staff entertainment'.

(e) Document 16 could most appropriately be given to whoever is responsible for cleaning or pinned up on a noticeboard.

(f) Document 19 could be thrown away, or else put in the auditors' file for 1999.

It would be sensible to close the old 'miscellaneous' file and either start a new one or else have a file for 'unusual orders', especially as the product is somewhat unusual.

Maintaining a single file for domestic orders seems sensible as these are likely to be 'one-off' purchases. However, it would be helpful if this were arranged alphabetically so that related documents (for example 5 and 18) could be quickly matched.

List of key terms and index

These are the terms which we have identified throughout the text as being KEY TERMS. You should make sure that you can define what these terms mean; go back to the pages highlighted here if you need to check.

BPP PUBLISHING

See overleaf for information on other
BPP products and how to order

Mr/Mrs/Ms (Full name) ______________________

Daytime delivery address ______________________

Postcode ______________________

Daytime Tel ______________________ E-mail ______________________

FOUNDATION (ALL £9.95)	5/01 Texts	6/01 Kits	Special offer	5/01 Passcards	Tapes
Unit 1 Recording Income and Receipts	☐	☐	All		
Unit 2 Making and Recording Payments	☐	☐	Foundation		
Unit 3 Ledger Balances and Initial Trial Balance	☐	☐	Texts and	£4.95 ☐	£10.00 ☐
Unit 4 Supplying Information for Mgmt Control	☐	☐	Kits		
Unit 20 Working with Information Technology	☐		(£80)		
Unit 22/23 Healthy Workplace & Personal Effectiveness	☐		☐		
INTERMEDIATE (ALL £9.95)		**8/01 Kits**			
Unit 5 Financial Records and Accounts	☐	☐	All	£4.95 ☐	£10.00 ☐
Unit 6 Cost Information	☐	☐	Inter'te Texts	£4.95 ☐	£10.00 ☐
Unit 7 Reports and Returns	☐	☐	and Kits (£65)		
Unit 21 Using Information Technology	☐	☐	☐		
TECHNICIAN (ALL £9.95)					
Unit 8/9 Core Managing Costs and Allocating Resources	☐	☐	Set of 12	£4.95 ☐	£10.00 ☐
Unit 10 Core Managing Accounting Systems	☐	☐	Technician		
Unit 11 Option Financial Statements (A/c Practice)	☐	☐	Texts/Kits	£4.95 ☐	£10.00 ☐
Unit 12 Option Financial Statements (Central Govnmt)	☐	☐	(Please		
Unit 15 Option Cash Management and Credit Control	☐	☐	specify titles		
Unit 16 Option Evaluating Activities	☐	☐	required)		
Unit 17 Option Implementing Auditing Procedures	☐	☐	(£100)		
Unit 18 Option Business Tax (FA01)(8/01 Text)	☐	☐	☐		
Unit 19 Option Personal Tax (FA 01)(8/01 Text)	☐	☐			
TECHNICIAN 2000 (ALL £9.95)					
Unit 18 Option Business Tax FA00 (8/00 Text & Kit)	☐	☐			
Unit 19 Option Personal Tax FA00 (8/00 Text & Kit)	☐	☐			
SUBTOTAL	£	£	£	£	£

We aim to deliver to all UK addresses inside 5 working days; a signature will be required. Orders to all EU addresses should be delivered within 6 working days. All other orders to overseas addresses should be delivered within 8 working days. * Europe includes the Republic of Ireland and the Channel Islands.

AAT Order

To BPP Publishing Ltd, Aldine Place, London W12 8AW

Tel: 020 8740 2211. Fax: 020 8740 1184

E-mail: Publishing@bpp.com Web:www.bpp.com

TOTAL FOR PRODUCTS £

POSTAGE & PACKING

Texts/Kits

	First	Each extra	
UK (max £10)	£2.00	£2.00	£
Europe*	£4.00	£2.00	£
Rest of world	£20.00	£10.00	£

Passcards/Tapes

	First	Each extra	
UK	£2.00	£1.00	£
Europe*	£2.50	£1.00	£
Rest of world	£15.00	£8.00	£

Grand Total (Cheques to *BPP Publishing*) I enclose a cheque for (incl. Postage) £

Or charge to Access/Visa/Switch

Card Number

Expiry date ______ Start Date ______

Issue Number (Switch Only) ______

Signature ______

REVIEW FORM & FREE PRIZE DRAW

All original review forms from the entire BPP range, completed with genuine comments, will be entered into one of two draws on 31 January 2002 and 31 July 2002. The names on the first four forms picked out on each occasion will be sent a cheque for £50.

Name: ______________________ **Address:** ______________________

____

____

How have you used this Interactive Text?
(Tick one box only)

☐ Home study (book only)

☐ On a course: college ______________

☐ With 'correspondence' package

☐ Other ______________

Why did you decide to purchase this Interactive Text? *(Tick one box only)*

☐ Have used BPP Texts in the past

☐ Recommendation by friend/colleague

☐ Recommendation by a lecturer at college

☐ Saw advertising

☐ Other ______________

During the past six months do you recall seeing/receiving any of the following?
(Tick as many boxes as are relevant)

☐ Our advertisement in *Accounting Technician* magazine

☐ Our advertisement in *Pass*

☐ Our brochure with a letter through the post

Which (if any) aspects of our advertising do you find useful?
(Tick as many boxes as are relevant)

☐ Prices and publication dates of new editions

☐ Information on Interactive Text content

☐ Facility to order books off-the-page

☐ None of the above

Have you used the companion Assessment Kit for this subject? ☐ **Yes** ☐ **No**

Your ratings, comments and suggestions would be appreciated on the following areas

	Very useful	*Useful*	*Not useful*
Introductory section (How to use this Interactive Text etc)	☐	☐	☐
Chapter topic lists	☐	☐	☐
Chapter learning objectives	☐	☐	☐
Key terms	☐	☐	☐
Assessment alerts	☐	☐	☐
Examples	☐	☐	☐
Activities and answers	☐	☐	☐
Key learning points	☐	☐	☐
Quick quizzes and answers	☐	☐	☐
List of key terms and index	☐	☐	☐
Icons	☐	☐	☐

	Excellent	*Good*	*Adequate*	*Poor*
Overall opinion of this Text	☐	☐	☐	☐

Do you intend to continue using BPP Interactive Texts/Assessment Kits? ☐ Yes ☐ No

Please note any further comments and suggestions/errors on the reverse of this page.

Please return to: Nick Weller, BPP Publishing Ltd, FREEPOST, London, W12 8BR

REVIEW FORM & FREE PRIZE DRAW (continued)

Please note any further comments and suggestions/errors below

FREE PRIZE DRAW RULES

1 Closing date for 31 January 2002 draw is 31 December 2001. Closing date for 31 July 2002 draw is 30 June 2002.

2 Restricted to entries with UK and Eire addresses only. BPP employees, their families and business associates are excluded.

3 No purchase necessary. Entry forms are available upon request from BPP Publishing. No more than one entry per title, per person. Draw restricted to persons aged 16 and over.

4 The decision of the promoter in all matters is final and binding. No correspondence will be entered into.